W. C. FIELDS

was born William Claude Dukinfield, son of a London cockney who migrated to Philadelphia in the late 1870's. At age eleven, Fields ran away from home . . . and became a pilferer, a jailbird, a juggler and—in the opinion of many—the greatest comic artist the world has ever known.

Pulitzer Prize-winning novelist Robert Lewis Taylor tells Fields' whole incredible life story, from his days as a knockabout street urchin to his heyday as the celebrity who hobnobbed with King Edward VII (a fact from which Fields' father never fully recovered).

Here's the man who drank two double martinis every morning before breakfast, wrote The Bank Dick and My Little Chickadee on the backs of envelopes, left his money for the establishment of an orphanage "Where No Religion Of Any Sort Is To Be Preached." Here is the one and only W. C. Fields—a man who successfully defied civilization for 67 years and became the beloved king of American comedy.

"His memory is so beloved of his fans that they would no more brook an author who treats him clumsily than Tiffany's would entrust its diamond-cutting to a blacksmith. Taylor, fortunately, is a skilled literary lapidary. The gems of Fields' comical exploits are neatly cut and polished in his hands. . . . We heartily commend it to anyone the least interested in reading of one of the most fabulous figures who ever lived."

—Luther Nichols, San Francisco Chronicle

Other SIGNET Biographies and Autobiographies You Will Enjoy

W. C. FIELDS

His Follies and Fortunes
By
ROBERT LEWIS TAYLOR

A SIGNET BOOK from
NEW AMERICAN LIBRARY
TIMES MIRROR

SIGNET TRADEMARK REG. U.S. PAT. OFF. AND FOREIGN COUNTRIES
REGISTERED TRADEMARK—MARCA REGISTRADA
HECHO EN CHICAGO, U.S.A.

SIGNET, SIGNET CLASSICS, MENTOR AND PLUME BOOKS
are published *in the United States* by
The New American Library, Inc.,
1301 Avenue of the Americas, New York, New York 10019,
in Canada by The New American Library of Canada Limited,
295 King Street East, Toronto 2, Ontario,
in the United Kingdom by The New English Library, Limited,
Barnard's Inn, Holborn, London E.C. 1, England

PRINTED IN THE UNITED STATES OF AMERICA

To Fields' great friend, Gene Fowler, in gratitude for his large-hearted help and advice during the preparation of this book.

BOOK ONE: *Part One*

CHAPTER ONE

THE LIFE of W. C. Fields is a striking endorsement of Shakespeare's thought, "Sweet are the uses of adversity." There is no reason to believe that the Duke's philosophical utterance, in *As You Like It,* was calculated to prepare the world for Fields, but a knowledge of Fields' career would certainly have made things easier for the Duke. From infancy Fields found life laborious sledding, and he took extraordinary measures to triumph over all. Nobody in our recent history absorbed such a buffeting as a child and emerged so relentlessly successful in after life. By the time of his death, on Christmas Day, 1946, he was widely acknowledged to have become the greatest comic artist ever known. In his tempestuous youth he had achieved comfortable billing as "the greatest juggler on earth," but the title irked him—he was determined to establish his mind on a parity with his hands. For ten years the theater's best entrepreneurs assured him that he was a fine juggler and refused him parts in shows. The overwhelming unanimity of these rebuffs convinced Fields that he was a comedian; he had come far by rejecting the opinions of others. His perseverance and his evolution into the funniest man in the theater, in the movies, and in radio, proved him right.

Many supporters of Chaplin have long resented Fields' notoriety. Perhaps the best testimonial to Chaplin's greatness is the fact that Fields was incapable of watching him perform for more than a few minutes. The virtuosity of the little fellow's pantomime caused Fields to suffer horribly. One evening, a few years before Fields' death, he was persuaded to attend a showing of early Chaplin two-reelers. At a point in the action where Chaplin suffocated a 300-pound villain by pulling a gas street lamp down over his head, the laughter rose in deafening crescendo, and Fields was heard to cough desperately.

"Hot in here," he muttered to his companion, who was fortified against the cooling system with a heavy tweed jacket. "I need air." Fields left the theater and waited outside in his Lincoln. Later, asked what he thought of Chaplin's work, he said, "The son of a bitch is a ballet dancer."

"He's pretty funny, don't you think?" his companion went on doggedly.

"He's the best ballet dancer that ever lived," said Fields, "and if I get a good chance I'll kill him with my bare hands."

Gene Buck, later the guiding spirit of ASCAP and once the principal assistant to Florenz Ziegfeld, picked Fields out of vaudeville in 1914 and hired him for the *Follies*. In a letter to a friend, after Fields died, Buck said, "Next to Bert Williams, Bill was the greatest comic that ever lived, in my book. He was amazing and unique, the strangest guy I ever knew in my lifetime. He was all by himself. Nobody could be like him and a great many tried. He was so damn different, original and talented. He never was a happy guy. He couldn't be, but what color and daring in this game of life! He made up a lot of new rules forty years ago about everything: conduct, people, morals, entertainment, friendship, gals, pals, fate and happiness, and he had the courage to ignore old rules.

"When I first met him he had taken a terrific kicking around in life, and he was tough, bitter, and cynical in an odd, humorous way. He was as good then as he was at his peak. His gifts and talents as an entertainer and comic were born in him, I think. Some guys learn through experience and practice being comics. Not Bill. God made him funny. He knew more about comedy and real humor than any other person with the exception of Bert Williams. I've had a lot to do with comics and their development, and assisted and transplanted many of them during my humble course, and I just want to say that when Bill left the other day, something great in the world died, and something very badly needed."

Despite Buck's curtsy to Bert Williams, the gifted colored entertainer of the twenties, Fields as a national comic phenomenon had no counterpart. He became a symbol of fun; the applied skill of Chaplin and other funny men delighted audiences, but lovers of comedy laughed at the mention of Fields' name. Sensing this curious state of the public's mind, William Le Baron, former head of production at Paramount, for whom Fields made some of his best pictures, conceived the idea of opening movies of the master by showing only his feet walking. There was nothing especially hilarious about Fields' feet, though a full rear view of him, with all its pomp and fraudulent dignity, was uproarious. Without exception, however, audiences responded with noisy appreciation to their truncated first glimpse of the star.

One of Fields' friends once said that this spontaneous merriment was due to the popular notion of his personal life. Fields' defiance of civilization, over a period of sixty-seven years, became an institution in which the public took pride. His work was indistinguishable from his life; when people applauded Fields' feet they were cheering his escape from the humdrum. Most persons, as a scholar has noted, harbor a secret affection for anybody with a low opinion of humanity. Fields' early grapples with things like hunger, frost, bartenders and police gave him a vast, watchful suspicion of society and its patterns. This feeling shaped his art. When, in *The Bank Dick,* he started uneasily upon seeing a teller in a straw hat, he was only harking back to his youth. Fields' first bank account was opened after a brief conversation with the president, who happened to be wearing a hat at his desk. The hat worried Fields for years; he kept checking back to see if the president was still on the job and the books intact.

Fields' last motion picture, *Never Give a Sucker an Even Break,* which he wrote under his pen name of Otis Criblecoblis, was in some measure illustrative of his outlook. "His main purpose," said one of the studio officials, "seemed to be to break as many rules as possible and cause the maximum amount of trouble for everybody." A brief synopsis of the plot, which Fields first composed on the back of a grocery bill and for which he successfully demanded that the studio (Universal) pay him $25,000 follows:

In the opening scene, Fields, as himself, is outlining an original story to a producer, in the presence of the ingénue and the leading man. After he explains that the action begins in a pool hall, with the ingénue wearing a false beard, they somehow appear to lose interest, and Fields wanders out to pick up his small niece, whom he has parked, for safety, in a shooting gallery. En route he stops to watch a group of disgusted urchins throw mudballs at a billboard advertising one of his movies. He exclaims, "Godfrey Daniel!" (which was as near as he could ever manage to "goddamn" and still get by the Hays office) and proceeds. Shortly thereafter his niece's mother, Madame Gorgeous, a circus performer, falls off a trapeze and is killed. Fields and his niece then leave by airplane for Mexico City, where he plans to sell wooden nutmegs to members of the Russian colony. On the way, he accidentally drops a bottle of whisky overboard and without hesitation dives over after it, landing on top of a mountain, where dwell a Mrs. Hemoglobin and her daughter, Ouliotta. Fields teaches the daughter a kissing game but leaps off the mountain when her mother wants to play. He continues to Mexico City, picks up his niece and several other members of the cast, who wander in and out at irrelevant times, and returns to the mountain, having heard that Mrs. Hemoglobin is wealthy. Although he woos her with seedy elegance, she is won by a rival wooden nutmeg salesman. Eventually, we learn that most of the foregoing was the story Fields was trying, in the first scene, to sell the producer.

The Universal heads, when presented with this $25,000 epic, successfully concealed their excitement. One man felt that the plot, though fascinating, was thin; another came out flatfooted and said that, in spots, it even sounded bizarre. Still another ventured to surmise that the title, *Never Give a Sucker an Even Break,* would fit onto no theater marquee known to be in existence anywhere in the world at that time. Fields declined their comments. He hoped, he said, that the title would prove unwieldy and that the announcement would be abbreviated, everywhere, to read, simply, "W. C. Fields—Sucker." As to the plot, he pointed out, with some justification, that it was every bit as powerful and realistic as his story *The Bank Dick,* which he wrote under his alternate pen name of Mahatma Kane Jeeves, and as *You Can't Cheat an Honest Man,* for which he received another screen credit under his third alternate pen name of Charles Bogle. The first of these creations hinged on his successful campaign to induce his prospective son-in-law, a bank clerk, to embezzle $500 for investment in a beefsteak mine, and the second was concerned with the efforts of Fields, as Larson E. Whipsnade, a circus owner, to get his show across a state line before the sheriff caught him.

"Bill only had one story," said Eddie Sutherland, who directed several Fields pictures. "It wasn't a story at all, really—there was just an ugly old man, an ugly old woman, and a brat of a child." Creatively, Fields was aloof from the formal story. He considered life a highly disorganized tale, at the best, and he was convinced that art should follow in its footsteps. In consequence, he assembled, for a "plot," a series of very distantly related incidents aimed to depict the most deplorable and humorous aspects of human existence. It was his continuing program, for example, to steer children into saloons; also, he underwrote many other enterprises of dubious standing, such as theft, arson, swindle, fraud, mayhem and murder.

One of the most uplifting scenes in *Never Give a Sucker an Even Break* found him, with his niece, Gloria Jean, drinking a whitish fluid in a saloon. Fields, with a look of belligerent ease, was hunched against the wood, his arresting nose not far from the slender fire of a brass cigar lighter.

"What kind of goat's milk is it, Uncle Bill?" asked the admiring tot.

"Nanny goat's milk, my dear," replied her old uncle, and as he breathed into the lighter a two-foot blue flame leaped out across the bar.

When he was approached about the straight part of Wilkins Micawber, in *David Copperfield,* Fields was charmed. He assured Metro-Goldwyn-Mayer, which made the picture, that he loved straight parts, and he enthusiastically signed a contract which required him to speak with an English accent. Later on, thinking the part over, he announced that, as Micawber, he believed he would do some juggling. Horrified, the studio heads vetoed the idea at once.

"Dickens made no mention of juggling in *David Copperfield*," one of them said coldly.

"He probably forgot it," Fields replied. Finding the producers adamant, he suggested a happy alternative: he would substitute an act in which he performed at a pool table and told an anecdote about snakes. He thought it would work in neatly following the funeral of Copperfield's mother.

Metro, to his indignation, still preferred the Dickens version, and he sulked for weeks. When the shooting began, his English accent turned out to be pure Fields, a high nasal mutter loaded with pretentious articulation. The studio railed in vain.

"My father was an Englishman, and I got this accent from him," he kept saying. "Are you trying to go against nature?"

CHAPTER TWO

IT WAS often difficult to trap Fields into telling the truth, but his father was, as he had said, an Englishman—James Dukinfield, a London cockney, whose family had emigrated to this country in the late 1870s. He settled in the Germantown district of Philadelphia and married a neighbor's daughter, Kate Felton. Their first child, William Claude, who later changed his name to W. C. Fields for professional reasons, was born on April 9, 1879. Both the Dukinfields and the Feltons were poor, and Dukinfield had to scramble to make a living. After weighing several professions, he invested in an elderly horse named White Swan and began to hawk vegetables and fruit. Years afterward,

Fields was to give various accounts of his ancestry. He told an interviewer for a high school paper that both his father and his mother had suffered from leprosy, a blatant falsehood. During one period he maintained, seriously, that his grandfather had invented a process for making imitation tortoise-shell combs, and, in attempting to come to America, had been shipwrecked off Glen Cove, Long Island. For years he attributed his artistic talent to a powerful theatrical strain in the family—an uncle, he said, had been a popular Swiss bell ringer at Elks' smokers and chowder parties. "I've got the theater in my blood," Fields used to say.

The Dukinfield household was dedicated to making ends meet, and there are grounds for the belief that Fields was dangerously bored by the time he was four. The family recreation consisted of listening to Mr. Dukinfield sing sentimental and religious songs, after he'd had a couple of beers. His favorites were "The Little Green Leaf in the Bible," "Annie Laurie," and "Oh, Genevieve," all of which Fields detested to his dying day. In fact, he worked up a strong fixation about vocal music, and would absent himself from any locality in which he believed song threatened. One of his mistresses, toward the end of his life, handled domestic spats by locking herself in his bathroom and singing at the top of her notable voice. Fields would howl, beat on the walls with a cane, and threaten to burn the house down with her in it. He went to the length, on one occasion, of firing some newspapers and holding them in such a way that the smoke curled under her door. She emerged, but she continued to sing till she reached the street, and Fields later conceded her a moral victory. "The girl's got guts," he told several friends.

The elder Dukinfield, who annoyed Fields from the start by dropping his *h*'s, was occasionally jolly around the house, but he was prey to fits of tyranny. He was an ardent devotee of the quick, disciplinary blow, leaning slightly to backhanders. He got to the point where he was punctuating sentences by whacking Fields. Dukinfield was missing the little finger of his left hand—a deletion he attributed to the Crimean War—and a backward cuff with that hand was, according to Fields, uncommonly painful. Though a good, loyal American, the father had monarchic sympathies. He was not entirely ready to accept the Revolution. "Would the King be proud of *that?*" he'd bawl at the boy, and administer a clout to remind him of his duty. Without doubt, Dukinfield would have been aghast to learn that, some years hence, his son would be chatting companionably with an admiring Edward VII.

Fields' mother, the former Miss Felton, was a hardworking housewife with an exceptional measure of native shrewdness. Her family for some generations had been occupied in the hauling line. From her, Fields borrowed much of his vigilance as well as the muttered asides that were later to convulse audiences. Mrs. Dukinfield had a habit of standing in her doorway and conversing with passers-by, meanwhile damning them in asides to her family. After the people had gone, she would mimic them with great comic skill. Fields studied these monologues. Years later, when he was starring in the stage play *Poppy,* he invited her to New York and established her in a box at the theater. "How'd you like my work, Mother?" he asked in his dressing room following the final curtain. Her answer was, "I didn't know you had such a good memory." Fields always said that he seldom knew whether his mother was being naïve or cute. Once, not long after he had brought her to see *Poppy* he was telling her about his travels among various aborigines, and he said of one tribe, "They invited me to dinner—a very excellent repast, starting off with whale."

"Goodness!" exclaimed Mrs. Dukinfield. "I should think that would make a meal in itself."

Mrs. Dukinfield and her husband addressed their son as "Claude," a name he was unable to stomach throughout his life. He was continually trying to use the name Claude for villainous characters in his plays and movies. As a boy, he preferred to be known as "Whitey," a nickname the children of the neighborhood gave him in recognition of his pale blond hair. Fields once petitioned his father to forget Claude and have the name changed legally to Whitey, but he received a moderate beating for his pains. In the ten years following his birth, the Dukinfields had two additional sons, Le Roy and Walter, and two daughters, Elsie Mae and Adele. From time to time, in his movies, Fields was to take note of these names. For instance, Fields felt that his young sisters were annoyingly consecrated to eating; in *The Bank Dick* he conceived the name "Elsie Mae Adele Brunch Sousé," for the character of his small daughter. It was a coincidence, he said, that in the course of the story he tried to brain her with a concrete urn. Toward the end of his life Fields began to sign dispatches to his most intimate friends, such as Gene Fowler, the writer, and Gregory La Cava, the director, with "Whitey Dukinfield."

In one of these, some notes that he wrote out for Fowler, Fields reminisced about the Philadelphia of his childhood: "The trolley-car parties or trolley rides took the place of the old hayrides in the summertime. A party would get together, engage an open trolley car, and adorn it with bunting. Noise ran rampant; the occupants would blow horns and make noises with rattles, and the smart alecks would make smart cracks at the ghillies who stood on the corners or who passed with their girls. Some would even make bad noises with their mouths.

"Philadelphians were fond of riding on cars or trains and singing—not that they ever produced any outstanding singer that I can remember. They would arrange parties, leave Philadelphia about 5:30 P.M. on either the Pennsylvania or Reading Railroad for dinner ('supper' they called it, the midday repast was referred to as 'dinner'). They would proceed on a private car to New York, see a show —probably Maurice Barrymore—and return to Philadelphia, everything included for a round sum. One of the swankiest things to do was dine at the Reading Railway Terminal or the Pennsylvania Station dining room in New York, same as people in Los Angeles a few years ago would drive to San Bernardino, a distance of seventy-five miles, to get a full-sized smidgeon of corned-beef hash."

In another reminiscence, also for Fowler, Fields touched on the saloon and bawdy-house situation in his home town. He later apologized for the sketchiness of these references, ascribing it to his extreme youth. "Saloons in Philadelphia," he said, "were closed at twelve o'clock Saturday night and opened at one minute past midnight on Sunday. There were queues formed at nearly all the leading ones, which did a thriving business until the early hours

Monday morning. Saturday night the saloons did a fine bottle business.

"Of course we had notch (nautch) joints all over the city and there were many reformers who wanted to blot them out altogether, others who wanted to have them concentrated in a certain section of the city. A fellow was afraid to whistle for his dog after nine o'clock at night, for fear of being hit on the sconce with a heavy door key. The low-ceiling price bazaar for sexual relief was a street called Middie Alley. You could barely get a pushcart through this avenue. Top price—twenty-five cents."

Fields enjoyed talking about early Philadelphia, partly, his friends suspected, because he liked to demonstrate his phenomenal memory. When in good form he would rattle off long lists of stray information, such as the fact that Philadelphians called merry-go-rounds "hobbyhorses"; that they called peanuts "ground nuts"; that small restaurants were called "oyster houses" or "oyster saloons" (though they sold no liquor); that Sunday entertainment was limited to band concerts at Willow Grove and Strawberry Mansion in Fairmount Park; that firecrackers were known as "shooting crackers," and that the city was known for Philadelphia Pepper Pot, Philadelphia scrapple, sticky-bottom cinnamon buns, and "Scotch cake," a flat cake an eighth of an inch thick and six inches in diameter, upon which Fields claimed to have broken several teeth in his fledgling years.

On one occasion Fowler's secretary took a secret shorthand record of Fields' nostalgic comments. They went as follows: "Well, sir, I remember those boat races on the Schuylkill—the river ran right through town. People used to ask what to see in Philadelphia and somebody would say, 'It's the greatest cemetery in the world.' Everything in town was run by contractors, nobody made a dime. The gas company sold out to a new electric company and we had electric lights. Well, the people decided this was a mistake, so damned if they didn't get a lot of old guns and pistols and swords and charge down to the City Hall yelling about how they wanted gas back. The charge was repulsed.

"Every year, you know, the city would allot so much money toward hoisting the statue of William Penn up onto the City Hall. Finally they got him up there, but they turned his tail end south and had him looking north. Well, the people on the south side set up a hell of a howl. There was a big fight. I was born on the north side, but I didn't care one way or the other—he looked just the same to me, both sides.

"Great town for breweries. These all had saloons in conjunction with them, owned and operated them that way, you see.

"Then there were those old-fashioned two-horse streetcars. They also had a man who helped pull the cars uphill. He sat on his horse, put a line on the cars, and with the other two horses took them up the hill. I remember one guy in particular, man named Stink Reese. He was a little runt, but everybody respected him because of his position and because he carried a whip. Mean, too—if he didn't like a driver he wouldn't help him uphill. They had cable cars on Market Street.

"Gilmore and Sousa were the bands that played in Willow Grove Park. There was a place called Lemon Hill Mansion, a tower with a circular staircase; get up there and see all around, maybe up to the City Hall in Germantown. The topic of conversation day in and day out was, 'We're up as high as William Penn's feet.'

"Everybody sat in the kitchen in the wintertime. It was so god-damned cold in the rest of the house you couldn't stand it. The kitchen was the only place with any heat. We used to make snowballs, dip them in some kind of flavoring, and have a party. There sure was lots of snow. One year we had a blizzard there, a big one. It went over the horses' heads. It was quite a thing to see the snowplow coming, and we'd go knock on the neighbors' doors and tell them it was coming. It had twelve horses."

Fowler: "That's very interesting, Willie. Thanks a lot."

Fields: "You're welcome, my boy."

Thus the Philadelphia of Fields' youth—a city then, as now, of high moral indignation and average morals.

As a small boy Fields was sensitive, mulish, humorous and independent. He was of medium size but possessed of uncommon constitutional and muscular strength. Because he also had an excess of both daring and aggressiveness, he held sway over all the other neighborhood children of his age, many of whom were a head taller than he. There were two girls in the group, Fields recalled later, who were grown far beyond their years. He had trouble, he said, whipping them without using a club. The best sources agree that Fields probably did have trouble with precocious girls; his shows were crowded with mentions of savage victories over the opposite sex. "You remember the time I knocked Waterfront Nell down?" he asked a fellow bartender in *My Little Chickadee,* and when the man replied, with some heat, "Why, you didn't knock her down—*I* did," Fields said, "Well, I started kicking her first." Among the children of both sexes he was known for isolated, meaningless acts of bravura; once he climbed a fifty-foot sandhopper and jumped off into a sandpile, the impact driving his knees into his eyes and blacking them vividly. His companions, one by one, climbed the hopper and stared at the ground, but they climbed back down and went home, while Fields stood carelessly by, massaging his eyes with a handkerchief. Almost from the time he began to talk, he spoke in the extravagant nasal drawl with which he was to become identified. This was substantially a gift from his father, who advertised his wares in a similar tone while following White Swan on the grocery route.

Dukinfield was a great believer in all the known adages about idleness, as they applied to others. He took energetic measures to prevent the boy Claude's mind from becoming a devil's workshop. As soon as Fields was able to walk comfortably, the father took him along on the hawking tours. In after life, Fields always said he felt "undignified as a three-year-old apprentice in the costermonger trade." For one thing, his father's adenoidal cry, minus the *h*'s, struck him as ludicrous. When the boy was called upon, a year or two later, to take up the chant, he applied himself mainly to burlesqueing his father. This led to friction. Fields also had a habit of publicizing vegetables the cart didn't carry, simply because the names pleased him. "Rutabagas, pomegranates, calabashes," he would yell, and the housewives would flock to his side. Dukinfield would explain that his son was new on the job and then cuff him as they bounced down the road.

Fields' schooling was brief—a circumstance that both-

ered him all his life. By adulthood he recognized this questionable lack in his equipment, and he set out, with characteristic zeal, to overcome it. He bought, among other
books, whole sets of Dickens, Thackeray and Stevenson,
and read them all. His taste, he once said in discussing this
period, was principally for funny characters, but he also
struggled manfully with the most bilious of the English romanticists. Fields remarked to a friend that he was "probably one of the few people outside an institution who can
outline the various plots of *Silas Marner.*" In his avidness
to learn he remembered everything. Producers at Metro-
Goldwyn-Mayer, who had forcibly restrained him from
juggling in *David Copperfield,* were amazed to hear during
a subsequent illness of Fields, that, while delirious, he had
quoted Micawber's speeches by the page.

A synthesis of Fields' declarations about his schooling
places the length of his attendance at about four years. The
figure may be a little high. One of his relatives believed that
he turned up for school one Monday in the autumn of his
sixth year but that he lasted till only around noon. He
never went back, the relative said. There were indications
that he found the classroom cramped and the teacher's
manner inadequate. Fields once told an actor that he had
taught himself to read, but he added that he had also gone
to school for four years. Then he eyed the man belligerently, determined to let him make what he could of the muddle. Another of Fields' relatives said that his first scholastic stint did, in truth, last one day but that he returned,
from time to time, for further tries. All sources have agreed
that, despite his father's unsatisfactory pronunciation, he
preferred a life with turnips and beets to the regimentation
of school.

One afternoon when he was nine, Fields sneaked into
the gallery of a vaudeville house and watched a performance of the Byrne Brothers, jugglers. He was electrified.
He ran home and, with several lemons and oranges lifted
from the cart, set up shop in the stable. Juggling, he found,
was a perverse enterprise. "By the time I could keep two
objects going, I'd ruined forty dollars' worth of fruit," he
told a friend later. Fields' homework with the fruit opened
new vistas of discord between him and his father. Their
mutual disapproval ripened fast. Dukinfield would crouch

in the stable, then, if he caught the boy bruising lemons, he would prance out and give him a hiding. A crisis was reached not long after Fields' eleventh birthday. He had left a small shovel lying in the front yard, and Dukinfield stepped on it. The handle flew up and banged him on the shin. Unfortunately, the father had barked the same shin earlier that day on a hubcap of the vegetable cart. He hopped around on one leg awhile, cursing, then, seeing Fields studying him in a detached sort of way, he picked up the shovel and rattled it off the boy's head. During the next few days Fields devoted himself to getting even. He said afterward that he rejected several plans certain to arouse the interest of the coroner and settled on a simple but effective reprisal. Holding a large wooden box poised aloft, he hid in the stable. His father came in, looking for trouble. Fields crowned him. Then he walked off down the road and never returned.

CHAPTER THREE

THE FIRST NIGHT of Fields' exodus he slept in a hole in the ground—a "bunk," covered over with boards and dug by his gang—in a field a mile from home. It was tolerably comfortable, as accommodations of this sort went, but toward morning the rain came down and the bunk began to leak pretty freely. By morning it had taken on the look of a hog wallow, and Fields began to be sorry he had left. When the sun rose over the treetops, he climbed out, after a couple of false starts, scraped away the topsoil, and lay down in the grass to dry off. He felt creaky and rheumatic, he said later, but the sun soon revived his prejudice against being hit with shovels. And now a new worry came up—he was hungry. After a while he crawled over behind some bushes near the road and awaited developments. Around nine o'clock a colleague known by the affectionate name of "Pot-head" Edwards came along on his way to school. Fields called hoarsely from the shrubs, explained his plight, and invoked aid. It was not long forthcoming. As they took their meals, the fugitive's friends, like Pip supplying the convict in *Great Expectations,* secreted a bun here and a parsnip there, and made for the bunk as soon as they escaped surveillance. They looked up to Fields. They were proud of his indifference to authority.

Fields' family made little more than a token search. His mother felt that, at eleven, he was young to set up on his own, but the problems of four other children diverted her mind. The attitude of Fields' father could perhaps be summed up by the handy phrase "good riddance." He took the stand that a boy careless with small shovels would likely grow up to be careless with large shovels, and that such a person was a menace. He trained another of his offspring to help out on the cart. For years thence neither Dukinfield nor his wife knew where their son had gone. Meanwhile, the boy had begun to enjoy himself. There being no other place available at the moment, he tightened the bunk's defenses against weather, stole a quilt off a neighbor's line, and bought some candles with a dime he had borrowed from an admirer. At the same time, his friends continued to bring food. Adequately housed, well stoked, and having no connection with vegetables and fruit save as consumer, Fields felt at peace for the first time in years.

The idyll was short-lived. The day he had fled, in March, was balmy for that season. Less than a week later the weather turned surly, and he found the quilt insufficient. To heat things up, he made a small bonfire in one corner of the bunk, but it caused such a smudge and hurt his eyes so badly that he covered it with mud. He spent one night wrapped in the quilt and huddled over a candle. When he surfaced the next morning it was snowing briskly. About this time, the participants in his food lift gave up, for the most part. The novelty had worn off, and several of them, caught greasy-handed, had been soundly trounced. Their loyalty to Fields was solid, but it fell short of corporal punishment. The time had come, Fields felt, to move into a better neighborhood. He discovered that it was a period in which the kind of housing he sought—free and removed from the scrutiny of police—was extraordinarily scarce. The only possibility, he found as he went over the ground, was another spa of his fellows, the Orlando Social Club, a benevolent group similar to the Innapenent Order of Infadelaty, which was organized some years later by Penrod Schofield and Sam Williams. The club had its headquarters over the shop of a compliant blacksmith named Wheeler. It was an informal room, suitable for the development of spartanism. The roof was patchy and the walls had been carelessly joined; the furniture included a three-legged table and five empty beer kegs. Into this new apartment Fields moved with his quilt, a can of pork and beans, and a resolve to face the future without flinching. His subterranean stint had given him the social outlook of a mole, he subsequently said; for several days life above ground made him feel like an imposter. Long before he was used to it, he was starving again, and he embarked on a career of petty crime.

There can be no doubt, in view of the evidence at hand, that Fields may now be regarded as Philadelphia's most distinguished vagrant since Benjamin Franklin. Franklin, at least by his own account, toiled in the path of righteousness; Fields, by his, committed every misdemeanor and small felony on the city's books. Though shy about his schooling, Fields was often voluble about things that he considered undamaging to his character, such as trespassing, theft and imprisonment. Throughout his life he heaped accounts of these triumphs on both his friends and his interviewers. One time he was chatting with Alva Johnston, who wrote masterly pieces about him for *The New Yorker* and the *Saturday Evening Post,* and several friends at Dave Chasen's restaurant in Hollywood. After describing a number of censorable adventures, Fields began a windy account of what he characterized as "one of the most romantic episodes of my life." It took place in the Solomon Islands, during a professional visit he'd made there.

"I had this Melanesian belle, a comely-looking lass," he said, "and I was headed for the shrubbery, which grows very lush in those parts. Well, her husband was following along behind holding a forefinger up in the air and crying, 'One dollah, one dollah!' "

The anecdote continued its ribald course, and when it was finished, Johnston had to leave.

As soon as he was gone, one of Fields' companions said, "Bill, you're a damned fool to talk like that to a man who's about to write you up. You ought to be more circumspect."

"Circumspect, hell!" Fields cried. "I don't care how black he paints me."

During his Orlando Social Club, or early larcenous, phase, Fields was anything but circumspect. The urge for self-preservation is strong in the human, and Fields, though he suffered, had every intention of surviving. He began by lifting commodities off such carts as ventured out in the still-winter weather. "Good morning, Mr. Giovanni," he'd cry, and after an exchange of amenities the man would drive off the poorer by three tomatoes. Because of Fields' work with the lemons, his fingers were practiced and nimble; also, he knew his way around a vegetable cart. As time went on he became painfully familiar to cart drivers, who would slash at their horses when they saw him coming. On his pilfering sorties, Fields wore a loose-fitting blouse, which he filled as he made his rounds. After a while vegetables palled on him, as vegetables will, and his mind turned to thoughts of a balanced diet. He worked up a device to obtain protein, but it involved traveling to an obscure part of town. With his face fixed in a timorous smirk, he would enter a butcher's and say, "Mama sent me for three pork chops." When the butcher produced these from the icebox, the boy usually added, "Oh, yes, and a pound of bacon." Then, as the butcher turned away, Fields would grab the chops and fly. Relating his adventures, in the years to come, Fields always apologized for the unimaginative quality of his meat thefts. He preferred to dwell on a system he devised for robbing Chinamen. Because he lived in the headquarters of a populous club, his whereabouts became known to all the members, and he enlisted their aid on occasion. A favorite sport, conceived by Fields during a night when the smithy rats were making things too warm for sleep, involved the use of one confederate. The friend would stand on a streetcar track in front of a laundry as an oncoming car set up a peevish clanging. When the noise was sufficient to drown out the China-man's bell, Fields would dash in and clean out his till. The system was nearly perfect, since immigrant Chinamen then spoke little English and few Philadelphia police were well grounded in Chinese. A fast boy could manage a neat start, and Fields was unusually fleet.

In the daytime, Wheeler's forge kept the barn warm, but toward midnight a chill settled on the Orlando Social Club. Fields spent the first few nights sleeping on the floor, then he removed a door and padded one side with burlap. As a bed, it had shortcomings, but it was, he felt, softer and much cleaner than anything available in the brother-hood's country place. So severe were the frequent cold snaps that Fields often strayed from the forge to seek shelter elsewhere. For a while he was lodged in a livery stable, occupying a Percheron's bran trough. He spent one cramped month in a barrel. A bartender let him sleep a few nights in a heated saloon; his bed was a stack of news-papers on the floor of a toilet. This reservation was can-celed by the saloon owner, who became fretful about the authorities. "The kid's in there drinking whisky all night," he told the bartender. "They'll close us up." Fields always denied this. The truth is that he never touched alcohol in this period, though his public utterances on the subject were afterward frivolous. "I never drank anything stronger than beer before I was twelve," he liked to tell reporters.

The boy spent several nights sleeping in a cellar that had a convenient, punched-out window. He would kneel outside until the owner had banked the fire, then crawl through and nest in a woodbox near the furnace. These were comfortable quarters, and he was chagrined when the window was suddenly boarded up. He finally deduced that the repairs were somehow connected with his sys-tematic abstraction of the housewife's preserves. "The thing taught me a lesson," he once told a friend. "You've got to know where to stop."

Despite his occasional nights out, Fields stuck for the most part close to the social club. He arose many morn-ings so stiff he could scarcely muster the agility to steal. One of his chief methods of thawing out was to sit with his back against a board fence. He found that when the sun came up, boards absorbed heat quickly and transmitted it pleasurably to his back. Fields conceived a fondness for high board fences that he never lost. Years afterward, during his travels, he was likely to spot a fence and sneak off to warm himself luxuriously. Also, he acquired a sharp fixation about beds. His principal aim, he said, was to reach a station in life in which he could sleep between clean sheets every night of the year. "To this day," he told an interviewer late in life, "when I climb in between clean sheets, I *smile*. When I get into bed and stretch out—god damn, that's a sensation!"

Fields' offhand larceny inevitably led him into trouble. The Philadelphia police came to regard him as a one-child crime wave. He was frequently seized and flung into jail, but always, he maintained, for something of which he was innocent. "They never got me for the right offense," he liked to say. In jail, he gave whatever name came handiest at the time and so patently enjoyed the city's bounty that he was usually released without delay. Notwithstanding his enjoyment, he complained bitterly about his couch, the menu, and the service, and hurt his warders' feelings. They viewed him as a corrupting influence on the other tenants and were glad to get rid of him. During one time of frequent jailings, Fields temporarily gave up stealing and subsisted on the free lunch in saloons. He would swagger in, buy ginger ale with a nickel he'd panhandled, and visit the free-lunch cage. The meal he managed to make in a few minutes' time, from hard-boiled eggs, pickled herring, cheese, bologna, liverwurst, onions and similar staples, was worth several times the price of his drink. Bartenders began to share the official police view of Fields; he had to distribute his patronage widely to avoid ejections.

The deeper he settled into his vagabondage, the higher he rose socially. Among the members of the Orlando group his prestige was unapproached. This kind of deference would turn the heads of most children, and it turned the head of Fields. He became downright snobbish. Amidst his contemporaries his attitude was lordly, and he was condescending to the blacksmith. His manner suggested that he did not wholly condemn toil but that it placed a barrier between him and Wheeler. His address in the smithy took on overtones of "My man" and "My good fellow." In these years Fields developed a grandiose air, shot through with fraud, that stuck with him like a plaster. He once said that his pre-eminence was gratifying, though it had drawbacks. Boys for miles around, envious of his glitter and easy ways, sought to devaluate him physically. He was beaten up several times a week. Representatives of other districts would waste a day's travel for the privilege of licking him. Nothing altered the fact that he stole for a living and was regularly jailed. Off and on during his life, Fields corresponded with a few of his boyhood friends. One became a Philadelphia stone mason; another succeeded to ownership of the family bakery, from which edibles once found their way into the fugitive's bunk.

The quality of freedom is never absolute, and Fields paid variously for his escape. Among other things, because of exposure, he suffered almost continuously from colds. His voice cracked, hoarsened, mellowed and re-formed on a note of permanent rasp. In a backward child this could have proved tragic; in Fields it seemed to complement his new demeanor. Neither he nor his companions knew it, but a national character was beginning to take shape. As a result of the beatings, his nose bloomed far beyond the ordinary. It was reduced to pulp so often that, in gaining scar tissue, it rapidly added dimension. Fields was right when, in reminiscing about his nose, he absolved whisky from part of the guilt. From his middle age onward he became aggressively sensitive about his nose. He sometimes resented whimsical allusions to it by his most cherished friends. One time, while on a deep-sea fishing trip with Gene Fowler and some others, Fields sat in a boat's stern for hours beneath a broiling sun. His nose, always tender, lit up like a Japanese lantern. Suddenly, Fowler said, he heard a popping sound, and he cried, "Uncle Willie's nose has exploded!" Fields was wounded; he went below and sulked until they reached shore. Later on he telephoned Fowler and said, "Who all have you told that damned story to?"

"Why, I don't know," Fowler replied. "Everybody, I think."

Fields cursed him vigorously. "You ought to be ashamed of yourself," he said at last. "You're making fun of an unfortunate man with an affliction." He calmed down when Fowler promised to call all the people he'd talked to and retract the news about Fields' nose exploding.

CHAPTER FOUR

THE SECOND WINTER after his departure Fields entered upon a time which was forever afterward distasteful to him. He tried to forget it. In interviews he skirted it nimbly, allowing his hobo triumphs to stand intact and untarnished. Only a handful of persons—relatives for the most part—knew his dreadful secret. The regrettable truth is, however, that for a space he backslid in a rather shocking manner. After one spirited dip of the temperature, during which Wheeler closed the forge and muttered vaguely about moving to Georgia, Fields went to live with his maternal grandmother. It is to be presumed that she informed the boy's parents of his whereabouts, but they made no recorded attempt to recover him. Persons close to the situation believed that, in the two years, they had made adjustments.

His cushioned residence was only a part of the compromise that Fields eventually came to regard as infamous. He accepted employment. His grandmother was opposed to children stealing for a living, and she said so, in robust language. Under her tutelage he got a job as "cash boy" at Strawbridge & Clothier's Department Store. His duties consisted of sprinting back and forth between departments, holding a leather cup containing change. He suffered terribly, according to one of the few friends he later took into his confidence concerning this low point in his affairs. "I had trouble passing the exits with the change box," Fields said. "Sometimes, without thinking, I'd go out one revolving door and come back in another. It was a difficult time for a self-respecting thief."

Like Huckleberry Finn at the Widow Douglas's, Fields made an honest effort to become civilized, but, as Twain's hero said, "it was rough living in the house all the time, considering how dismal regular and decent the widow was in all her ways." Fields got fidgety in the evenings; occasionally he slipped out and went to a saloon. The garnering of fifty cents' worth of free lunch for a nickel ginger ale usually put him right—it restored his faith in himself. During this season of his employment he was aware of a basic anxiety that hung over him like a thundercloud. He felt that his fingers, despite the free lunch, were apt to grow rusty through the interruption of his stealing. In his spare moments he again took up juggling, which had been a latent passion with him since his visit to the Byrne Brothers. In his grandmother's back yard, in barns, in stables, in any place where he might work in peace, he kept the objects flying. Cut off as he was from Dukinfield's supply of spherical edibles, he sought other things to juggle. On Sundays he hung around the municipal tennis courts. When a ball sailed over the backstop, Fields grabbed it and ran. He begged cigar boxes from tobacconists, he lifted croquet balls from quiet lawns, he borrowed Indian clubs from gymnasiums, and he dug utensils out of scrap heaps. It was priceless training, for he was learning to juggle objects of every possible shape. Through the dark hours of his regeneration his practice never flagged.

There came a day at the beginning of the spring thaws when Fields' grandmother recognized the inevitable truth—the job was too big; the boy couldn't be civilized. They parted, on amicable terms, and Fields returned to the gutters. He was free once more, but soft living had left its mark. Again as in the case of Finn, "I liked the old ways best, but I was getting so I liked the new ones, too, a little bit." Fields had been making two dollars a week at Strawbridge & Clothier's, and though they offered to raise him to two-fifty, he decided to better himself. Also, he was looking for something a little less formal, a little less stigmatized. His first employment after leaving the store involved racking balls in a pool hall. It was congenial work and offered, besides a bed on a table, a chance to juggle billiard balls in the evenings. This was a significant connection for Fields. He found himself studying the absurd, solemn mannerisms of pool-hall habitués, those tense, pale victims of a hard, ancestral rite. He observed the cautious choosing of the cue, the inelastic placement of the chalk, the hush before the fateful shot, the low aside. In general, this all struck him as perhaps the funniest thing he had ever seen, and he stored it up for future reference.

History has no record of pool-hall employees who were not experts at the game. By practicing on idle tables, Fields became, in the professional phrase, a "shark." He got so good that he began to represent the house in matches against customers looking for sport. Also, he made, by betting, a fair amount of money on the side. He was adept at the ancient poolroom trick of hustling—of playing badly for a game or two, then hiking the bet to a plushy level and turning on his best form. This sort of artifice, though common, is looked upon as unethical in the best billiard circles, and Fields was frequently thrashed. Because of his long experience with colds, he found the ever-present chalk dust of the establishment a source of annoyance, and he at last resigned, fearful of contracting silicosis. Before he left, however, he conceived a love for the game that he never got over. In his after years, when he lived in big houses, Fields always had an expensive pool table, generally in the living room. He used it not only for recreation but to promote rest during periods of insomnia. As a ball racker, he had taken a fancy to the pool table for sleeping purposes, and he often turned back to it in his later, wealthier days.

At the conclusion of his billiard phase, Fields planned his next move very carefully. Although his life at this stage appeared aimless, he was beginning to exhibit the foresight that later characterized all his actions. "There is very little luck," he was to write a lady friend fifty years thence. "Almost everything must be thought out." His objective, in the professional line, was a job which left him plenty of leisure time in which to juggle. In addition, since it was now summer, he wanted something cool. Finally, he preferred a position that would excite the envy of the young. He thought it out and luck was with him. Within a week he was signed on as assistant to a man named Gomer Wheatley, who drove an ice wagon. Fields was first attracted to this employment while reading an ad in a newspaper. Struck by the name "Gomer Wheatley," which was in ten-point type, he was compelled to read the eight-point text it accompanied. Wheatley said the run took only a few hours, neglecting to add that it started around 3 A.M., at which time there was a minimum of shrinkage. At the outset, Fields was appalled, but he was case-hardened and got used to it. Wheatley was keenly interested in juggling. He pressed his helper to teach him a few tricks. Of this venture Fields later wrote an acquaintance, "I did my best, but I could only teach him how to juggle his accounts."

The partners enjoyed themselves. Wheatley had a leisurely bay horse, and he was a fairly leisurely man himself. He and his assistant took turns filling the orders, as the horse clumped idly down the darkened streets. It was a summer of good weather; Fields had chosen wisely. The cicadas sang in the trees, the night wind was fresh and cool, dogs complained sleepily, without meaning anything in particular, and an occasional light showed where somebody had a wakeful baby or an early job. Just before daylight the birds arose with a noisy clatter, and not long afterward the first children began to chase the wagon. In general, Fields took care of the twenty-five-pound and fifty-pound cakes, and Wheatley carried the others. On especially heavy orders, for stores or restaurants, they worked together, each taking a handle of the prongs. Mostly, a proprietor would give them a little something at times like these—a sandwich, some cookies, a bottle of Bevo. As salary, Fields was getting three dollars and fifty cents a week and all the ice he could eat; he made out comfortably. He had a room over a tailor shop. It cost him five dollars a month.

Each morning the job was finished by ten. Then they would visit some bartender customer who was preparing the free lunch for the day. Wheatley would buy beer, Fields ginger ale, and they would eat their fill of the lunch. Fields took all of his meals in saloons that summer; late that summer, too, he switched from soft drinks to beer. In the afternoons he juggled steadily. It had become an obsession with him. Around this time he had begun to know that he had an extraordinary talent and that a career awaited him. But he was in a hurry. The grim and dedicated aspect of his practice was awe-inspiring to boys who came to watch him. He refused all temptations to be distracted. Many days he persisted until time to go on the ice route. Years later, discussing this with a fellow worker at Paramount, for which he was making *The Big Broadcast of 1938,* Fields said, "I still carry scars on my legs from those early attempts at juggling. I'd balance a stick on my toe, toss it into the air, and try to catch it again on my toe. Hour after hour the damned thing would bang against my shinbones. I'd work until tears were streaming down my face. But I kept on practicing, and bleeding, until I perfected the trick. I don't believe that Mozart, Liszt, Paderewski, or Kreisler ever worked any harder than I did." In a few months he had mastered all the feats of the Byrne Brothers and, within the limits of his paraphernalia, had invented new ones. He was never satisfied; he drove himself savagely. For a child of thirteen it was a demonstration of almost superhuman will, and it marked the inner compulsion that separates the genius from the mediocrity. This inexplicable fire is always a little frightening.

In the autumn the ice business dwindled, and he and Wheatley reluctantly parted. Their time together had worked a tonic effect upon Fields. Many children would have found his early-morning stint onerous, but he felt that his life had become ordered at last. He had tucked away a rather neat nest egg, of six dollars and fifty cents, and he had brought his juggling a long way since the Dukinfield lemons. Though jobless, alone, stung by weather, ill-clothed, badly fed, pursued by bullies and harried by the police, he faced the future with contentment. To guard his savings, he took, as a stopgap, a job selling papers on a busy corner downtown. He realized that this was a descent from the ice cart, but dug in and made it go. Between sales he was able to work in various kinds of juggling, by folding the papers this way and that. Because of the running show he put on, he pushed his sales higher than those of nearly anybody in the district. He sold papers with an élan which has perhaps never been equaled in the news-hawking profession since then. "He had the flourish of a grand seigneur," said a relative who knew him in that period. "He had a trick of somehow handing out papers as though he were distributing alms." Also, Fields was probably one of the first newsies to call out any details of the day's events. This practice became commonplace in later years, though the majority of its exponents stuck pretty closely to the headlines. Fields handled things differently. He was beginning to develop a fascination for odd names, and he searched his wares through for catchy examples. As a result, his reports on the news showed, from a journalist's standpoint, poor editorial judgment. "Bronislaw Gimp acquires license for two-year-old sheep dog," he'd cry, and add, "Details on page 26." Many citizens of Philadelphia bought his papers out of simple curiosity.

Fields' revenue from the news business provided him with enough money to live on, and he regretfully gave up stealing. He had, he said, established an enviable record as an independent shoplifter, unbacked by either syndicates or kleptomania, and he hated to throw away all he had built up. But he recognized that he was getting too old to continue; the first flush of his speed was past and the police were likely to tuck him away for a long stretch. Although he actually went straight, Fields contended that he remained a thief at heart. His case in a way was similar to that of an elderly ballplayer, of whose unsuccessful attempt to steal a base Arthur "Bugs" Baer said, "He had larceny in his heart, but his feet were honest." All his life Fields bragged spaciously about his wayward youth. He made himself out to be somewhat more vicious than Fagin's shiftiest charges. Once, during an interview by a breathless girl reporter, he outlined a whole calendar of his youthful iniquities, and she said, "Tell me, Mr. Fields, now that you've become rich and famous, how do you feel about stealing and all that sort of thing?" "Young lady," said Fields, fixing her with a reproving stare, "there is nothing more contemptible than a thief."

For a short period Fields became fed up with the bustle and roar of downtown news hawking, and he took a paper route in the suburbs. This turned out to be an injudicious decision. "In the words of my friend John Barrymore," he once said, "it was the winter of my discontent." The trouble could be laid to dogs. Fields once estimated, after careful work with a pencil, that he was bitten on an average of every six houses. He added that the figures were misleading, since only one out of every five or six houses harbored a dog. Dogs would knock off their dinners, taking chances of losing bones to transients, and cross the street to bite him. They would detour around people vastly more substantial in order to fall upon the boy. Alva Johnston, in his profile on Fields in *The New Yorker,* offered what is doubtless the accurate explanation of this prejudicial treatment. "Fields can give the impression to men that he is a highly respectable fellow," Johnston said, "but he cannot give that impression to dogs. Once a tramp always a tramp, as far as dogs are concerned. Looking right through his fine clothes and synthetic dignity, they see the former hobo."

Fields made a studied attempt to cultivate dogs, largely in the interest of self-preservation, but it failed miserably. He tried every known method to avoid irritating them. He let sleeping dogs lie, but they bit him during bad dreams. He ignored barking dogs, and they bit him in the middle of sentences. He found dogs with bad names consistently dangerous. Dogs picked on Fields throughout his life, but he never gave up hope of an entente. One time, when he was in a California sanitarium and vastly bored, he read a newspaper item about a dog that had been "arrested" for drunkenness. The pet lived in the back end of a saloon and, prompted by some frantically whimsical customers, had fallen into careless habits. One evening, after the dog had been hitting it up, a customer, for a lark, called a patrolman, who led it off to jail. Fields phoned the saloon and expressed concern over the dog's plight. "Bring it out here to the sanitarium," he said to the saloon owner. "I want to enroll the poor fellow in Alcoholics Anonymous." When the owner and the dog arrived, several reporters and a *Life* photographer were in attendance. After downing a highball, Fields lectured the dog sternly, while the reporters took notes and the photographer recorded the lesson for posterity. But the pictures never appeared in *Life;* Fields' illness had been so severe that he was unphotogenic.

Later, when he recovered, the incident disturbed his sense of humanity. He arranged to have the dog adopted by some friends in the country.

CHAPTER FIVE

FIELDS ENJOYED TELLING about his first juggling engagement. He said the episode prevented him from becoming a Methodist. He said further that it illustrated what could be bought in Philadelphia for fifteen cents in 1891.

He and a boy he'd hired as stooge attended the annual outdoor strawberry festival of the First Methodist Church, which had promised to pay him thirty cents if he would do some juggling tricks. Approaching the neighborhood, Fields, with an air of professional elegance, was carrying a cane and the stooge was carrying the paraphernalia—three hats, five tennis balls, and three cigar boxes. A brisk rain started in as they sighted the church, and at the door the elder deacon told him that the festival would be held inside. Fields generously agreed to these arrangements and started in, followed by his porter.

"I'm sorry," said the deacon, "but you'll have to leave the cigar boxes behind."

"Why is that, my good fellow?" Fields asked.

"Because smoking is a sin," said the deacon.

"The boxes are empty," said Fields, opening the lids and showing him.

"That makes no difference to the Lord," replied the deacon.

"If you'll pardon us a moment, your worship," said Fields, withdrawing to the sidewalk, "my associate and I will confer." They put their heads together, and a few moments later Fields looked up and said, "If it will patch things up with the Lord, these boxes never contained tobacco—they were made especially for me."

The deacon thought it over, then admitted them. In the course of the evening, following recitations of "Crossing the Bar" and "The Gypsy's Curse" by a daughter of the organist, Fields did his juggling. Afterward, catching the deacon stoking at the refreshment table, he asked for his thirty cents. "Not now," said the deacon. "Later." Four additional times in the next two hours, Fields caught up with the deacon, tugged at his frock, and requested payment. The answer was always, "Not now. Wait till after the benediction."

Finally, a little impatient, and determined to limit his future church work to Baptists, Fields got his stooge and went out to the foyer, which was filled with umbrellas. Nobody noticed the boys, since a basso was rocking the building with a rendition of "Asleep in the Deep."

"Let's collect our wages," said Fields, and began to load up. Between them they carried out thirty-one umbrellas. Fields was considering a second trip, but the stooge maintained that the head deacon, though overweight, had the rangy build of a stepper, and they decided not to take a chance. An hour later they sold the thirty-one umbrellas at a downtown hockshop for a total of a dollar twenty cents. Then they boarded a streetcar, rode to the end of the line, entered a restaurant, and had the following meal for fifteen cents apiece: Steak, chicken, potatoes, beans, applesauce, peach pie, cheese, milk and coffee.

Fields could never tell this anecdote often enough. When he reached its end, he would dwell lovingly on the itemized dinner. Then, incensed at the appalling change in conditions, he would retire to the kitchen and bawl out his cook, having somehow become convinced that the whole thing was her fault.

Early in the spring after his fourteenth birthday, Fields read a notice in a Philadelphia newspaper about the opening of an amusement park, variously called "Plymouth Park" and "Flynn and Grant Park," at nearby Norristown, Pennsylvania. According to the ad, the management was negotiating for some of the most celebrated talent on two continents. Fields interpreted this as a clear call to action. He spent sixty cents for a round-trip ticket on a carline, and rode out to make application. He said later he was by no means surprised that the management hired him promptly. However, when he inquired about his salary, the manager fell into a violent coughing fit, and Fields withdrew. He returned in two weeks for the gala opening and performed several tricks he had perfected. "I was nervous," he wrote a friend long afterward. "I wasn't sure Norristown was quite ready for me." His contribution was well received, and the park retained him on an indefinite basis. At that time Fields' routines were similar to those of the Byrne Brothers, whose act he had frankly imitated. Among other things, he juggled five tennis balls, periodically pretending that one was getting away from him, and catching it, with comic gestures, as it flew off at an angle. Another trick involved the use of three hats, which he kept putting on his head, knocking off, and spinning into the air, meanwhile fixing his face in alternate expressions of abstraction, bafflement, dismay and belligerence, as the hats seemingly refused to obey.

Fields, by now, had become practiced at a phase of juggling whose value rested more upon humor than on skill. In this period he was a remarkable all-around juggler and he had also learned an elementary but significant truth: though juggling was enjoyed by nearly everybody, it had to be different to be memorable. Fields introduced a fresh note into his tricks: he made them funny. He developed a genius for the conscious error, the retrieved blunder. As the San Francisco *Examiner* was to note, a few years afterward, "It is impossible to tell whether Fields makes real or fake mistakes in his juggling. He will drop a hat apparently by accident in the middle of some difficult feat and then catch it by another apparently accidental movement. It is all so smooth and effortless." Though he was to carry juggling to heights previously unknown, he never lost his fondness for fumbling. Many years later, when giving large dinner parties, Fields liked to stand at the head of his table and serve. After filling a plate, preferably a comparative stranger's, he would start to hand it down the line, and then drop it, provoking a loud, concerted gasp. With consummate nonchalance he would catch it just off the floor, without interrupting whatever outrageous anecdote he was relating at the moment.

A good many of Fields' juggling stunts, during his Norristown connection, involved flipping up a slender object, such as a yardstick, and catching it, balanced by one end, on a finger, a foot, or his forehead. As a result of the painful, man-killing practice he often described subsequently, Fields at fourteen was probably as good at this form of juggling as anybody in the world. The cigar boxes, which he had first taken to using only because they were available and free, were far from conventional juggling material, but they were to become symbolic of his art. At this time he had only begun to exploit them; later he was to perfect a routine with cigar boxes that nobody else was ever able to duplicate.

Most of Fields' materials were makeshift. "I evolved a trick to use small cups on the ends of rods," he told one of the Paramount publicity men in 1926. "I caught small balls in the cups and continued juggling in the meantime. If I'd had any money I would have bought this kind of stuff in places that supplied professionals, but I had to improvise. I made the rods out of pieces of broomstick. I stole the cups off an oil burner—they had them on there to cap the flames. A friend of mine who lived in a foundry drilled holes in the cups and fastened them to the broomsticks. All my equipment was put together in this same general fashion."

At the end of his first week at the amusement park, Fields received details about his salary. The manager called him in, complimented him on a brilliant performance, and produced five dollars. The manager added that, despite the deceptively large crowds, business had been slow. While Fields was unsuccessfully trying to resolve the logic of this statement, the manager deducted one dollar and fifty cents from his salary as "agent's commission." Fields went to a dressing tent to do some ciphering. At length he worked it out that, if he excluded meals, he was losing only ten cents a week on the engagement, counting carfare and commission, and that, barring some emergency like illness or apprehension by the Methodists, he could juggle professionally nearly all summer. As to the nest egg, he figured he would be spending it in a good cause.

Before Fields had exhausted his capital performing at Plymouth Park, he had a stroke of fortune. On the bill with him were two Germans, teeterboard experts, who had taken a fancy to his work. In the middle of the summer they quit to accept an offer from Fortescue's Pier, in Atlantic City, and they urged Fields to go along. Fortescue's was a pleasure dome of imposing grandeur, compared to Plymouth Park, and Fields was reluctant to take the step. Among other things, he complained that he had no costumes, or even a change of clothing, except for a hunting shirt that had formerly belonged to the blacksmith. The Germans offered to buy him an alternate pair of trousers, but he refused to accept charity. In the next few days Fields pondered this opportunity. Then he hit on a shift in billing that would solve everything. He would drop his simple title of "Whitey, the Boy Wonder," alter his name slightly, and bill himself as "W. C. Fields, the Tramp Juggler." In this way he could walk onto any stage without having to change clothes.

The Germans agreed that this was an inspired idea, and Fields bade farewell to the Norristown manager, who retained the balance of his salary, a dollar and eighty cents, under the heading of "severance commission." Before he left Philadelphia, Fields had another inspiration. He decided to notify all his friends of his impending flight from the town of his nativity and hold a monster benefit for himself. He paid a hostler two dollars for the use of a stable; then he went to work on the invitations. Fields never slacked any chore that was likely to pay off, and he concentrated with real vigor on the benefit. Not only did he inform his friends, his acquaintances, and a number of near-strangers, but he passed the word to bullies who had whipped him, bartenders who had regularly tossed him out of saloons, and a good portion of the city's police force, whose knowledge of Fields was confined largely to his heels. The evening arrived, and the benefit went off on schedule. Everybody agreed that it was a whacking success, and somewhat out of the ordinary as benefits went. Fields juggled a lot of equipment he had stolen from members of the audience, made several speeches in which he ran Philadelphia down mercilessly, laying squarely on its shoulders the blame for losing him, and peddled a kind of punch he had made out of tap water, rotten lemons, and two quarts of peach brandy he'd found in a cellar. Then he passed the hat. The audience responded with surprising generosity. Although his

friends sprang forward loyally, the heaviest contributions
came from the bartenders and the police. They'd had so
much trouble with him that several of them sentimentally
declared they would be glad to send him a weekly remit-
tance if he'd put up guarantees never to return. Fields
thanked them for coming and, as they filed out, shook
hands with each and every one. He said afterward that the
closing minutes had netted him two watches, a gold pen-
knife, and fourteen dollars in change, but he later denied
this. In any case, he took in, altogether, around a hundred dollars, which was the most money he had ever seen.
For 1893, it was a sensational benefit, and Fields discussed
staying on a week longer and holding another, but the hostler said he didn't think it would be safe.

The acquisition of sudden wealth made it possible for
Fields to consider fancy costumes for his act. He went
into several stores, to inspect different combinations, and
finally decided to buy a new street outfit and cling to
the tramp idea for juggling. Though the ensemble he selected cost him eight dollars, he felt that he had picked up
a bargain. It included a black-and-white checked suit, a
pair of light tan shoes, and a gray derby of peculiarly low
and rakish design. The secondhand clothing store in which
he located these items was indifferently lighted, and when
Fields came out he cleared up the continental aspect of
the derby—it had apparently been sat on by some person
of excessive tonnage. In another shop he bought an enormous piece of yellow luggage, and when he had gathered up
his few other belongings, such as his cane, his tennis balls,
his cigar boxes, and his hunting shirt, he left for Atlantic
City, riding in a day coach and smoking a big black cigar.
Philadelphia's loss, as he had hinted at the benefit, was
the world's gain. A great comedian was on his way.

When Fields reached Fortescue's Pier, which housed a
beer garden and a restaurant, he searched out the Germans and made application for a job. Looking him over, the
management was dubious. The boy was a colorful sight,
but he seemed young for the big time. By happy chance a
friend of the Germans', Sliding Billy Watson, already a favorite and soon to become legendary, was on the bill. The
Germans arranged a meeting, and Fields went through his

routine. "You've got a great act, my boy," Watson told him. "You're going to be famous." Fields agreed, and awaited developments. On Watson's advice, the manager of Fortescue's signed the juggler on, but with reservations. His duties transcended ordinary juggling; besides doing his tricks, he was required, by contract, to swim out and drown several times daily. "Iss a great chance," one of the Germans told him. "You haff arrived." Though skeptical, Fields accepted the job. He soon found that major-league vaudeville was not child's play. By comparison, the stint at Plymouth Park seemed like a vacation. At the end of his first day's work, he was in a state of near collapse. Activities on the Pier had begun early, with the arrival of the first swimmers on the adjoining beach. Fields and his colleagues went through their routines a couple of times, and then interest slacked off. At this point, prodded by the manager, Fields changed to a bathing suit, swam out about a hundred yards, sank, arose, thrashed around, and began to bawl for help. Fortescue's life guards were prompt and efficient; he was towed in fast and the bilge pumped out. The incident attracted large crowds, and shortly afterwards Fields resumed juggling. A drowning appeared to have a salutary effect on the Atlantic City crowds; it made them both hungry and thirsty. Fields' double-barreled offering was repeated every hour or so until late in the evening, at which time he staggered damply to a room he'd rented and fell into a troubled, aqueous sleep.

One of the inducements of this job, in Fields' eyes, had been the substantial salary of ten dollars a week and, in the trade term, "cakes." All in all, it looked like a pleasant situation, and the employees were an agreeable group. Fields and a cornetist in the band, a youngster named Frank Tinney, met frequently to discuss their ambitions. Each assured the other that he would become famous, and, as it turned out, they were both right. The fare in the beer garden was digestible; also, the artists, including the drowner, were permitted to gorge at will. Do what he would, however, Fields was unable to pry any cash out of the manager. Like the head of Plymouth Park, the man wailed steadily about business, which seemed, at least superficially, to be bustling. "I need a dollar to pay for my room," Fields told him at the end of a week. "If I had a dollar clear, I'd hire another drowner," the manager replied. Then he promised to settle up by the next week-end. When that time rolled around, Fields was in reduced mental and physical circumstances. For one thing, he was annoyed about the absence of pay; for another, his co-ordination had gone sour. The trouble was easily diagnosed: briefly, the boy was too waterlogged to juggle. His situation looked desperate, and when the manager welshed again, he quit. For two days Fields dried out in his room; then he went down the boardwalk a short way and got a different job. The pay was nominally the same, and his duties were entirely landlocked.

His experience at Fortescue's made Fields permanently hostile toward swimming. He also liked to say it turned him against water in general. He once told a reporter, inaccurately, that he had never taken a drink of water after his last encounter with the life guards at Atlantic City. "I didn't need any more," he said. "I had it stored up, like a camel." During the last quarter of his life, Fields occasionally rented houses that had swimming pools. He kept the pools filled for company, but he never went near them himself. When people inquired about this curious behavior, he'd say, "I once drowned twelve times a day for two weeks. Would *you* like to swim if you'd drowned one hundred and sixty-eight times?"

CHAPTER SIX

FIELDS' NEW JOB was at a neighboring pier which was also a kind of staging point for traveling troupes. The proprietor lacked the progressive ideas of Fortescue, operating, for one thing, without a drowner, but he was deployed over a wider area. He tried out acts at the pier, then, if he could talk them into it, he sent them on the road. His employment of Fields opened up new and dismal adventures for the boy juggler. The pier was, in a way, a springboard, though situated, as it were, beside a dry pool.

Rested and dehydrated, Fields was an immediate success in his new situation. His co-ordination returned and his spirits brightened. It was not long before he was tapped for a road tour.

"You're too big for the pier," the manager told him. "I'm going to put you in one of my traveling burlesque companies. Very high-class, artistic-type entertainment."

Exhibiting the business acumen that had caused him to score so heavily with the benefit, Fields replied, "What's the salary?"

"Eighteen a week, transportation, and the best of lodgings," said the manager. "You'll be booked out of my New York office."

Fields joined the company in New York and the members headed in the general direction of the Middle West. For people in a glamorous profession they were not overly imposing. The company manager was a ferret-faced little man named Hawkins, who, Fields said later, was never able to look him in the eye. Impartial accounts indicate that, in this matter, Hawkins is deserving of some sympathy; during the weeks they spent together, Fields tried to look him in the eye every ten or fifteen minutes, to complain about conditions. The villain of the troupe, an elderly wreck named Harley Gibbons, was generally too drunk to go onstage, and Fields took his part, appearing in a mustache fashioned from dyed hemp, and carrying a blacksnake whip. Various other members of the company were often indisposed, for one reason or another. The ingénue, Fields said, was frequently held up through the absent-minded misplacing of her upper plate. She probably did not have, as he usually added, her two grandchildren along on the tour. Somewhere in New Jersey, the woman who played the mother parts was jailed on an immorality charge, and Fields also took over her role. If tired, he spoke her lines with his usual wheezy twang and was occasionally critically assailed in communities of outstanding culture. Throughout most of New Jersey this criticism took the form of overripe tomatoes; for some reason it switched to cabbages as they entered Ohio.

It was often difficult to separate the chaff from the wheat in Fields' reports of his travels. The best authorities agree, however, that on his first road tour he did a great many things besides juggle. Contrary to many published reports, he accompanied his tricks with a monologue in this period. It varied from day to day, depending on his luck at stealing jokes. In small towns he cultivated a practice of visiting public libraries and reading up on humorous literature. When he ran across anything worthwhile, he added it to his patter. Also, he said, he lifted jokes indiscriminately from rival acts. When confronted with these thefts, as he frequently was, Fields would draw up with such injured truculence that the accuser usually retired in confusion, unconvinced as to who was actually guilty. "Bill, stole a good many of his later vaudeville routines from Harry Tate, the London comedian," said Gregory La Cava, who directed several of Fields' early movies. "He would steal any act he could get away with, but if somebody tried to borrow something from him, he went crazy." Once, in the *Vanities*, Fields stood in the wings watching Ben Blue, who, warming up to his work, unexpectedly went into a routine he'd done years before. When he came off the stage, Fields grabbed him by the collar and knocked him down. "You stole that from me!" he roared. Blue called him a liar and got witnesses to vouch for the originality of his material. Fields then realized that Blue was merely stealing back something Fields had originally stolen from him, and he made no further fuss.

On the tour, Fields complained steadily until they reached Kent, Ohio, where the manager abandoned the company and returned to New York. "I'm going in for a conference," he told the players, whose salaries had not been paid since they left. "Your hotel bills are taken care of until I get back." Half an hour after his departure, the hotel clerk came up with a bellboy and put the company's luggage in the street. He said the manager had left an unpaid bill of fifteen dollars and seventy-five cents. Once again Fields found himself adrift in cheerless surroundings, but he reported later that on the whole he was glad; he said he had been playing so many different parts that he was beginning to develop a split personality. He had taken to muttering fragments of dialogue to himself as he walked along the streets. He would pull up on a busy corner, cry, "Oh, you will, will you?" hiss, "And who's to stop me?" then continue, with the crudest kind of gestures:

"Oh, you rotter, you unutterable cad!"

"Sticks and stones may break my bones, but names will never hurt me."

"Oh, God! if my brother, Ellsworth Boynton, the heavy-weight wrestling champion of the world, who, if you recall, was mentioned in Act One as being expected back momentarily from London, were only here!"

"Ha, ha, ha, ha, ha, ha!"

"Help! Police! Police!"

Fields often collected quite a crowd with these inadvertent scenes, and he sensed that professional-looking men, with satchels, occasionally eyed him speculatively. He felt that the time had come to return to pure juggling. Though he was relieved to be free, his situation was critical. He had started the trip with a tidy stake, the remnant of his benefit fund plus a couple of weeks' salary from Atlantic City. But he had been lending money, at usurious rates, to the manager, who was expecting a large check from New York at each stop. A business plunge of this kind was foreign to Fields' principles, and he was both financially and spiritually hurt by its failure. "The bastard offered me 50 per cent interest," he related to a friend. "It was a shabby way to treat a boy in his teens."

Fields never forgot the lesson he learned in Kent. In after life nobody could borrow from him. Now and then he gave some needy person money, on the quiet, but he would not lend as much as fifty cents to his closest friend. One afternoon on the Paramount lot, William Le Baron told a number of movie actors about a once-popular star who was currently down and out. Then he took up a collection. Fields withdrew to a shady corner, sat down, and watched the proceedings with a disapproving eye. Everybody expressed sympathy and contributed generously, Maurice Chevalier and Bing Crosby handing over a hundred dollars apiece. When Le Baron reached Fields, he said, "How much shall I put you down for, Bill?"

"Not a dime," snarled Fields.

"Why not?" said Le Baron. "If you're that damned cheap, I'll put up a hundred for you."

Fields was so annoyed by Le Baron's generous stand that he finally came forward with a hundred dollars. But he grumbled about it all the rest of the week.

Another time one of his best friends, Charley Mack, of the blackface team of Moran and Mack, somehow found himself detained in Syracuse for nonpayment of alimony. "Please send me $500," he wired Fields. "I'm in jail up here." Mack waited eagerly for his old pal's reply, which arrived with heart-warming promptness. "If it's a good jail, I'll join you," Fields told him.

Stranded in Kent in the dead of winter, with six dollars, Fields appraised his situation carefully. His findings were negative; the situation had nothing to recommend it. He borrowed a sled from a group of boys coasting on a hill, and hauled his baggage from the hotel to the railroad station, a distance of half a mile. Then he went about trying to sell an overcoat he had recently acquired in another second-hand store. A pimply youth in a saloon, with many a leer and wink, bid two dollars for the coat on condition that Fields introduce him to the company's ingénue. Fields explained this situation to the lady, who agreed to help him out. Either her presence or the beer he had been drinking exerted a keen aphrodisiac effect on the youth, for as soon as he met her he tried to drag her upstairs in the hotel. Fields was obliged to knock the fellow down, thus forfeiting the sale of the coat. Later, quizzed about the cause of the trouble, Fields said, "He was trying to get her to adopt him."

Back in the saloon, Fields at last sold the coat, for two dollars, and proceeded to the station. And there he had an experience that affected him profoundly. When he reached the ticket window, he asked the fare to New York, and the agent, an elderly, gray-haired man wearing steel spectacles, quoted it at ten dollars and a few cents.

"Well, I guess I'm stuck," said Fields (as he repeated the conversation in later years). "I've got eight dollars."

"Aren't you one of that play-acting bunch?" asked the agent.

Fields replied that he was, then awaited the familiar sneer.

"People don't put much trust in you folks, do they?" said the agent.

"We're used to it," Fields told him.

The agent closed the window and came around into the waiting room, where he took a ten-dollar bill out of his pocket. "Son," he said, handing the bill to Fields, "I've always wondered what there was to that story. When you get a little ahead, send this back."

It was one of the few acts of gratuitous kindness Fields could remember in the fifteen years of his life, and it pierced his case-hardened shell. He sat down on a bench and cried.

Despite his most persevering efforts, it was two years before he could repay the debt. On Christmas Eve, 1896, when he had just received an advance of twenty dollars from Fred Irwin, the manager of a reputable road show, he mailed two ten-dollar bills to Kent. In an accompanying, grateful note, he explained that one was for interest. Then he went to a free soup kitchen on New York's west side and stood in line for a Christmas dinner.

CHAPTER SEVEN

"FOR A COUPLE of years after I made my start, I was dead broke practically all the time," Fields told an interviewer for the *American* magazine in 1926. He was referring to his middle teens, years that most boys later look back upon as their happiest. It would be hard to exaggerate the wretchedness of Fields' life in this period. He tramped to the booking offices, he starved, he froze, and he became so threadbare he was ashamed to ask for jobs. Having an understandable prejudice against the outfit that had disconnected him in Ohio, he avoided its office for weeks, hoping for something better. Once during this interval he signed on with a cheap circus, but his niche was ignominious. The management had a juggler, a very jealous man, and Fields, the erstwhile darling of Fortescue's, the most prolific drowner in the memory of Atlantic City, and the majority of a road-show cast, took work as a peg boy. His duties consisted mainly of having his fingers crushed by roustabouts swinging mauls. His hands were heavily bandaged; he wore gauze as Eskimos wear gloves—constantly and with resignation. By nagging his bosses, he finally ascended to drum carrier, and his fingers healed. His enjoyment was intense when he wangled this job, but he found that it, like holding pegs, was imperfect. The trouble was that the circus manager was a rhythm lover and, though exceptionally stingy, had gone all out for a drum. It was quite an instrument—huge, weighty, resonant, an easy standout in a rackety band. In eastern New Jersey, on a clear day, according to Fields, its booming was clearly audible across the Hudson.

In a short time the boy was able to hear only disturbances like thunder, explosions, and collapsing buildings. His sleeping became spotty; at night, though the songs were ended, the drum continued to boom. After two weeks of this, he concluded that neither deafness nor lunacy was preferable to mangled hands, and he volunteered for a comedown. The management, rhythm-happy but understanding, assigned him to a trio of discontented elephants. Throughout his life Fields never really cared for elephants, and he felt that the three he met in the circus were especially difficult. Also, he said, despite their size they were narrow-minded. Fields had a trick of absently releasing mice in their area, and the elephants took it personally, retaliating in various ways. They tripped Fields as he was carrying water; they doused him when he'd spruced up for a date with the snake charmer; they gulped water steadily and blew it on the ground; and, worst of all, they kept nudging him. Walking between them with a pail, Fields would be rocked off balance by the bull; then one of the females would close in and bounce him back. A moment later he would find himself dangerously bracketed, and he would bawl for aid. The association grew into a continuous series of practical jokes, with Fields, as he acknowledged, both outnumbered and outthought.

Studying them, Fields decided that the elephants were professional expatriates; also, he believed they didn't like show business. "Why don't you go back where you came from if you don't like it here?" he said he used to yell at them. Both he and the elephants were elated when the show's juggler found himself, in addition to his working materials, with a case of measles on his hands. Fields, through almost tearful persuasion, succeeded to the post, even though his equipment was stored in a New York loft. He juggled alone for three weeks, then he was joined by the stricken performer, who had dropped the measles. After that they juggled together. One time, trying to recall those days for an interviewer, Fields said that his act had centered on his juggling a lamp, a silk hat, a cigar, two white mice and an orange. He added that in some New Jersey city the S.P.C.A. had made him give up the mice. He was always loyal to old friendships, he said, and he freed the mice near the elephant pen.

It was getting along toward the cold weather now, and the show holed up. Without much reluctance Fields returned to New York. He liked the circus' air of unqualified fraud, but he considered the business a dead-end for a juggler. In later years, however, he set up as an authority on both circuses and carnivals and used material from them in his work. In doing the stage show *Poppy,* which had a carnival story, and in making the pictures *Sally of the Sawdust* and *Poppy,* both of which grew out of the play, Fields was a terrible nuisance about expounding carnival lore. When he first walked onto the movie set of *Poppy,* he examined an equestrian ring suspiciously and called for a yardstick. Then he took the ring's diameter and yelled, "This thing's a yard too wide. Pull it in." The production group went into annoyed conference. "The diameter of circus rings in ancient Rome was fourteen yards, nine inches," Fields said testily. "That size has prevailed everywhere in the world since then, and we're not going to depart from it. It's a matter of universal superstition. When the corrections are finished, you'll find me in my dressing room." A group of disgusted carpenters rebuilt the ring, and the cast re-convened.

Fields' untriumphant re-entry into New York found him no wealthier than he had been when he left. In fact, except for a pair of mohair trousers which he said he had stolen from the half man, half woman (who was currently dressing feminine) he was in precisely the same condition. He made a quick round of the booking offices, was offered a job, at no salary, as understudy to the rear end of a skin act, and finally dragged himself to the office of his former employer. The man was glad to see him; he reminisced about the good times in Atlantic City and expressed regret over the recent incident in Ohio, ascribing it to a knavish unit manager. The man had left the firm, he said, and Fields would be welcomed into another wandering troupe, with a three-dollar salary advance. There was no mention of back pay.

The players left town in a week, this time taking a more southerly route. Fields juggled, played small parts, sang, danced, lectured, filled in for absentees, and, by degrees, found his job almost identical to his last stint with the company. But the new unit manager was vastly more satisfactory than the fugitive from Kent. Although he never paid anybody any salary, he looked Fields in the eye without flinching and his manner was frankly larcenous. He put the players at ease; they knew he was going to rob them and wasted no time in idle speculation. His real talent, then, lay in his ability to remove worry from the unit, leaving the emphasis on artistry. He was popular with all hands. "A capital fellow, Shawn," they'd say. "A real, dyed-in-the-wool rogue, a skunk of the old school." Several of the cast, including Fields, placed wagers on Shawn's probable desertion, one fixing it near Trenton, another making it Reading, and a third declaring in favor of Pittsburgh. Fields kept piling change on Punxsatawney, a town whose name he liked (and which he used, intermittently, forever afterward), and lost heavily. The manager did not, in fact, disappear until they reached Wheeling, and then only after he'd bought a new suit, a certain giveaway of his intentions. Everybody agreed that it was a sporting gesture, and, using the past tense, as of a cadaver, they spoke highly of him.

Fields got back to New York by riding the rods of the Baltimore and Ohio Railroad. It was an uncomfortable trip, for winter, and in one place, at least, he came within a shade of freezing. The train hit a flooded spot in Pennsylvania, and the boy was drenched. Since the train was doing fifty or sixty miles an hour, there was no opportunity for him to get down, and when he did, a couple of yardmen had to chop him down. He was taken to a railroad shack, where he eventually thawed out, although for a couple of hours a local physician was talking enthusiastically about amputations. Arrived in New York, Fields made another swing of the booking places, and this time he had better luck. A berth was open at the old Globe Museum, on Third Avenue; the headless lady, while walking on the icy pavements, had fallen and fractured her skull. Her stall was fitted up for Fields to juggle in. While the alterations progressed, he had additional good fortune. A heavy snow fell on the city, and he obtained several days' work shoveling, at twenty cents an hour.

Life in the museum was stimulating and congenial. He worked in close association with a ventriloquist, a bearded lady, and a fire-eater. The four took lunch together, generally going to a nearby Mexican restaurant to accommodate the fire-eater, who favored warm, spicy foods. They talked over plans for success, agreeing that, no matter where fate directed them, they would continue to keep in touch and write round letters at Christmastime. A reporter, moved by this story, once asked Fields if they had stuck to their resolve. "None of us ever sent so much as a post card," Fields told him.

In one way the museum was troublesome: it was inadequately heated and the fire-eater was the only one of the performers who could stay comfortable. Fields was getting ten dollars a week for his tricks, and collecting it, but he was so continuously frostbitten that he finally moved up to a flea circus on Fourteenth Street, which had a coal stove. There, in comparative warmth and battling the fleas for pre-eminence, he practiced his delicate art. He was developing into a master juggler, but he was, he felt, at a financial stalemate. Notwithstanding the low scale paid to fleas, which were then unorganized, the circus's profits were modest, and Fields could never jockey his price above the

standard ten dollars. When an opportunity came, through
an impresario named Jim Fulton, to join another traveling
burlesque, he snapped it up. Altogether, it was a substantial rise; the salary was twenty-five dollars a week and
was actually paid now and then when business was unusually flush.

Like the managers of most Eastern road companies, Fulton took his troupe into the Middle West. He was a man of
some artistic integrity, a fact that militated in favor of
Fields. Whereas on previous hauls the boy juggler had
been required to supplement his tricks by acting in various
capacities, he was now relieved of these additional duties.
After one performance, in Zanesville, Ohio, when Fields
was asked to fill in as the love-smitten daughter of a hardware merchant, Fulton gave it up as a bad job. As nearly
as Fields could diagnose the trouble, his raucous bellowing
that "I must think of my father—I must! I must!" sounded unconvincing. Also, Fulton indicated, the fake yellow
curls looked odd in conjunction with Fields' nose, which,
though not unlovely in this period, was recognizably mascu-
line. Added to this, at a point in the action where the
daughter had nothing much to do, being required only to
stand by while her father had it out with a yarn salesman,
she pulled three cigars out of her tunic and accomplished
some extremely spirited sleight of hand, misplacing the
scene's emphasis, in the opinion of the manager.

Fields spoke of his work at this time to a reporter, Mary
B. Mullett, in the middle 1920s: "You see, although my
specialty was juggling, I used it only as a means to an end.
I didn't just stand up and toss balls, knives, plates, and
clubs. I invented little acts, which would seem like episodes out of real life; and I used my juggling to furnish
the comedy element.

"Somehow, even though I was only a kid, I had sense
enough to know that I must work my mind and not just my
hands. If I hadn't realized that, I'd be laid on the shelf today. People would be saying, 'Bill Fields? Oh, yes! he used
to be a juggler, didn't he?'"

Although his role as all-around understudy was ended,
Fields sometimes took part in burlesque skits involving
several comedians. Fulton's "burlesque" was unlike the burlesque of later years; more properly, his unit could have

been called a repertory company. Its usual presentation was an ordinary two- or three-act play, one of the damp, anguished melodramas then in flower. Between acts, Fields did his specialties. As a change of pace Fulton on some nights gave a series of comic skits, out of which general entertainment grew the muscular, ribald burlesque of today. For the most part, his players were quiet and well-behaved. Fields' personal life in this time of his eighteenth year alternated between sequestration and public expansiveness, the latter usually accompanied by beer. From taking a glass of beer as an excuse to gorge on free lunch, he had grown fond of an occasional session during which he drank quite a few glasses in a row and eschewed the food. Fields was to know stretches late in life when he insisted on eschewing food thoroughly; he sometimes eschewed it for days on end. With Fulton, he either sat in his room and read books or repaired to a saloon and foregathered with the local bloods. If the troupe had a rosy, accommodating ingénue, Fields also devoted many evenings to dalliance; he was fond of girls and was, in turn, popular with them, although they often complained about his stinginess. As a general thing, when a girl in Fields' presence expressed a desire for refreshment, he took it to mean beer, or water, and he had no compunctions about dining, à deux, in a dog wagon. His ceaseless bout with privation had given him great respect for money. To a man in the Fulton company who inquired as to his ultimate ambition on earth, Fields replied, "To make a thousand dollars a week." As he said it, his eyes were fixed on that bright, personal horizon and he seemed to know that he would be there, on some secret schedule of his own, a few years hence.

Early photographs of the young juggler reveal him as almost handsome, with a full head of light-colored hair parted near the middle, a firm, self-contained, indomitable line of a mouth, and humorous, quizzical eyes. Only in Fields' eyes could one read the vast, pervasive sense of the absurdity in humans that was to shape all his work; in the rest of his face was written the hard score of his fight for survival. Fields grew to be quite vain about having his picture taken. He was often peremptory with photographers about which exposures he wanted developed. In general, he liked views that glamorized him and rejected ones that had a searching or definitive quality. A print that he gave to close friends during his Hollywood years shows him holding a cane somewhat in the manner of the late Jimmy Walker, flawlessly barbered, and exhibiting the filmy stare of a young actor approaching the worn balcony of the Capulets. "Is that the cane you used in your juggling acts, Bill?" a recipient of the print once asked him, and Fields replied with considerable heat, "Juggling, hell! That stick's been in the family for generations." Fields' touchiness about pictures grew out of the fact that he was repeatedly caricatured in his tramp costume. As a rule the artist wrote some such caption as "The Tramp Juggler" or "Skillful Comic," but too often, in Fields' opinion, the picture carried the simple identification—"W. C. Fields." It made him look as if he'd just rolled into town off a cattle train, and he was convinced that people took it as his habitual state of dishevelment. "This kind of thing might get back to Philadelphia and ruin me socially," he once said.

It was on Fulton's tour that comic juggling got its first real impetus in this country. Like his namesake with the steamboat, Fulton was to open new vistas with a traveling unit. Whereas Robert had gone upstream with the *Clermont,* Jim moved overland with Fields. During their association, which lasted eighteen months, Fields became popular out of all proportion to his theoretical salary and his billing. "The best act in the first part of the program last evening was that of W. C. Fields, a juggler with a nice, quiet manner, a relief after the noisy and laborious team of Greene and Werner," read an item of the period in the Cleveland *Plain Dealer.* Critics everywhere showered praise on the boy, and he began to sense a gigantic maladjustment. Back in New York, after the tour, he took steps to correct this. When Fred Irwin, whose road shows occupied a comparatively exalted standing in the theater, offered him a job, Fields said, "I'll have to have thirty-five dollars a week."

"Why, that's outrageous!" cried Irwin. "You haven't been getting anywhere near that."

"I was getting twenty-five dollars with Fulton," said Fields, "and my work has improved exactly 40 per cent."

"Yes, but there's a difference," Irwin told him, and added, with familiar theatrical logic, "you see, I pay my salaries. Everybody knows that. You ought to take less."

"Thirty-five a week," said Fields, secure in the knowledge of his new popularity.

Irwin capitulated, but he was marked for further woe. He and Fields had no contract—a system that managers of that era favored. With Irwin, it was a precaution against an act's failing to come up to snuff; with other managers, it was a hedge against the awful possibility that a performer might turn unruly and demand to be paid, at which point he would be released for insubordination. Working conditions among players could scarcely have been worse. They were housed in the meanest of lodgings and fed at the boarding tables of parsimonious widows; they dressed in wind-swept cubbies overrun with rats; many nights they sat up in dingy coaches and did shows all the next day. Their social position was roughly similar to that of a condemned baby strangler—"decent people" drew aside to avoid touching them on the sidewalk. A popular joke of the time, conceived by an insensitive but humorous juvenile and destined to be much used, in variations, went as follows:

MOTHER (*to returning prodigal*): And what have you been doing all these years, Otis?

SON (*drawing himself up defensively*): I've been employed as an actor, Mother.

MOTHER (*with a loud shriek and near fainting*): Oh, my God! This is terrible! Your father and I thought you were a burglar!

As managers went, Irwin was a shining model of benevolence. But the time was the managers' heyday, and the best were none too good. Deserting a company of paupers in an unfriendly hamlet was regarded, at the worst, as mildly rude, or thoughtless; there was no real point of ethics involved. A manager's promise of salary was like a weatherman's promise of rain—sometimes it rained, more often it didn't. In any case, it was nobody's fault. Players accepted their lot stoically. They were in the business for the love of it, and, by and large, that's all they expected to get. This viewpoint, though widespread, could not accurately be applied to Fields. He stands up well among the great money-lovers of his day. In fact, few persons in any profession have ever had a more wholesome regard for a dollar. He realized that if audiences were cool to his act Irwin would drop him without a qualm, and he planned his campaign accordingly. As punishment for his greed, Irwin decreed that Fields should lead off the bill—an impossible spot for a juggler. Stragglers and program rustlers blurred those delicate climaxes so vital to the appreciation of precise sleight of hand. However, of the opening performance, in Newark, a critic wrote, "Easily the best act on Irwin's bill last night was the opener, an up-and-coming youngster named W. E. Fields. We'll keep an eye on you, Mr. Fields!" Fields was undisturbed by the fact that the critic misfired on his middle initial; it was five or six minutes after the paper hit the street when he appeared in Irwin's office.

"Seen the reviews?" he said pleasantly.

"That's a hard edition to make," said Irwin. "Most of the boys have to leave real early."

"It's here on page five," continued Fields. "Man says, 'Easily the best act——' "

"This is the minor league," Irwin assured him. "The real critics come later."

"I didn't get to finish," Fields said. "What I was about to say was, I need fifty a week."

Irwin howled like a man stricken, but he had little choice. He agreed to the fifty, and the tour proceeded. It went smoothly as far as Cincinnati, where a reporter for the *Inquirer* wrote, "Fields was a scream. Irwin has a real find there."

A few minutes after edition time, Fields, heavy with papers, sought out the manager again.

"Looked over the news, Fred?" he asked, having decided, democratically, on the given name.

"I never read the papers," said Irwin. "It gives me indigestion."

"Man says, 'Fields was a scream. Irwin has a real——' "

"What's on your mind, Bill?" said the manager, who believed in cutting to the heart of a situation.

"Seventy-five dollars," said Fields.

"You're a goddamned bandit," Irwin told him. "This is the last raise you get, if I have to disband the unit."

Fields clamorously affirmed that he had no further financial ambitions, and harmony reigned for weeks. In December of 1898 he wrote his mother a letter—her first news of him in eight years—and enclosed a ten-dollar bill. Thereafter, despite his monetary caution, he sent his mother at least ten dollars every week for the rest of her life. Many times on the road, he once said in a moment of rare confidence, he brooded about his former home life, feeling the greatest compassion for his mother in her rigorous grind. Besides sending her the ten-dollar allotment, he was to brighten her life in many ways during the next few years. And, as is not uncommon in hard-boiled people with a soft streak, he did it on the sly, loudly denying that he would lift a finger for his family.

In Akron, Ohio, near Kent, Fields telephoned his old benefactor, the ticket agent, and invited him to attend a performance. The man came over, bursting with pleasure and vindication, and took a strong paternal interest in the entire evening's proceedings, calling Fields "son," lending counsel to the manager, and escorting the girls back and forth between wings and their dressing rooms. "His pride in my success couldn't have been greater if I'd been his son," Fields later told a friend, Jim Tully, the writer. "Different members of the troupe entertained him and made him feel glad that he had once been kind to a member of their fraternity." For years afterward, whenever Fields was playing near Akron, he looked up the agent, and so did other show people. The risky benefaction proved to be reciprocal. Because of his connection with Fields, the agent got to be a big man in his town, the confidant of celebrities. Citizens of Kent having trips to make or freight to transport gave the railroad preferential treatment, mainly to catch up on the theater news. The town became a key point along the line, and the railroad raised the agent's wage.

Irwin's unit played to big business all through the Middle West. The troupe was a good one, with several skilled performers, some good material, and even two or three pretty girls. Irwin knew that he was rarely blessed; he had, besides these assets, a star without star billing—a youngster who was destined for greatness. As a boon of this kind, Fields gave mixed satisfaction. He was a restless boon, unconvinced that it was better to give than to receive. After a performance in Denver, when his act had been especially telling, a man for the *Post* wrote, "Fields was a knockout last night, a comic who reaches the heights of juggling perfection . . . it is said that the engagement of three days will be all too short for everybody to see this consummate artist."

"Fellow in the newspaper here was talking about the show," said Fields, when he reached Irwin. "Says 'Fields was a knockout last night, a comic who——' "

"No," said Irwin.

"I need some new equipment," said Fields. "I was thinking maybe if I had a hundred a week I could——"

"No," said Irwin. "We settled this thing in Cincinnati. You're not going to get another damned dime out of me!"

Fields found that, with a salary of a hundred dollars a week, his standard of living greatly improved and his outlook freshened. But he fell victim to the law of compensation. Though he could now afford many things previously denied him, he had a new set of worries. It was the old story of the uneasy head with the crown, the frightened Croesus. His money bothered him. He took to examining bills to make certain they were not counterfeit; further, he became suspicious of the Treasury. What if the Government fell? Would his greenbacks stand up under the new regime? Would they be viewed as tender in another land? Weighing everything, he found currency dubious and decided on conversion. After exchanging what bills he had, at the nearest bank, he asked Irwin to pay him in gold henceforward.

In 1896, on a dark night in San Francisco, with $210 in gold secreted in various recesses of his attire, Fields walked toward his hotel, much easier in his mind. As he rounded a vacant corner, he was struck with some heavy, blunt instrument—as the police later described it—and he slumped to the pavement. When he awoke, half an hour later, he found himself stripped of ore. There were drawbacks, he observed, even with the mother lode. In the words of a Nebraska orator of that year, he had been crucified on a cross of gold. Next payday he opened a small bank account, the first step in what was to develop into the most outlandish savings program in the history of banking.

Fields' days of want were over. The waif was behind him, caught up and transformed in the harsh converter of ambition. He was to have wistful moments about his boyhood, but it had slipped by without ever actually having existed. Almost from the beginning, he had known nothing but hardship and abuse. While his contemporaries frolicked through the leisurely time of their youth, he had fought for his life. That he came through at all was singular; that he came through with humor was evidence of courage and genius. But in the human a process of hardening can seldom be undone, and Fields was to keep his scars. The day never arrived when he was free from the ghost of poverty. And as is common with others, he wasted his worry on the least of his troubles, for his financial stress was ended, though his artistic and personal problems had scarcely begun. His tours with Irwin were the last of his nondescript connections. Vaudeville beckoned—the unknown road of a new medium stretched before him. For Fields it was a golden road and led to fame and fortune.

BOOK ONE: *Part Two*

CHAPTER EIGHT

AMERICAN VAUDEVILLE, the counterpart of English "variety," was somewhat younger than Fields, having been born in Boston in 1883. The circumstances of its birth are of moderate interest, as obstetrics goes. A circus employee, Benjamin Franklin Keith, growing tired of bouncing from town to town in wagons full of freaks and carnivora, rented an empty candy store in Boston and hung out a sign, "Gaiety Museum." His only excuses for this enterprise, his sole attractions, were Baby Alice, a midget weighing one and a half pounds, and a stuffed mermaid. Bostonians, a seafaring people, are presumably blasé about mermaids, for they gave the dummy very little time, but they flocked in with petty cash to see the midget. Keith was much encouraged by the success of his theater; he soon added to his cast a pair of comedians, Joe Weber and Lew Fields, and a chicken with a human face.

The bill being thus balanced, his theater continued to prosper. Keith was a restless, inventive man, and he branched out rapidly. He launched the idea of continuous performances, making it possible to pay stage entertainers more money than they could get in revues, and he took every step to beguile into his new medium all the talented performers of the day. In addition to being progressive, Keith had a bias against smut; as the new acts poured into his office, he gave them a good dry cleaning, then turned them over to Boston. This was partly instinct and partly caution. The city was, and is, known to be handy with its bans, and would doubtless have frowned on the smallest jokes about sex, even if uttered by a pound-and-a-half midget.

In 1885 Keith formed a company with Edward F. Albee to present at popular prices the startling new musical plays of Gilbert and Sullivan. The next year they began the real estate acquisitions that were to lead to the largest chain of theaters in the world. Their first purchases were the old museum in Providence, Low's opera house there, and the Bijou Theatre in Boston. They built a theater in Philadelphia. Their new form of amusement caught on and swept the country; by 1911, when Keith died, vaudeville was by a considerable margin the most widely attended stage entertainment in both this country and Canada. In 1928 it was estimated that, in the two countries, more than one thousand vaudeville theaters showed their acts to two million people daily. The Keith chain eventually grew to include theaters in nearly every American city with as much as 100,000 population.

Simultaneously with the first success of the Keith circuit, other chains sprang up in different sections of the country. In Chicago, Kohn and Middleton established a theater for vaudeville performances late in 1886, and in that same year Gustave Walters was ready with his Orpheum Theatre in San Francisco. Other names, most of them in the New York area, came to be identified with vaudeville before the turn of the century: F. F. Proctor and his Twenty-third Street Theatre; John J. Murdock with the Masonic Temple Roof; Oscar Hammerstein and his Victoria Theatre, at Forty-second Street and Broadway; Alex Pantages and his Northwest Vaudeville Circuit. In Ohio, Gus Sun started a statewide circuit in 1905. Keith and Proctor combined forces in that year to form the United Booking Company, which emerged as more or less the clearing house for all bookings. Owners and managers everywhere joined this organization, to standardize the business, and in 1916 the performers, protecting their interests, organized "The Vaudeville Artists Association." By 1928 it had more than 15,000 members.

Working conditions improved, salaries increased, and further stars of the opera, the circus, and the dramatic stage ventured into the entertainment. Some of these were Sarah Bernhardt; Maurice Barrymore and his children, Ethel, Jack and Lionel; the Four Cohans, of which George M. Cohan became the best-known member; David Warfield; Mr. and Mrs. Sidney Drew; Nazimova; William Faversham; and Lenore Ulric. As performers continued to be converted, talented comedians began to grace the vaudeville stage, among them the Ritz Brothers, Sliding Billy Watson, Joe Jackson; Willie West and McGinty, the Marx Brothers, Ted Healy and his Stooges; Sweeney and Duffy; Lou Holtz; Wheeler and Woolsey; Clark and McCullough; Joe Cook; Robert Emmett Keane; Nat Wills; and Ben Welch.

For the most part, vaudeville rested on songs, dances, short dramatic sketches and acrobatic turns. The acts followed one another in quick succession, with no continuity and only a token effort at arrangements. It was the custom to open a bill with "a dumb act," one which involved no spoken lines, such as tumblers or teeterboard specialists, so that the noisy, late entrance of patrons would have a minimum disturbing effect. In general, similar acts were spaced apart, and some attempt was made to build the show toward a climax by weighting the latter part of it with the most effective performers. The large theaters had a bristling complement of sets and properties which were available to all the visiting artists, but most acts carried the bulk of their own mechanical devices, special scenic effects and additional decorations. In and out of the stage doors of these glittering palaces passed a continuous parade of gigantic trunks, boxes, crates and other luggage, plastered all around with names and labels that seemed to the crowd of ever-present stage struck in the street to be the very epitome of glamour.

Fields' enthusiasm over the prospect of changing his employment was dampened only slightly by the knowledge that quite a few others bearing his last name were seen regularly on the bills, threatening possible confusions and detractions. Besides the famous Lew Fields, of "Weber and Fields," there were Ben Fields, like himself a former newsboy from Pennsylvania; Harry Fields, a comedian dealing in Hebrew dialects; Mrs. Nat Fields, a singer and dancer; Joe Fields, a comedian and impersonator; and perhaps most popular, as her name suggests, "Happy Fanny" Fields, a well-molded dramatic star. It was a spangled company and a competitive world, but after thinking it all over, Fields stepped onto the colorful scene with optimism and nonchalance. He had been through too much to be fretful over failure. By now he knew he was good, and he protected his gift with hard layers of self-confidence. His first vaudeville booking came from Keith's, which operated the most successful existing circuit. A talent scout had seen Fields in the Irwin show on a night in Chicago when the audience had been especially stimulating. By a happy chance Irwin's tour was scheduled to end there several days later.

The scout, who was also one of the owners of the circuit, called at Fields' dressing room. The boy juggler was removing his make-up, and the man was aghast at his youthful appearance. "Why, you're only a kid!" he said.

"State your business, my friend," said Fields, carefully folding a putty nose into a handkerchief and placing it in a drawer. The Keith's man replied that he had watched Fields' turn and had found it (as Fields later reported) "a fair attraction." Gaining confidence in the presence of an obvious stripling, he then offered Fields sixty-five dollars a week. But he had sadly misjudged his man. When he asked what Fields was getting with Irwin, Fields replied, "A hundred and seventy-five a week," a gross lie.

Staggered, the scout expressed an opinion that the figure

represented twenty-five or thirty dollars more than Irwin himself was making.

"A very equitable arrangement," Fields said.

After a great deal of haggling, during which the Keith's man grew increasingly nettled and began to wish he were dealing with an older and mellower head, a salary of $125 a week was agreed on. But when the scout turned to go, Fields indicated that the conference was not quite over.

"About the billing," he said.

"Why, we take care of the billing," exclaimed the scout.

"Only in a general way," said Fields. "The fact is, I've decided to be billed as 'W. C. Fields, the Distinguished Comedian.'"

"We bill you as a juggler," said the unfortunate from Keith's. "Damn it all, you couldn't be a day over nineteen. What do you mean, 'Distinguished'?"

"Good day," said Fields, lighting a cigar.

"W. C. Fields, the Distinguished Comedian," cried the scout, and ran out of the room like a rabbit.

Fields was pleased with the new announcements. He clipped several from newspapers and sent them to his boyhood friends, who had not heard from him in years. "Vanity can be excused when you are young," he once said of these communications. The truth is that Fields was eternally grateful for his friends' succor in the black time of his flight. As the years wore on, he began to realize that he might literally have starved had the boys not kept him supplied in the first difficult months. One of the samaritans, when an old man, wrote Fields asking for a note to show that they had been friends in Philadelphia. He mentioned the Orlando Social Club, alluded to the "bunk" where Fields had crouched miserably, and ended on the rather wistful note that he wished he'd sought out a bunk of his own. Fields wrote his old chum a long, nostalgic letter rapturously affirming their friendship, and signed it, with a grandiloquent flourish, "Whitey Dukinfield."

Fields' vaudeville opening took place, for some reason, in Columbus, Ohio. He juggled a number of tennis balls and hats, nearly dropping several, as the audience saw it, but comically retrieved them, to great applause, just in time. He balanced some sticks on his toes and fingers, and then did the act he had been working on with the cigar boxes. As one writer viewed the latter routine, it was "his masterpiece—a trick of juggling twenty-five cigar boxes, end on end, with a little rubber ball on top. First the ball was dropped and caught in his other hand; then each box followed in succession, the top one falling with machine-like precision without disturbing the boxes beneath it. It was a wow!"

Although Fields had previously appeared in Columbus, the town had never seen him juggle. It was acquainted with his work in a different capacity, that is, as it was brought to bear on the role of a rascally sawmill operator. During his first road tour, the man who normally played the part had suffered an attack of poisoning, in a saloon, and Fields took over, temporarily foregoing the juggling. For once he was splendidly effective as a straightaway dramatic performer. In the scene, a notably luscious ingénue found herself strapped to the usual conveyor belt of the period, and Fields, as the rogue, was intent on dividing her into slabs of a more convenient size. It happened that the girl in question, offstage, had not only consistently repulsed Fields' advances for weeks, but had once threatened to summon the police. Fields handled the saw with finesse. It was only of wooden construction, with no teeth worthy of the name, but it unquestionably would have raised hob with her skin. The girl's shrieks, as she lay strapped to the plank, were heart-rending; more than once the audience thanked heaven it was all in fun.

Receiving, as he now did, $125 a week, a gigantic sum for a boy of nineteen in those days, Fields was vexed with his old trouble about idle cash. He already had one bank account, in California, but to go out and back was obviously too long a trip to make a deposit. Worried and remembering his unhappy experience with the gold, he finally devised a scheme. He would open a bank account everywhere he went. He began with the large cities, placing twenty dollars here and ten there, and worked on down to banks that occupied, perhaps, a corner of a feed store in a crossroads village. Sometimes he hopped off trains and opened an account while an engine took on water. He piled the bankbooks in a corner of his wardrobe trunk, and, for the most part, forgot them. As it turned out, it was a curious program, for the time was never to come, as long as he lived, when Fields was to need any of the deposited money. On two or three occasions only, he went over the books, cleaned out many accounts, and concentrated the money in larger banks, but he never changed the system as a general savings plan. At one time he had, he said, 700 accounts in banks all over the world. After his death his executors located thirty accounts. Some of his friends, such as Dave Chasen, Gene Fowler, and Billy Grady, who acted as Fields' agent for fourteen years and then became casting director for Metro-Goldwyn-Mayer, thought that thousands of dollars of Fields' money continued to lie fallow in banks under spurious names. "I think he lost at least $50,000 in the Berlin bombing," Fowler said. "He had bank accounts, or at least safe-deposit boxes, in such cities as London, Paris, Sydney, Cape Town, and Suva. I do not know this for a fact, but I think that much of his fortune still rests in safe-deposit boxes about which, deliberately or not, he said nothing."

There were two reasons for Fields' banking system. Primarily, he saw it as a way to discourage thievery, a breach of the moral code he detested in others. Second, he was, he felt, building up safeguards against being stranded. By now he had the full-fledged phobia about poverty that remained with him to the end of his days. He often had a dream, he once told a friend, in which he found himself penniless and starving in an unfriendly wayside settlement. "I'd stolen some bread or something," he said, "and everybody was after me—police and dogs were coming and there was a big hullabaloo. I used to wake up in a cold sweat. But then I'd see it was a dream and I'd say to myself, forget it—you've probably got a bank account in that town."

As a rule Fields opened the accounts and took the safe-deposit boxes in his own name, but he was known to hint darkly about scattered riches controlled by such people as Figley E. Whitesides, Sneed Hearn, and Dr. Otis Guelpe—names for which he sometimes expressed a fancy in other connections. Throughout his life, Fields rarely spoke of his accounts to people other than his secretaries or his lawyers, and then only if necessary for business reasons. The occasions were few and far between when he even mentioned his possessions to friends. Once, he told of his infrequent visits to a small bank in Iowa, which had an exceedingly gullible and friendly teller. Fields liked to drop in every three or four years to add a small deposit to his capital. The teller, a middle-aged, myopic man, greeted him with warmth and curiosity. "Account of Professor Curtis T. Bascom?" he'd say, and squint at Fields. "Why, dear me, Professor Bascom! Delighted to see you again. Now, tell me, where have you been this trip?" Thus provided an opening, Fields would dilate entertainingly on his recent expedition up the Amazon after an almost extinct species of three-legged ostrich. The teller would listen raptly as he dwelled, in detail, on the expedition's struggles with cholera, head-hunters, crocodiles, women, ticks, witch doctors, booze, quicksand and missionaries. When Fields had concluded, the teller would ask respectfully about the next trip. "We're going into the Arctic," Fields would tell him. "We've fitted out an expedition to hunt the northern Mexican hairless—for scientific purposes, of course. See you around 1906, if we come through."

"Good-by," the teller would cry, much affected. "The best of luck, Professor Bascom!"

In this phase, Fields, at nineteen, enjoyed talking, and especially lying, offstage. Perhaps this was because he had quit talking onstage. With Fulton, and part of the time with Irwin, he had not only talked in dramatic roles but had accompanied his juggling with patter. When he began to get the upper hand of Irwin, he abandoned the patter, for some reason he never cleared up. One of his public utterances on the subject, in 1926, was ambiguous and elliptical: "When I began, I used to do what we called a 'dumb act.' That is, I didn't talk: it was all dumb show. Then I started using lines to help get the laughs. For I want to emphasize this point: even when I seemed to be just drifting along, without any particular purpose to guide me, I did have a definite desire." His desire was, of course, to become a comedian, but why he decided to approach it silently, around the turn of the century, none of his friends knew. The best guess is that Fields, who, as he said, was always looking into the future though he seemed to be proceeding haphazardly, had his eye on a European tour. International bookings were denied to many kinds of American vaudeville, because of the difference in languages;

straight juggling obviously carried no such handicap. "The important post of closing the first half fell to W. C. Fields, a 'dumb act,' " said *Variety* of one of Fields' early vaudeville appearances. "Why Mr. Fields does not speak is quite simple—his comedy speaks for him."

In the next few years Fields' act became one of the most popular vaudeville was ever to know. It was the period of his swiftest development. With the warm praise of each fresh audience his touch grew surer. He knew where he was going, and he was in more of a hurry than ever. On the road tours, with a little money for the first time, he permitted himself some well-earned relaxation, squiring the ladies and throwing the saloons a little custom now and then. Upon his start in vaudeville he returned to his man-killing practice. In the evenings, in his room, he took up the laborious polishing that had made his work distinguished. Often he stood beside his bed and tossed objects into the air until he fell over, in a sort of coma, and slept the night through without extinguishing the light. "Usually," he said, "I could tell when to quit. When I got so tired I began to drop everything, the person below beat on the radiator and I knocked off."

Once, in a Pittsburgh hotel, Fields, still in his street clothes, was on the point of mastering a difficult feat and continued after the warning thumps. The trick involved a sizable crockery jar which he had found in his room, and there were indications, he said, that as it kept falling it jarred considerable of the plaster loose down below. The hour was around 3 A.M., and there can be no doubt that sleep, on the lower level, was, for anyone with normal hearing, awkward. Presently, the subordinate tenant, a giant of a man, sprinted upstairs in his nightshirt, whacked on Fields' door, and accosted him bitterly. Fields had thrown the door open with his usual injured fury, determined to bluff it out, but his first glance told him that this was no ordinary mortal. Expecting to be floored, if not actually murdered, he stepped back promptly, but the man's expression changed as he said, with a certain deference, "Ain't you the feller that was juggling to the the-ater tonight?" Fields replied in the affirmative, then asked him how he knew, saying, "As you see, I haven't got my tramp costume on now."

"Oh, I don't know," said the man in an admiring tone. "Somehow, you look like you still got it on."

Fields' feelings were hurt, but he agreed to teach the visitor a juggling trick, choosing a simple one that called for two paring knives. "I hope he worked at it," Fields said afterward, "because if he did, he was almost certain to cut himself very painfully."

CHAPTER NINE

Not long after he entered vaudeville, Fields had an experience which disturbed him profoundly. Walking the streets of a Midwestern city, between shows, he saw a movie marquee luridly advertising an epic film on venereal disease. Although, as is usually the case with these offerings, the letters screamed the pitfalls of sex, the lobby photos of half-dressed women were downright attractive, if not bothersome. Bosomy madames lounged in unlighted hallways, teen-age girls drew sailors toward the fatal couch, and there was evidence of gay, subsidiary sins, such as drinking and smoking. For the authorities' sake, the message was indisputably present, but on the outside it rang of a harmless bacchanal.

Fields immediately bought a ticket and went in, hoping to see some naked women. His first view fell somewhat short of his expectations, being concerned with an elderly male wreck in the last stages of syphilis. If the fellow was one of the sailors in the lobby, Fields concluded, he had indeed descended far and had much better stuck to his ship, or played chess at the Seamen's Hall. None of the women ever turned up, or, if they did, they looked different, no longer emphasizing the well-turned breast or alabaster thigh but exuding, now, a very real menace. Fields was disgusted; he had paid forty cents for a seat down near the front and felt that he had been skinned. He started to leave, but the next caption froze him in his spot. "You, too, can wind up in a place like this!" it said, and he leaned back, thinking maybe they were coming to the brothel. But it was a hospital room, containing a man, a formerly well-to-do merchant, so the screen said, who, in a moment of weakness, possibly after surveying a lobby display for a venereal-disease film, had visited a bawdy house and was now in an outrageous condition and past any hope of salvage. Fields stayed on. He hadn't any place else to go, so he traveled the whole celluloid trail, from one clinical horror to another. He was, finally, impressed, not only by the eroded state of the people involved, but by the alarming statistics. Since the discovery of sex, some years ago, venereal disease has offered the statistician a highly enjoyable meadow for exercise. Within an hour or so Fields was pretty certain that his case had been covered by one of the broadsides, which went, in a very general way, "Eighty-two per cent of all white, Protestant males between the heights of five feet two and six feet eight are exposed to syphilis on an average of eleven times a year in public drinking places," and "Three out of every twenty-seven Chinese coolies past ninety who arrived in San Francisco from 1862 to 1864 showed possible symptoms of inherited gonorrhea." When Fields came out of the theater, he hurried past the lobby display without looking back. "I was afraid of turning to saltpeter," he said later. Years afterward, he told his secretary in Hollywood, Magda Michael, about seeing this picture. Though he described it lightly, he admitted that it permanently altered his outlook. So vivid was the experience that he even recalled the incidental music that played during the scenes. "It was from Tschaikovsky's *Swan Lake,*" he said. "I could never hear that damned thing again without wanting to take a Wassermann."

Before he saw the movie, Fields had never been a promiscuous youth, fixing his attentions on one girl at a time and then only if she weren't likely to interfere with business or cost him anything. Afterward he became notably chaste. During his vaudeville years he was often "going with" some girl, invariably an actress or other theatrical performer, but he never pursued women indiscriminately. Fields was, in fact, far from a lecherous man. Despite his brassy latter-day publicity as a gaudy spirit and all-around rip, he had many quaint and old-fashioned ideas about women. For instance, he preferred that women wear petticoats. One time when he was ill and hospitalized at Las Encinas Sanitarium, in Pasadena, he took exception to his nurses' attire. Lying in his bed, and keeping a watchful eye on what went on around him, as was his custom, he had taken note of various patches of pelt when the young ladies leaned over for a swab or a bottle of pills. He called in the superintendent. "See here," he said, "I'm paying this place seventy dollars a day and I want you to put all the nurses that come into this room in petticoats. My mother wore them, and her mother before her—it's the only decent garb for a woman." The sanitarium agreed, and his nurses self-consciously bundled up.

Fields was always embarrassed whenever anybody told off-color jokes in the presence of women. Dirty stories bothered him at any time; he considered further that a reliance upon manufactured anecdotes of whatever kind was positive indication of a crippled wit. His face underwent awesome changes at the accursed social preamble of "Here's a hell of a funny story I picked up the other day." In a mixed gathering, if some man, stimulated by gin and the dubious charm of his own narrative style, began an uproarious sex joke, Fields often retired to the bathroom, or began a vacant search for matches. He could never abide loud, vulgar women, and he was vastly uneasy around a woman who drank. Invariably, when a woman, whether a cotillion leader or a fishwife, entered a room he was in, he performed the pretty rite of standing up. Once, his old friend and former agent, Billy Grady, called at Fields' home, bringing a lady he wished to present. The day was warm, and Fields, at the moment, was upstairs behind his table-high desk, entirely nude. Grady and his lady came up without knocking or ringing the bell. When they burst into the study, Grady began, "Bill, I want you to meet——" then stopped, furious. Fields was rising slowly, wearing only an expression of regal punctilio. He executed a courtly half bow and said, "Pray come in. I'm delighted to see you." Relating this anecdote, another of Fields' friends

said, "Bill was full of scruples about women, all right, but
he never allowed anything to take precedence over
humor."

His regard for humor infrequently led Fields to introduce a *double-entendre* into his work, but it could scarcely have been objectionable to the fussiest censor. He liked
to contrive situations wherein he and a sexless crone exchanged pleasantries of an amorous and slightly appalling
kind. When he and a dowager entered a game room in
You Can't Cheat an Honest Man, she asked, with an arch
look, "By the way, how *is* your ping-pong?" and Fields replied, in a mildly bragging tone, "Pretty good, how's yours?"
The notion that anything might come of this was, of course,
rejected by an audience as preposterous beyond the
dreams of vulgarity. Fields' tête-à-têtes with Mae West in
My Little Chickadee reached such absurd heights of hyperbole that they were effectively removed from the romantic.
The truth is that Fields always viewed romance in a pretty
comical light. In *Chickadee* he enjoyed a scene in which he
climbed a ladder to Miss West's boudoir, disguised as her
masked lover. "I played it straight," he told an inquisitive
friend who hadn't seen the picture. It was a sensitive and
venturesome meeting, in the classical spirit of Leander
paddling toward Hero. Ascending the ladder, Fields had
trouble with his mask, which kept slipping, and when he
entered the room, the eager maid rushed forward just as
he poked his rather chilling nose through the gap and began a series of low-comedy endearments in a hoarse, asthmatic whine. This scene pleased Fields, but he preferred
a later one in which, again through mistaken identity, he
reclined in the half dark with a goat.

In the beginning, in vaudeville, Fields played, besides the
Orpheum Circuit, such places as Henderson's Coney Island, Brighton Beach, and Custer and Black's Music
Hall, all in New York, and Poli's Circuit, which extended
into New England. After his first success with Keith's, he
was booked, off and on, by the William Morris Agency,
which, together with other agencies, kept him gainfully employed. Unlike many vaudeville performers, Fields managed, by skillfully juggling both agents and managers, to
avoid delays between bookings. He conceived a horror of

the brotherhood's familiar lament, "Between Engagements," or "At Liberty," that showed up in pathetic brevity all too often in the theatrical publications *Billboard* and *Variety*. Even when he was middle-aged, wealthy and famous, he became furtive and uneasy if unemployed for long. Idleness always revived his old fears, returning him to his starvation days—never a very long trip, in his mind.

In San Francisco, again with Keith's, he had some imposing professional pictures made at Bushnell's, which was the most popular shop of its kind in those days. As pointed out by John Chapman, in his newspaper features about Fields, Bushnell's was rated above New York photographic shops because it showed that a performer was important enough to travel. Pictures inscribed "Bushnell's, San Francisco" and standing outside a theater lobby gave an artist special distinction; other artists, who didn't have pictures from Bushnell's looked up to him. In San Francisco, Fields also bought a diamond ring, an acquisition he had planned for some time. It was a good-sized stone, costing several hundred dollars, and showed up well, on a sunny day, for two or three blocks. Fields wore it with a princely air, somewhat tempered by his fear of having it snatched. Entering a high-class restaurant, he would exhibit the ring in a series of dazzling, flamboyant gestures, then eat with his ring hand tucked into his waistcoat, meanwhile darting quick, suspicious looks here and there, with particular reference to the waiters.

As the money rolled in, Fields cultivated manorial tastes. He had fed on things like saloon herring and ditch water so long that he welcomed an opportunity to be fastidious. While other vaudeville people reposed in humble, traditional lodgings, Fields put up at the best hotels. Not for him the crowded trough of the boardinghouse, the shabby resorts of the theater. From town to town he dined richly, in the favored cafés of the bourbons. With his inborn pomp and fakery, he rapidly became a master at the impressive nuances of table skill. Customarily languid diners nudged one another in admiration of his style. He was patently born to the purple, and his manner was condescending. "This sauce," he would cry, waving toward a resplendent casserole. "Has the chef by some mischance omitted the paprika?" A waiter, stung, would bow low, and the gourmet's neighbors, eying their Newburg, would nibble and test in confusion. Fields always said that, in this era, he didn't believe he was making out too well with the waiters. They complied, but they gave him searching looks. He felt, also, that they emphasized "Sir" a little heavily and, on occasion, bowed *too* low. Like dogs, waiters seemed familiar with his past.

In the first months of his vaudeville, Fields had an urge to expand his act, and he remembered his former employment in the pool hall. At the same time, he recalled an act he had seen in recent years, in which a Professor Devereaux performed with trick billiard devices. The professor, Fields now understood vaguely, had retired. After a good deal of figuring with a pencil and a notebook, he consulted a manufacturer of vaudeville equipment in New York. The upshot of this visit was Fields' celebrated pool table, which, with its owner, was to convulse audiences all over the world. It was built in sections, to be easily transportable, and had an ingenious system of invisible strings, to provide the master perfect control over the balls.

For several weeks Fields spent nearly all his waking offstage minutes practicing with the table. He added equipment as he thought of it. At first he had intended to work with an ordinary cue, but a few weeks later he had a better idea—he would use one full of twists and bends, in a condition roughly comparable to that of a shepherd's crook. As a ball racker, he had witnessed the ritual care with which the customers took their cues down from the rack, hefting them, rolling them on the table, and sighting down their length, to be sure they were true. It was his purpose, he said, in addition to being merely funny, to present the ultimate commentary on pool-hall mannerisms. There was a possibility, he admitted, that some members of his audiences, such as cloistered ladies and others who had not had all the advantages, would be unfamiliar with pool-hall behavior, but he hoped that, when they saw him, they would hasten to repair their education. "We must strive to instruct and uplift as well as entertain," he told a manager who timorously questioned the social worth of the pool table.

After long sessions of pruning and polishing, Fields opened with his new act at the fashionable Orpheum in

Boston. It was a risky tryout, because the average upper-class Bostonian, as is well known, spends comparatively little time in pool halls. Nevertheless, Fields' trick table was received with thunderous, low-bred applause. From the moment he walked on, in his rags, and selected his ridiculous cue, he was reassured about the value of esoteric parody. He rolled, or attempted to roll, the cue on the table, but it only bumped and clattered. Then, perplexed, he held it to his eye, his expression indicating an incipient awareness that the stick was not altogether straight. His manipulation of the balls seemed uncanny. At one prodigious whack from the unlovely cue, they would scramble over the table and dive into the pockets like rats. Or, again, as the old New York *Star* said of a subsequent performance, the way he made them "carom around the table and land in his capacious hip pocket is an amazing revelation in the art of billiards."

Despite his back-alley garb, Fields' gestures were majestic as he pursued the significant game. No stylized flourish escaped his attention. He stooped low as he studied the lie of the balls, he broke off his aim to shift, ever so slightly, the irrelevant position of the chalk, and he dropped all holds to flick a disturbing ash off the end of his splayed cigar. Over a period of forty-five years, he was to alter the act constantly, in little ways. Basically, it remained the same—a burlesque, or parody, or satire, or caricature, or travesty, dealing with a thoroughly unimportant institution. The last performance of the act was in the wartime movie revue, *Follow the Boys,* which was released in 1944. When first approached about redoing his old sketch for the film, Fields was reluctant, even crotchety. He didn't like movie revues, he said. They turned out to be meaningless hodgepodges, with strings of imposing names, and were rattled off with such machine-gun speed that audiences reeled away glassy-eyed and exhausted. When he was told that the act would be a fine morale builder for American boys in places like El Alamein and Guadalcanal, he capitulated. Sitting beside his radio, he had followed the war from day to day with choleric and profane interest. He asked the studio (Universal) to engage Eddie Sutherland, who had directed several of his movies, to direct the shooting of his pool act.

On the set, Fields decided that, to recapture his old vim, he needed an audience, and the scene was rigged so that, in the story, he was performing for a roomful of troops. By special dispensation of a post commander, the troops used were actually men from a nearby army camp. Fields found this situation congenial and stimulating. As the cameras ground, he walked onto the set, wearing a frayed business suit and an antique straw hat from his own wardrobe and absently humming an unmelodic air. He started when he saw the audience, as if something had been put over on him, and took down the warped cue with his familiar look of persecuted dismay. Then he went about trying to poke the end of the cue through a loop formed by his left forefinger and thumb. With his face hideously contorted, he chased the needless loop around the room, finally cornered it, and settled down to sawing for his aim. As in former years, he interrupted this several times to move the chalk, whose position offended his sensitive eye. Then, having fixed on the precise angle, he lunged forward, tripped, and opened a two-foot rip in the fabric. Muttering indistinct threats against various fictitious persons, he began to thrust at the balls savagely, shooting them all in with a single, unlikely blow on two or three occasions. At last, clearing the table of all but three balls, he announced to the audience, with delicate enunciation, "A difficult massee shot." As he hauled himself up on tiptoes and raised his cue to the vertical, his expression clearly revealed that the troops were in the presence of a great moment. Then, after a dramatic pause, he drove violently downward, knocked a sizable portion out of the center of the table, and jammed his arm in up to the shoulder. He viewed the disaster with mild, baffled concern, and the curtain fell.

So enthusiastic were the troops, at the conclusion of his old act, that Fields came back for several curtain calls, in the best vaudeville tradition. As he removed his straw hat for the last applause that was ever to greet, in person, one of the most celebrated funny routines in the history of the stage, Fields' eyes, according to a bystander, were "suspiciously moist." "He seemed to know he would never do it again," a studio employee said.

"Bill had slowed up the act about a third since I first directed it," Eddie Sutherland recalled. "But, even so, we finished shooting in a day and a half." As Fields left the lot, several people thanked him for his fine patriotic effort and said how much good the scene would do. He shook their hands with self-conscious pleasure, went to the cashier and collected the $25,000 he had agreed on, then shuffled off toward his car, whistling a soundless tune, his eyes fixed on the distant horizon.

CHAPTER TEN

IN 1901, after a brief but wildly successful apprenticeship in American vaudeville, Fields had an offer for a European tour. He was much pleased. For some time he had looked forward to getting away from this country. Born with a compulsive urge for flight, he felt happiest when he was out in front of some imaginary pack. As his ship, the old White Star liner *Ivernia,* drew away from the wharf, he knew that his pursuers of a hungrier era—dogs, police, Chinamen, barkeeps, irate householders, bereft butchers, and an occasional father—would have the devil of a time catching him now, and he relaxed. "I had the feeling that I was leaving my troubles behind," he told a friend. Although Fields no longer had any critical troubles, he still harbored the uneasy notion that somebody was after him. In the complex garden of his mind stood a bothersome weed patch of guilt—the harvest of his multiple transgressions. As he grew more successful, the guilt flourished, and he became proportionately more suspicious of his fellows.

His first foreign engagement was at the Palace in London. He used a modest billing, a compound of his favorites: "Wm. C. Fields, the Distinguished Comedian & Greatest Juggler on Earth, Eccentric Tramp." He added the "m" to his first initial, he said, as a kind of overseas fillip, for dignity. The English audiences received him with the greatest generosity. By American standards, and most others, the average Briton's idea of humor is a fairly dark and embarrassing business. One of England's best-loved critics reviewed Mark Twain's *The Innocents Abroad,* upon its publication, in a perfectly sober and disgusted vein. The book was full of exaggerations, the critic said, and was, in his opinion, worthless as a travel guide. He took exception to Twain's finding, in the Colosseum at Rome, a yellowed program of an evening's entertainment, giving a line-up of Christians about to face the lions, and other events. It was unlikely, said the critic, that any such bill could have survived all these years in the Colosseum dust. An American publisher later printed the criticism, together with Twain's sulphurous letter of reply, in an anthology, where they will remain for all time as an interlocking tribute to the literal mind.

Fields had been forewarned about Englishmen and humor, and he approached his first performance in a taut condition. But his worry was energy wasted; everything he did was received with gusty appreciation. In fact, the English were so nice to Fields, both on stage and off, that the law of diminishing returns started to set in. Their politeness bothered him; daily it grew more onerous. At length he took a short trip to Ireland, where he'd heard that people were occasionally rude.

When he returned, Fields could no longer resist his impulse to take advantage of the English. Strolling about, he had observed dressed fowls hanging outside poulterers' shops, a negligent form of display, he reflected, that would have meant certain bankruptcy in his old Philadelphia days. He bought a cheap but commodious knapsack and began to take walking tours. His line of march was concentrated in the areas heaviest with poultry shops. Wending his friendly way, he carefully filled the sack, abstracting a hen here, rejecting a partridge there—making, all in all, a pleasant and profitable holiday. It was a kind of processed poaching, and done at a time when the British poaching laws were severe. Fields himself said he sat in a courtroom where a woman was given a stiffish sentence for poaching eggs. Fields had no particular need for the fowls; stealing them merely represented, in his mind, another foolproof method of staying ahead. He had graduated from larceny several years before, but he did not consider lifting poultry from Englishmen stealing. The fowls were obviously hung outdoors to be removed, he said. Ignoring them would have been an implied criticism of British advertising methods, and he did not wish to offend. Out of sentiment, he kept the knapsack all his life; it was made the subject of a Paramount publicity release in 1933.

The lopsided romance between Fields and the English continued, off and on, for years. On subsequent tours, at each unusual expression of their good manners, he worked out some compensating mischief. Notably, he devised a complicated scheme to beat stationmasters out of the fee for excess luggage. Fields was traveling with two wardrobe trunks at the time, and it irked him to cough up funds outside of his fare. In America one could occasionally check any amount of impedimenta on a single ticket. He always enjoyed bragging about tricking the stationmasters, explaining, somewhat unclearly, that the economy had involved his buying the official a glass of beer while some confederate shoved the cases into a baggage car. "It saved me many a pretty penny," Fields used to say.

In reminiscent humors he related that he had made a profound study of English psychology. While on the tours he had often demonstrated his knowledge to some unbelieving companion. Once, preparing to board a train with another American, he discoursed at length on the Englishman's courteous inadequacy in the face of bad manners, and went on to prove his point. Asking the American to stand by, he entered a first class compartment marked "Reserved for Mr. Ashcroft." Fields unhooked the sign, tossed it on the floor, opened a newspaper, and sitting down, began to read with an attitude of imperial nonchalance. A moment later a trainman came along and said, "I'm sorry, sir, but this space is reserved."

Without glancing up, Fields waved him away.

"It's reserved, sir," insisted the trainman. "The sign's fallen on the floor."

"I'm reading," said Fields. "Go along, now, and don't interrupt."

"If you wouldn't mind, sir," said the trainman, "I think I'd better summon the conductor."

Fields continued to read. The conductor arrived and said, in a familiar vein, "Beg your pardon, sir, but this space is reserved."

"What's the meaning of this outrage?" demanded Fields, quivering with indignation.

"There's been some mixup," said the conductor. "The space is reserved for Mr. Ashcroft. Tall man with a yellow goatee."

"This is my seat!" cried Fields. "Bought and paid for. Leave! Be off!"

The conductor removed his hat and mopped his face; then he said, "I hardly know what course to take. Perhaps I'd better summon a constable, sir. This is a little out of my line."

With a look of pious vindication, Fields returned to his paper.

A couple of minutes later the conductor returned, with the trainman, a constable, and the unhappy Ashcroft. A general consultation was held, while Fields, deep in concentration, caught up on an item (he said) about a Hyde Park matron who had suffered a gastric setback after gorging on tainted kippers.

"See here," sputtered Ashcroft at last. "You've got my seat, you know."

"The sign's right there on the floor," added the conductor, pointing.

"Most irregular," agreed the constable.

"Depart!" cried Fields. "Vacate my compartment immediately! Why, damnation, I wouldn't be surprised if this was actionable!"

The group drew off to inspect him in bewilderment. The conductor was nonplused, and so was the constable; neither could remember a case drawn along exactly similar lines.

"By your leave," said the trainman to the conductor, "there was that matter three years ago in Dulwich—green-grocer in the second-class coach next to the rear."

"Not the same," said the conductor, with asperity. "Not the same thing at all!"

"Before my time," said the constable. "Unless mistaken I was in Brixton then, or was it Norwood?"

"It's a puzzler, all right," said the trainman.*

In a little while they trailed off to find Mr. Ashcroft another seat. Still reading the paper, Fields waved his companion in, and shortly afterward the train left on its journey to Edinburgh.

As Fields grew older and mellower he loved to talk about the English. They were a hardy and inexplicable race, he felt, and full of admirable, civilized qualities. Sitting in Dave Chasen's restaurant, with a few close friends, he would expound the anecdote about Mr. Ashcroft and the train seat, speaking in expert dialect and illustrating his talk with what struck him as typically English gestures. His philosophy of "Never Give a Sucker an Even Break," which he often stated but seldom practiced, gained its first real impetus in England.

Fields had acquired the philosophy in the first place from a well-known American confidence man of the period, "Doc" Atterbury, whose eminence in his chosen line was comparable to that, later on, of One-Eyed Connolly in the gate-crashing dodge. Atterbury had a manner which he had borrowed jointly from the Czar of Russia and Ghengis Khan. His assumptive, princely arrogance seemed to Fields, on the few occasions when the two had met, the very crest of elegance. All children have their heroes, and Fields tried to model himself after the doctor, whose claim to the professional title, incidentally, derived from the fact that he had been widely jailed in connection with peddling a nostrum compounded, according to United States agents, of kerosene, spring water and lye, that was guaranteed, if applied either locally or internally, to clear up things like tuberculosis, fractures, and pregnancy.

Fields' experiment with Ashcroft was largely an imitation of an English encounter that Atterbury once had, in Fields' presence. Atterbury had taken a seat on a train and lit a cigar, in violation of the rules, as stated clearly in every car. A stranger on the opposite seat demurred, pointing to the sign. Gazing serenely out of the window, At-

Note: This dialogue, reconstructed later by the comedian for an article, may be approximate.

terbury continued to smoke, pausing only to flick off his ash.
The stranger became increasingly upset and argumenta-
tive. At length he pulled out a card and cried, "Perhaps
you don't know who I am, sir?" Atterbury's scrutiny of the
landscape was undisturbed, but the complainant succeeded in forcing the card between two of his fingers, after
which Atterbury put the card in his vest pocket. At this
moment the conductor arrived, and the stranger, arising,
burst into an impassioned protest. When he had finished,
the conductor began a reproachful lecture. Atterbury, still
studying the countryside, abstractedly drew out the card
and handed it over. "Oh, that's different, sir," said the conductor, and led the stranger away, promising to find him a
seat elsewhere.

Fields maintained that his own heckling of the English
was done in no spirit of meanness or contempt but was
actually a form of reverence. "I was merely acknowledging
their breeding," he said. "You don't think I would have
stolen chickens in the Balkans, do you?" he sometimes
added in an injured tone. Distinctions were often very fine
with Fields; his friends had to hop nimbly to avoid insult-
ing him. Upon occasion he took note of the English in other,
milder ways. In London, during one of his performances,
Edward VII sat in a box. Forewarned of the King's coming, Fields, with the help of the stage manager, expanded
the act slightly. Three different times in the course of his
routines, the tramp juggler looked up at the royal box,
seemed to recognize an old friend in the King, and started
toward him with hand outstretched. As the audience
howled, the curtain rang down each time just before Fields
reached the box. In later years, relating this incident, he
would say, "I can still see the King smiling." As Fields was
leaving the theater that evening, the manager, much agitated, approached him and said, "Mr. Fields, a gentleman outside wishes to greet you." It was Edward VII, accompanied
by a retinue of friends. "I want to thank you and congratulate you on creating so much merriment at my expense,"
said the King, and, with a genial smile, he wrung Fields'
hand. "In my opinion, that Edward was a majestic man,"
Fields always said afterward, and meant it.

King Edward was genuinely impressed by Fields' work
and went to see him several times. Once, after an especially

droll performance, the King invited, or commanded, him to appear at a garden party the following Saturday at the Palace.

"King's having a party here at the Palace," said Fields, reading the note to his associates.

"He means Buckingham Palace, you silly fellow," said a cockney acrobat, and Fields began to make plans. He was toying with the idea of borrowing an imposing uniform from some theatrical friend and renting a few decorative orders, but the King sent additional word by a courier that he would like Fields to appear in the tramp suit.

The day arrived, and Fields appeared, deposited at the palace door by a highly disapproving coachman. It was a gala function, even by regal standards. The flower of English knighthood rambled over the formal gardens, sipping, munching, chattering, and pinching silverware in traditional style. The King greeted the juggler with effusion, although, Fields said later, a couple of nearby earls and a bishop were seen to shift their pocket watches. Their attitude changed, he went on, when it got about that he had come by invitation. The King's command, though inherently condescending, in the manner of royal invitations, was an emphatic compliment. To entertain the guests, Fields was to share honors with a French actress, one Sarah Bernhardt, who recited at length from *L'Aiglon,* a sad play of that period about a young Frenchman who had got in a jam and had to leave his country.

Aside from the brilliance of the fete, the day was not altogether successful for Fields. By an unhappy coincidence, he had his old trouble with dogs. A maharajah, glittering with gems bestowed upon him by his worshipful but pauperized subjects, turned up accompanied by a pair of peevish, well-fed mastiffs. The dogs were plainly bored by the affair, as is frequently the case with foreign mastiffs at an English garden party, but they were rewarded by Fields. While most of the guests were only amused by his tramp costume, the dogs took it as authentic. From the moment they saw, or sniffed, him, they began to draw snobbish lines. Each time Fields stacked up his cigar boxes, the dogs rushed in to destroy him. Though he worked hard, his timing was bad and his morale was shaken. For several minutes, he said later, he concentrated on a trick with a loaded cane, hoping to catch one of the dogs on the jaw. But they were spry, for mastiffs, perhaps because of their colonial upbringing, and he never even nicked one. The King at last persuaded the maharajah to tie the dogs to a tea table, and Fields ran through a number of tricks with all his old skill.

Notwithstanding his cavalier treatment of England, Fields liked many things about the country. He was one of the few foreigners, at the time of his death, who had learned to savor English food. While he admitted that the vegetables often tasted as though they had been boiled in a strong soap, he took a fancy to such standard British preparations as Yorkshire pudding, roast beef, mutton chops, dressed fowls hanging outside poulterers' shops, and kidney pie. Also, he approved of the English custom of reading good literature. He found a noticeable difference in the quality of reading matter favored by Americans and Englishmen. Whereas most Americans, in his opinion, were content with best sellers and the stories in popular magazines, even relatively uneducated Englishmen stuck pretty close to material of classic dimensions. Patriotically determined to raise his own cultural level, at least, to that of the English, Fields bought a huge trunk and transported it in a hansom to a secondhand bookstore.

"Serve you?" asked the proprietor with politely concealed astonishment when Fields and the driver staggered in under their burden.

"Fill her up," said Fields, pointing to the trunk.

"Anything particular the gentleman desires?" asked the proprietor (according to Fields). "Books? Nice bunch old magazines?"

"Books," said Fields. "Fill the trunk with books."

"Gentleman favor any particular color? A nice red looks uncommonly well in a trunk. *Ferd!*"—here he raised one hand and snapped his fingers at a scrawny youth in the rear—"bring up the Bidwell folio! Man was recently took up on suspicion of scuttling," he went on. "A Folger E. Bidwell, in the shipping line, and they consolidated certain of his effects. Now here's books!" he said with pride as the boy wheeled up with a cartful of wreckage. "Here's volumes as will set well in a trunk—record of incoming and outgoing vessels, together with tonnage, since 1832—

twelve volumes in a nice mock-leather binding and hardly a hole punched out. Knock the offering down to two pound ten."

"There seems to be some misapprehension," said Fields. "I want the best books you've got, the finest authors in English literature." *

After some skirmishing about the price, Fields filled the trunk and repaired to his hotel room. For months following he dug into the volumes, reading, studying, memorizing. Many of them he had met before, when he began his self-imposed education in America, but now he broadened his scope, digesting and enjoying writers whose output, earlier, had seemed prohibitively erudite. Among the authors represented in his new collection were Shakespeare, Sir Thomas More, Bacon, and Milton; and Virgil, Homer, Chaucer and De Maupassant in translation. At the same time he acquired additional works of Dickens that, to date, he had overlooked. From the moment of their first acquaintance, Fields had felt an especial affinity for Dickens, in some of whose characters he saw strong traces of himself. Another thing militating in Dickens' behalf, for Fields, was the frequent appearance, on the same bill as himself, of a performer named Owen McGiveney, a popular vaudeville artist of the time, who specialized in Dickens impersonations. McGiveney had a real feeling for Dickens, and Fields always went out front to watch him after his own act was finished.

"Gentlemen," Mr. McGiveney, as Micawber, would cry from the stage, "you are friends in need and friends indeed. Allow me to offer my inquiries with reference to the physical welfare of Mrs. Copperfield in *esse,* and Mrs. Traddles in *posse*—presuming, that is to say, that my friend Traddles is not yet united to the object of his affections, for weal and for woe."

And Fields would listen and muse, perhaps divining the day, some thirty years forward, when he himself was to utter the delightful, stilted phrases, while Dickens, in whatever corner of heaven is reserved for genius, must surely have applauded.

---

* Note: It is impossible not to recall a scene from *Great Expectations* in reading this report of Fields.

Like several of Mr. Dickens' cockneys, Fields enjoyed dropping into a pub after working hours. A gradual transition was taking place in his drinking habits. Heretofore, he had occasionally permitted himself a few rounds when in a carnival mood; now, he was beginning to find that a quiet drink or two settled his nerves. The agonizing strain of deadly, sustained precision was driving tiny cracks in his spectacular constitution. In his early twenties Fields was reaping the first destructive rewards of his lust for fame. Days and nights, year on year, of bringing his will to bear on the fantastic demands of his craft were exacting the toll that is always levied upon ambition. He was winning his fight for perfection, but he was losing something along the way. "After a tough performance I'd have trouble settling down," he said of this phase. "I was on edge, overstimulated. Often I'd be able to read, or walk it off, but sometimes it took a few beers to calm me down." It seemed, at the time, a harmless system. "Happiness means quiet nerves," he was to tell his household years later in Hollywood. But by then he knew that he would never have it.

CHAPTER ELEVEN

ONE of Fields' cardinal rules for success was to disregard advice. He had established early that jugglers can out-juggle non-jugglers. He generalized this curious view and clung to it, with one or two lapses, throughout his life. It was his belief, for example, that Harvard lawyers are not necessarily statesmen, that writers can out-write editors, and that most critics, to be taken seriously, should be able to create as well as criticize. He had become aware, when very young, that for every artist there are several hundred persons with a profounder, and louder, understanding of his artistry than any mere artist could possibly have. He had read of the keen critical rejection of failures such as Wagner's operas, Lincoln's Gettysburg Address, Walt Whitman's poems, and Christ's Sermon on the Mount, and he was sensibly impressed. Late in life Fields divided critics broadly into two groups: those who were ignorant but pretentious and thrustful, in the interest of making a living, and those whose pronouncements were distorted by prejudice or jealousy, such as Nicholas Rubinstein, whose blistering report on Tschaikovsky's piano concerto, though he himself was a perceptive musician, damned the work as "worthless, impossible to play, clumsy, awkward, poorly composed, and shot through with obvious and shocking thefts." Rubinstein, a critic suffering from jealousy, would no doubt have been horribly chagrined to know that the concerto was later to be recognized by a famous band leader named Freddie Martin, bolstered up by a lyric dealing with Love, and sung in some of the best dance halls in the world.

One of Fields' most notable lapses regarding critics took place in England. The man who engineered the incident, a contributor to a London newspaper, was kind to Fields but suggested what a pity it was that Hazlitt, who had written learnedly about Indian jugglers, had not lived to see the American visitor. By some chance, Fields happened to read the criticism, and in spite of himself he started to worry. The word "learned" stuck in his mind. Was there more to juggling than he thought? Was he exploiting his gift to the full? Would Hazlitt have approved? Very much worried, he went to a library, unearthed Hazlitt's works, and read the piece on juggling. He acknowledged that it was a revelation; Hazlitt clearly explained that juggling was a matter of precision, mathematics, co-ordination, muscle control, breathing, relaxed nerves, and several other imposing things, some of them in Latin. When Fields went away, his head was spinning. He only hoped that he could remember the ingredients of successful juggling long enough to put them into practice.

The following day at the theater he took up his usual stance, but his thoughts were on Hazlitt. He tossed several balls and hats into the air and concentrated heavily on precision, mathematics, co-ordination, muscle control, breathing, relaxed nerves and the things in Latin. All about him balls and hats tumbled to the floor. He picked them up and heaved them aloft again, chanting the learned phrases. On this try he almost caught one hat, he said, but it slipped through his fingers just as he got to "co-ordination." All in all, it was a trying evening for Fields, but it was worse for his audience. The awful shade of Hazlitt hung black over the hall. Fields kicked his cigar boxes, tripped over his cane, dropped a billiard ball on his foot, and probed the air for hats. Day after day he battled Hazlitt, juggling like a man with arthritis. At one point he decided he was through. But in due course his natural feeling about critics returned, and he resumed his work without assistance. "I was almost put out of business by a well-meaning corpse," he remarked later.

The experience taught Fields a lesson. It reinforced his disinclination to accept counsel; thereafter he was rarely known to listen to anybody about anything. Not long after the tussle with Hazlitt, he appeared in Edinburgh and became ill there. He ran a temperature, lost weight, and looked unnaturally rosy in the cheeks. An Edinburgh specialist, summoned by the music-hall manager, visited the sick man and took soundings. His examination required two or three visits and involved a number of tests which struck the patient as annoying. Fields took a notion, not entirely foreign to him in other cases, that the doctor was trying to badger him for some mysterious reason of his own. This notion was, he felt, more than justified when the specialist presented a bill for four guineas and handed down his diagnosis. "You're a very sick man," he said to Fields, who was regarding the bill with a look of stupefaction. "You'll have to be hospitalized for a long period and kept on a careful diet. If not, you won't live six months." As soon as the doctor left to make arrangements, Fields dressed, went out and bought a bottle of whisky; then he returned to his room and had a very decent time for an hour or two, after which he boarded a boat for Paris.

Twenty years later, when he was appearing in the stage play *Poppy,* he felt a little down again, and the management, as in Edinburgh, called a physician.

"We'll have to take you to a hospital for some tests," the

physician said to Fields, who was in his dressing room surrounded by worried members of the company.

"The hell with it," cried Fields, nervously remembering the four guineas. "Take them in here."

"But we have equipment at the hospital," insisted the doctor, as he removed a glass of medicinal rye from the patient's fingers.

"Then bring it over," said Fields. "I'm not leaving the room."

Instead of taking X rays, as he wished to do, the physician and several assistants from a piano factory brought in a fluoroscope and stripped the patient to his waist. It was a pretty scene, one that might have tried the humanity of Hippocrates. Fields, wearing a straw hat and standing more or less behind the fluoroscope, carried on a high, senseless monologue about the benefits of disease and the perfidy of doctors, while the company giggled and the physician and the manager pleaded for co-operation.

"Can you stand over a little to your left, Mr. Fields?" the physician would say. "We've only got the end of one collarbone in the picture."

"—down there in the New He-brides group," said Fields, resuming an anecdote he'd started a minute before, "and came down with a painful rash in the region of my *latissimus dorsi*——"

"To the left, Bill," said the manager. "That's your right —you're out of the picture entirely now."

"Had this rash in the region of my *latissimus dorsi*," said Fields to the company, "and they called in a native witch doctor——"

"Could the patient stop thrashing his arms?" called out the doctor in a querulous voice. "It seems to give a shimmying eff——"

"Beg your pardon," said Fields. "Well, this witch doctor made up a brew out of bats' feet and missionaries' teeth and listened to my heart with a conch shell. Then he——"

"Come on, Bill," said the manager. "You can have a drink later. The doctor's trying to look at your chest."

"Could the patient get behind the fluoroscope again?" asked the physician.

"Upshot of it was," continued Fields, "that the witch doctor turned to me and said, 'I'm sorry, but you've con-

tracted beri-beri, botts, and that dreaded of all diseases—
mogo on the gogogo.' He handed me a bill for thirty-two
beads and three yards of yellow ribbon."

After some time the physician actually made an examination. Then he said, "Mr. Fields, have you ever had tuberculosis?"

"Naw," said Fields, employing his favorite rejoinder.

"My examination shows that about twenty years ago you
had a very clearly defined case," the physician went on.
"The extensive scar tissue proves it beyond a doubt.
You're having a mild recurrence."

"Well, I guess it was that incident in Edinburgh," said
Fields at length. "But it healed right up. Tuberculosis is
nothing to worry about. Alongside of mogo on the gogogo
it——"

Nonplused, the physician signaled to the piano movers,
who picked up the fluoroscope and they all left. Fields put
his shirt back on, and *Poppy* proceeded as advertised. He
felt all right again in a few days. There can be no doubt
that the exposure and privations of his childhood had made
him easy prey to tuberculosis, but after the setback during *Poppy* he never had any further trouble with the disease. Later in life Fields had various explanations for his
singular recovery, most of them centering on whisky, a tuberculosis specific that probably would not withstand medical scrutiny. People who knew him best believe that he defeated the disease through the exercise of his extraordinary will power. Fields often overcame illness by ignoring
it. Like a horse, he considered himself well if he was on his
feet.

The European tour was good for Fields; he added self-
confidence to an already abundant supply of that quality, he
acquired culture in sizable doses, and he saved money,
secreting it in such banks as looked trustworthy. On this first
foreign tour he averaged $150 a week. His expenses were
small; in most countries, the exchange was favorable to
Americans, and living was, besides, relatively very cheap.
A situation of this kind was attractive to Fields, who believed in taking advantage of whatever windfalls the Lord
provided. When he returned to America, flushed with enthusiasm, he promptly took steps to book another tour. He

laid out a plan whereby he would share himself in equitable parts with the nations of the world. As the Pittsburgh *Gazette* reported his program, not long after the turn of the century, "He makes it a condition of all his contracts that he shall play one season in America and two seasons abroad consecutively. Hence he is perhaps the most extensive traveler on the stage."

Fields was, in fact, becoming a great international favorite. People who saw his act remembered it in detail years later. Notwithstanding his heartwarming natural receptions, he devised a simple scheme, in this period, to assure himself of ovations. When he entered a new town, he would send out a messenger to round up some boys. These he would employ, at moderate prices, to form a Fields claque. Other performers were often astonished, on a night that found the public generally limp, when the appearance of Fields evoked hosannas. The boys pitched in with such vim that it caught on around the house; people who, for one reason or another on certain occasions, felt disinclined to applaud anything, set up a thunderous roar for Fields, and managers duly took note. The latter action was largely superfluous, since Fields, after a hearty claque, usually looked in on the manager to describe the racket and ask for a raise. Once, headlining a bill at the Tivoli, that pleasant outdoor playground in Copenhagen, he organized his paid disciples and remained in his dressing room, after the show, to square up. One of the group, a curly-headed youngster in the throes of honest hero worship, refused the money and asked for a photograph instead. Fields, much pleased, gave him one, signing it with a grand flourish. Many years later, in California, he became acquainted with a Danish actor named Carl Brisson, who occupied a dressing room next to his on the Paramount lot. Fields invited him to dinner, and during the relaxation after dinner, Brisson offered to entertain. He stood up and imitated several of the juggling tricks, with familiar gestures, that Fields had featured in the days of his old European tours. Then Brisson produced the signed photograph Fields had given him at the Tivoli. Fields was touched and flustered.

Twice at the Folies-Bergère, in Paris, Fields had top billing. Charles Chaplin, a young Englishman just getting started in show business, was on the program both times but in a subordinate niche. Chaplin's contribution at these shows consisted principally of sitting in a box, like an ordinary patron, and shooting putty wads at the actors, a form of intramural entertainment with which Fields was not wholly in sympathy. Several of Fields' friends thought that he saw the stirrings of greatness in Chaplin very early, and grew hostile accordingly. "I hope Chaplin's picture [*Monsieur Verdoux*] is as bad as everybody says it is," he was to write one of them not long before his death. Fields never saw the film and so was happily unaware of the many fine moments it contained for Chaplin followers. Also on his bill at the Folies-Bergère was a young song-and-dance man named Maurice Chevalier, who was then appearing anonymously and rather contentedly in the chorus.

During his second foreign haul, Fields went from London to South Africa, which at that time was unsettled by the civil strife known as the Boer War. He was in Johannesburg when the trouble reached there, starting with a series of strikes. To a London friend he wrote, "The town is under martial law and we all must be in bed by eight o'clock each evening. The music halls are closed and two companies are lying idle. There is an epidemic of jugglers here. The outbreak includes Valazzi, Frank Le Dent, Silvo, Selma Braatz and myself! I have suggested an all-juggling bill. The place is full of grim-looking Boers with double barreled guns and thickly bearded faces. They pass the lonely hours waiting for trouble by vying with each other to look the dirtiest.

"It is now eight o'clock and the quiet is absolutely appalling. Not a soul on the streets except soldiers and policemen with guns slung over their shoulders. They stand about in groups and remain perfectly silent. The railway was guarded by burghers all the way from Cape Town. I am beginning to like Jo'burg, though, and am glad I did not commit *felo-de-se* on the boat coming out. I enclose you a Post-impressionistic sketch of me by a local artist. I didn't know whether to sue for libel or get him deported."

In a Cape Town saloon Fields met a young American cowhand, Will Rogers, who had shipped there with a herd of range ponies, hoping to sell them to the Boers. He showed Fields a lot of fancy rope tricks and said he wouldn't mind getting into show business himself, when he got rid of his stock. Later, in Durban, Fields again ran across Rogers, who by then had joined a small circus. In the years to come, their paths were to cross many times; they were to co-star in the *Follies* and appear together on many other bills. Rogers always had the greatest reverence for Fields, and Fields reciprocated the feeling, with his usual periodic reservations and suspicions. For a while, for example, he felt that Rogers' fame was becoming unwieldy and bothersome. Despite occasional snubs, Rogers continued throughout his life to think that Fields was the funniest man in history. Once, when Fields was ill at Las Encinas Sanitarium in Pasadena, Rogers went out to visit him, taking various goodies that he believed might be on the proscribed list. At the gate he was informed that Fields was too ill to receive callers. Rogers nodded politely, drifted down the wall a couple of hundred yards, climbed a sapling and dropped over, then pushed forward from bush to bush, as if stalking wild ponies, to Fields' room. They had a rousing reunion, while Fields' nurse, a girl in her teens, gave awestruck co-operation.

When Rogers had gone, the nurse assisted Fields to a couch and said mistily, "Isn't he a *wonderful* man? I just love that voice!"

"The son of a bitch is a fake," said Fields. "I'll bet a hundred dollars he talks just like anybody else when he gets home."

Fields met another American cowboy, Tom Mix, in South Africa during the Boer War. When Fields asked Mix what brought him down, he said carelessly, "Oh, I thought I'd get me in on this fuss."

Fields was impressed by what struck him as dangerous nonchalance.

"Is that so?" he asked. "Which side are you on?"

"Either side," said Mix. "I haven't had a chance to check up on what they're fighting about. It's all one to me, anyhow."

Fields never forgot Mix's offhand view of life. He took a strong proprietary interest in the cowhand's later film career, frequently telling about the South African meeting and saying that, so help him, there was *one* movie Westerner who was a hundred per cent genuine.

CHAPTER TWELVE

ONE DAY, Fields was visited at his hotel in Berlin by an American friend who, when he got in the room, began to skip around in a very trying manner. He looked under the chairs, behind the bed, and in the closet. Fields demanded an explanation, alert, as always, for trouble.

"Shhh!" whispered the friend. "There's a man in this room."

Automatically, Fields muttered, "The house dick!" and started to frame a denial of everything.

"My dear fellow," said the visitor, breaking off the joke. "It's you—you're twenty-one. This is your birthday!"

Fields sometimes gave out his birth date to the press (though generally lying about it, for no apparent reason except perhaps to keep his hand in), but he had small taste for birthdays himself. He seldom remembered when the fateful day rolled around. More often than not, he was in some place, at the time, where he knew nobody well and where a celebration would have had limited appeal.

On his tours and in this country, though he often saw friends (who were largely theatrical connections), he had wretched sieges of loneliness, when he aimlessly wandered the streets, sat reading in his room, or sequestered his thoughts in some quiet, uninquisitive bar. Realizing the solitary incompleteness of his life, he tried to develop hobbies. For a while he devoted himself to sketching—an artistic urge that seems to find lodgings in a good many actors. John Barrymore began his career as a cartoonist, his brother Lionel was a painter of exceptional diligence. Numerous toilers in the Hollywood vineyard now range their crisp, dried hills with brush and easel. Starting with a pencil and a notebook, Fields sought the elusive line. He sat in parks and studied the genus homo. His findings were unflattering. The species emerged as grotesque, its faces clownish, its figures warped. As his talent sharpened, he moved to pen and proceeded to crayon, slandering his fellows in bold, black lines. At length, in an impartial humor, he turned viciously on himself. The stockpiles of artists are rich in self-portraits. With any creative person, the present indicative is important, with the actor-artist it sometimes reaches an obsession. Van Gogh captured the saffron spirit of Arles, but he was equally content with the spirit of Van Gogh, frayed ear and all. Fields reproduced himself in caricature many, many times, and several of the works survive. They are deft and humorous, with real feeling for disparagement. The line is sharp, arresting, strong with animation.

Mainly, he drew himself in tramp costume. To an adroit reporter he finally acknowledged his new enterprise, and gave over a sketch of himself for publication. Thereafter, many papers printed Fields' caricatures of himself, in connection with interviews. Commenting on Fields' life in this period, the Cleveland *Plain Dealer,* for example, said, "How a man of the routine imposed upon W. C. Fields at the Hippodrome makes to be lonely when his activities in the theater take up most of the afternoons and evenings is surprising. Nevertheless, Fields confesses that he is one of the loneliest of men. When good books are not available, Fields makes time merrily pass by drawing sketches. Strolling along the streets and through the parks, he draws all and sundry. And his talent at this endeavor is almost up to his juggling, and that is saying quite a deal!" The confidential nature of this dispatch is astonishing, when it is considered that Fields seldom revealed his true status, of whatever kind, to any reporter. In no other known interview of the time does he mention being lonely. On the contrary, he often described his offstage commitments as being somewhat more social than those of the Astors. The *Plain Dealer's* report must stand, in the light of what Fields later told a few close friends, as a fine tribute to an enterprising, anonymous and long-forgotten reporter.

Vaudeville old-timers always remembered Fields as a solitary man. Marty Lynch, a juggler of that period who practiced his art long thereafter, wrote in a letter to a friend: "No one ever knew him [Fields]. I was playing in London a long time, and so was Fields, at different theaters, and all the performers used to gather after their shows at the German Club, on Lisle Street, in back of the Hippodrome. Fields would be there, too, but all alone always, sitting at a table reading and drinking, all alone.

"I would ask different actors if they knew him. Well, I met a few that played on 'bills' with him, but hardly anybody knew him, to speak to."

Fields' loneliness presumably reached such a pitch that, soon after the turn of the century, he contracted an alliance that will probably remain the cloudiest aspect of his history. He took a bride, a Miss Harriet Hughes, of 423 West Twenty-fifth Street, New York City. The liaison marked the beginning of a wrangle that continued until Fields' death. In fact, it was still in recent, lively progress, in California, where the widow continued the fuss with the late comedian's shade, trying, contrary to his wishes as expressly stated in his will, to gain control of his fortune. Fields and Miss Hughes met while she was dancing in a New York musical show. Fields had been engaged to do a specialty act during the show's New York run. She was a pretty girl, with a striking figure, and Fields at the time was both handsome and glamorous, if the tramp costume can be discounted. Miss Hughes' father was a respectable, hard-working wholesale grocer (Fields once remarked later that for a good portion of his life he seemed to have been pursued by vegetables) and her mother, a former resident of New Orleans, was a French Creole.

Fields himself was always vague on the subject of his wedlock, feeling that it "dated" him. The former Miss Hughes, who later lived at 123½ North Gale Drive, Beverly Hills, was never very co-operative with the press. In the interest of breaking the will, however, she announced through her attorney that the date of her marriage was "on or about the eighth day of April, 1900," and that the place was California. Relatives of the families have recalled a few details of the match. After the ceremony, the couple accompanied the show on tour. Then, back in New York, they lived for a while with the bride's parents. As seen by a member of the circle, Fields was considerate of his moth-

er-in-law and treated her with kindness. At meals, for example, he often tried to brisken up the gathering with little
mannerisms he had developed during his professional life.
Of these, Mrs. Hughes perhaps cared least for his habit of
dining with a beer bottle balanced on top of his head.

As one result of the marriage, Fields became reconciled
with his own family. After an absence of more than a decade, he returned to the Germantown hearth. On this visit he
took his wife and her sister Kitty, who had been a well-
known child actress and was still appearing in Broadway
plays. Kitty Hughes afterward married a Japanese-Ameri-
can, George Kurimoto, and lived in Jackson Heights. At
first, back home, Fields was nervous, lest his father might
remember the box and take further steps with the shovel.
But the quarrel was forgotten; the mood was genial. Fields'
brothers and sisters, like their parents, were eager for details of his career, and he expounded it by the hour, dwelling on his entrances into all the big American cities, to
ticker tape and mass cheering, and the strong comrade-
ship that had sprung up between him and European royal-
ty. The implication was strong in his reports that he had
the run of Buckingham Palace, and he was heard to remark that some of the bedrooms were "drafty." He spoke
affectionately of the King, whom he referred to as "Ed," or
"Eddie," and recalled with pleasure their nocturnal ram-
blings about the London cabarets. Needless to say, his family was spellbound; Dukinfield in particular seemed almost
unhinged with astonishment. He went into a mild shock
from which he never really recovered.

Fields found that Philadelphia revisited was a sunnier
place. He retraced the rocky trail of his fugitive youth. The
old bunk, where he had lain in muddy anguish, was tumbled in, its walls eroded, its bottom weedy. On the far end
of its lot a house was going up. Fields passed the time of
day with a workman, remarking that he had "once looked
into the lot as a possible residential site." The workman
replied, with unconscious appropriateness, that the neighborhood was growing up pretty fast and that it was always smart to get in on the ground floor. Fields agreed,
and strolled on toward the smithy. In his later accounts to
a friend, he seemed nostalgic about his homecoming. Just
as the bloodiest battlefields finally become places of ineffa-

ble charm, so did the ugliness fade from the scenes of his youth. Trudging over the trail, warm and friendly in the summertime of his visit, he wondered how it could have seemed so hostile in the years before. The forge was closed; Wheeler had apparently made good on his threat to move to Georgia; nobody appeared to know for sure. The barn was refurbished, occupied now by a newcomer, a beefy, red-faced steam fitter. As to the Orlando Social Club, its quarters were gutted and its members scattered. The steam fitter, who was sitting outside on a three-legged stool, taking the sun, mentioned the burned-out quarters when Fields approached.

"You the insurance adjuster?" he said sourly.

"Why, no, I can't honestly say that I am," Fields replied.

The man evidently failed to hear him, or paid no heed, for he went on, "Well, that second story up there, that's quite a mess, now, ain't it?"

Fields, looking up and seeing the scorch marks on the outside, murmured sympathetically.

"You been shinning around amongst the neighbors?" asked the fitter, with a keen look.

Fields stared blankly, and he continued, "There's been some talk that I fired it. I may be dumb, but I got ears."

Fields was about to congratulate him on a clever ruse when the man said, "They lie, that's how! There's slander laws, and so they'll find. I wasn't nowhere near. I was out on a boiler job—man blowed a sleeve valve and scalded two stokers two mile north of Cheaptown. So that's that, and you can investigate all you please, and be damned to you!"

Fields had been on the point of asking to see his old apartment, but in view of the steam fitter's vehemence he changed his mind and made off down the road, at a fairly brisk rate. Later on, he said the incident (as he related it in literary detail) had cheered him up. "I finally felt at home," he explained.

He visited the stable where he had reaped the golden harvest of the benefit. The place had changed hands and nobody knew where the former owner had gone. The new man, a lugubrious beanpole, was apathetic toward Fields' reminiscence about the benefit, interrupting continually with complaints that a client named Osborn had "lathered up" the establishment's best mare. "It isn't as though he'd selected Pondicherry Nell," he said. "She's wind broke already. Nothing but the best, he says, and points out Sadie. Tell you what," he added ferociously, lowering his nose to a point an inch or so from Fields', an unfortunate juxtaposition that placed him at a lively disadvantage, "I think he's putting her to commercial use. If I find out he's been drawing and hauling I'll——"

Fields left before learning the nature of the revenge likely to be visited upon Osborn. It was good, he reflected, to get back to the earth, to shake off, for a while, the problems of artificiality and reacquaint himself with the burdens of his audience. And always, as he proceeded, he studied the foibles of the race, taking mental notes, storing up for the future. He passed the house whose basement he had occupied on the nights when the first glacial blasts of winter had proved the inadequacy of the blacksmith's. There was a new basement window; the prohibitive boards were gone; the house had a fresh coat of paint. Fields was momentarily tempted to come back, window or no window, and spend the night sleeping in the woodbox. He felt the old urges; for a space he had the sharpest curiosity about the housewife's current store of preserves. But the hard-won luxury of clean sheets prevailed. He put down the rising, deodorized tide of old sensations and continued on his way. He was at last, he decided, almost civilized, and he returned to his waiting bride.

"I remember seeing him at the old Keith's Union Square, not long after the marriage," a distant relative said. "Hattie was helping him out in the act. She was dressed in pretty white tights and she looked ravishing. As Claude—we all called him Claude—did his tricks, Hattie handed him the equipment, standing by and smiling, you know, the way they do. We went around to the stage door and he came out, keyed up and perspiring but very polite. He asked us how we had liked the act and he seemed awfully pleased when we said it was funny."

In the first months of the marriage the couple lived in various furnished apartments. Then they took a suite at the old Bartholdi Hotel, on Twenty-third Street across from the Flatiron Building, in a district then distinguished by the pre-eminence of its architecture but today humbled by the loftier eyesores uptown. Though there is generous support for the belief that Fields was finally a difficult husband, he was at first docile, and stuck close to home. His evenings were devoted mainly to study, a member of the family recalled. He had a prolonged session of rereading his favorite authors—Dickens, Swift, Mark Twain.

So domestic had Fields become, after his season of wooing, that he invited his family to accompany him and Mrs. Fields on a professional trip to Europe. His brother Walter accepted, and the three sailed together on a sunny morning in May. Fields was, as stated, domestic, but his firmly rooted caution about money had hardly disappeared. It developed that he and the bride were to travel first-class and Walter was to join the mediocrities in second. During the voyage Mrs. Fields expressed concern over her brother-in-law's welfare; she persuaded her husband to investigate. Her worry was commendable but baseless. "Walter Fields was as good-looking a young man as any matinee idol, what they called in those days 'a regular Gibson type,' " said a female friend who knew him then. "He was tall and well-made and very blond, like most of the Dukinfields. Women used to pause and stare whenever he passed."

Fields and his wife picked their way into second class for the investigation and found Walter hobnobbing with a countess, the ship's only celebrity of the first magnitude. He nodded democratically but made no gesture about an introduction. Later on, it came out that the countess had spotted him from A deck with a pair of binoculars she carried for the purpose and had sought him out promptly.

Walter's position on the tour was not wholly that of guest. He also functioned as his brother's secretary. The work was not heavy, though Fields found many little tasks, annoying in the aggregate, to delegate from time to time. Once, in Fields' dressing room, when Mrs. Fields found a gayly scented letter on his table and demanded an explanation, he backed Walter into a corner, pressed a twenty-dollar bill into his hand, and cried in angry tones, "How many times have I told you to stop using my name?" The explanation, said Fields, was actually quite simple, though he somehow didn't feel up to relating it at the time—a young lady sitting in a box had merely sent him a warmly affectionate fan letter.

It was inevitable that marriage for Fields should fail. His years of fighting life on his own terms had diminished his adaptability. Even if he had married a girl with the patience of a saint, he would have been chafed by the double harness. There was, between him and Mrs. Fields, a difference in religious conviction. The bride was a responsive Catholic, given to sturdy dawn expeditions of worship. Fields' religion was less formal, less capable of definition. In general, he felt that the average minister should be unfrocked immediately and prevented, by force if necessary, from communicating any ideas to persons under thirty-five. He considered, further, that Methodists especially, having, as he had been told, a theological bias against nicotine, needed the most vigilant kind of watching. In the light of maturer statements from Fields, one gathers that he had a sort of religion of his own but that it was disassociated from the church. Never in his lifetime did he establish a rapport between himself and any of the Lord's agents on earth; his divinity was practiced wholly within the temple of his mind.

The little things that disrupt marriage became much in evidence during the few years that he and his wife lived together. The greatest sympathy may be felt for a woman whose choicest bric-a-brac was frequently describing a course between her husband's fingers and the ceiling. On days when Fields' timing was bad, she suffered acute and understandable shocks. With a figurine of the Virgin crashing here and a painted shell from Atlantic City dissolving there, she found it hard to read, or attend to her sewing.

On a second trip to Europe, Mr. and Mrs. Fields took Mr. Dukinfield along. The father had a nostalgic urge, as Fields said he put it, "to take another look at old Ben afore I die." His wife stayed home to mind the family, aided by a generous subsidy from her eldest son. Dukinfield's wish was gratified; shortly after they arrived in London, Fields put him on an omnibus that ran right by the big clock. On this tour Mrs. Fields notified her husband that she was expecting a child, and sometime before its arrival was due, she and Dukinfield returned home. She had remembered, perhaps, that an American boy born outside the country's limits is disqualified from becoming President. Her child was as she had anticipated, a male; he was recently an attorney, practicing in Los Angeles and living in Beverly Hills; an upright, mildly corpulent man in his early forties, astonishingly similar, physically, to his father, with the familiar resonance of voice, and vigorously devoted to his mother. "The two have always felt," said an acquaintance, "that they have been a very great comfort to each other during the long, hard years when Mr. Fields was receiving his vulgar publicity."

The boy was named W. C. Fields, Jr., a fact that he never presumed on; he has gone as anonymously as possible, by the name of "Claude," which both he and his mother favored. Mr. and Mrs. Fields separated a few years after Claude was born. The critical reasons for their disharmony will remain, appropriately enough, a family secret, since Fields never discussed the marriage, but his friends believed that the separation had a salutary effect on both of them. From the moment of his departure, Fields began to send his wife a weekly check, starting with twenty-five dollars and working up to around sixty dollars toward his death. Sometimes, when the fit was on him, he reduced the amount, occasionally with an explanation (which usually centered on "hard times") but more often without. Mrs. Fields took her son to Brooklyn, where they lived for a while; then they moved to a flat at Ninety-fourth and Amsterdam in Manhattan, and after that to Academy Street, where Claude grew up. He attended public schools, Evander High School, and finally Columbia University. At the latter place he showed his mettle—working his way through by playing the saxophone, stolidly refusing support from his illustrious father. Mrs. Fields, an energetic and thoughtful mother, had insisted that Claude, when quite young, take piano lessons, and it developed that the boy had considerable talent. In his high school phase, however, he succumbed to the syrupy bleats of the saxophone, which was then at the crest of its vogue. Gaining a decision over the saxophone, he organized his own band at Columbia. Claude had a successful undergraduate career. At its conclusion he ditched the horn and took up law. In Beverly Hills, he has always been regarded as a dedicated church worker.

Back on his own, Fields returned to Europe, again with his brother Walter. He expanded his itinerary, penetrating deeper into the Continent, exploring new areas of juggling appreciation. Of these, Spain was perhaps the most fruitful. In an interview a few years later, Fields remarked to an American reporter that if he had to choose another nationality he would make it Spanish. "They have a fanatical reverence for masters of legerdemain," he said, according to the writer, "and cherish Agoust, Severus and Cinquevalli almost as much as they are supposed to like El Greco." This statement was charitable of Fields, considering his first reception in Madrid. The manager of the theater had billed him after Fields' usual taste in those matters—that is, as "the greatest juggler," "greatest comedian," and several other superlatives, on earth. However, feeling was still pretty high as a result of the Spanish-American War, and the manager received word that an American juggler would be warmly greeted, perhaps with things like old tamales, garlic and Spanish mackerel. His communicant added that Fields would not need a round-trip railroad ticket, as the audience would almost certainly ride him out of town on a rail, in accordance with American custom. The manager got in touch with Fields and altered him, without immigration folderol, into an Englishman. When Fields, sensing an easy social improvement, suggested a title, the manager responded with native Spanish courtesy, and Fields appeared as "Sir Cuthbert E. Frothingham, S.B.," the name being the juggler's own creation, together with the initials.

Mack Sennett, for whom Fields was to work some years later in Hollywood, recalled a Fields engagement around this period in Hamburg. Before arriving in Germany, Fields said, he had developed an act in which he juggled six balls, a master feat in the juggling business. He was filled with confidence and, at the theater—the old Hippodrome—decided to stand in the wings and watch a few other acts, something he seldom did. His comfortable reverie was interrupted by the act that preceded his. It turned out to be a dwarf who juggled fourteen balls while riding a horse.

Fields was outraged; he forsook his pallid six-ball routine and substituted one that featured hats. But he was so angry he kept dropping the hats; he couldn't seem to get under them. He was unused to German audiences at this time and had no idea how things were going, but he fancied that they could scarcely be worse. At last, with another hat down, he stepped forward in a perfect rage and kicked it far out over the footlights. The spectators were charmed. They had been interested in but unstimulated by the dwarf's presentation. A knack for detail—grinding lenses, organizing drills, devising booby traps—was commonplace in German life, and they yearned for something new. "Ya, iss gute," "Oh, fonny!" and "Ha, ha, ein mann vill kicken der hat!" were among the pleased cries that floated up to Fields, and forever afterward, when playing in Germany, he made a big point of kicking hats (provided by the management) all over the house.

CHAPTER THIRTEEN

In the years between his marriage and the first World War, Fields followed the vaudeville trail. He played all the best houses of the day, and his salary grew. He had a singular financial reputation among managers, agents, and other middle men of the theater. It was, in essence, "No matter how smart you may be about money, Fields can outsmart you." He was cautious and patient, like a brilliant military tactitian. He never charged a hill without sufficient artillery support. In the matter of demanding a raise, he would wait until the house was leaning primarily on his act. Then, with flinty unction, he would appear in the manager's office. According to witnesses, the exchange (a variation of his old approach to Fred Irwin) always went about as follows:

FIELDS: Afternoon, Sam (*or George, or Ned, or Bert, or Homer*).

SAM: Oh, hello, Bill. Glad to see you.

FIELDS: How things going, Sam?

SAM (*guardedly*): Why, not too bad, Bill. Tough week for sets—had to put on three extra men.

FIELDS: Runs into money, hey, Sam?

SAM: Expenses are terrible just now. Worst I can remember.

FIELDS: Box office steady, I hope?

SAM: That *is* one thing. Business hasn't fallen off any, so's I can notice. Maybe Tuesday night.

FIELDS: Might even be building up a little, you suppose, Sam?

SAM (*much more guardedly*): Tell you the truth, I haven't seen the figures. I been so worried about expenses I haven't had time.

FIELDS (*concerned*): You ought to cut down your overhead, Sam. My four weeks are up tomorrow. I'd better go on back to Keith's.

SAM: Why, no, Bill. I said we might hold you over, and we'll do it. I'll take the slice out of my end.

FIELDS (*emotionally affected*): You're a square shooter, Sam. But you can't help hard times. I'll go on back to Keith's.

SAM (*in a slight change of voice*): I've got four hardware conventions coming in town in July. You know how they feel about juggling.

FIELDS: Recommend Oroso the Magnificent. You seen that wonderful new turn of his with one Indian club? The boy's coming along.

SAM (*almost screaming*): *Boy!* That son of a bitch is a hundred and fifty years old. He couldn't catch a basketball with two extra hands.

FIELDS (*with the far-off look*): Oroso the Magnificent. Working at present, I believe, through Finkleberg and O'Malley, 2750 Broadway.

SAM (*calm now and quite sour*): How much, Bill?

FIELDS: Four-fifty straight.

SAM (*deathly pale*): Four weeks and option for four hundred and two.

FIELDS: Four-fifty straight, and six.

SAM: By God! I'll——

FIELDS (*rising*): Keith's——

SAM: Four-fifty straight. And let me say that for a thieving, low-down, infernally——

FIELDS (*leaving, with an expression of offended dismay*): See you, Sam.

He shifted back and forth across the country, over to Europe, back again—always on the move, always in a hurry, and endlessly planning for the future. It was a desperate, uneasy kind of life, and all down the line it took its count. "I had the feeling," Fields once told a friend, "that although I didn't actually have anything right now, I was working to have something soon. I think that was the part that got next to me—all was going fine, but I didn't *have* anything, somehow. I was on a train rushing toward a good place, but I couldn't seem to get there."

He was never satisfied; he never slept soundly. He conceived an urge to appear in a different kind of show, and he wangled a part with McIntyre and Heath, two famous blackface comedians of the day, in a hybrid production of Klaw and Erlanger called *The Ham Tree*. It had a sort of story line but was essentially a vaudeville show. Dramatically, it did little for Fields, since no sooner had he got the part than he set up a clamor to juggle. McIntyre and Heath, if we may believe their friends, had never before encountered a performer of Fields' persuasion. Within a few weeks after the opening, in New York, he was virtually running the show. McIntyre and Heath had to dig vigorously to keep on the pay roll. Fields stayed with *The Ham Tree* for its New York run and on the road through the years 1906 and 1907, but he never gave his employers a peaceful moment. By now his standing with the press was solid, and he gave out interviews all along the route that made pointed mention of richer offers elsewhere. Over his theater there hung always the sinister threat that he might bolt.

An Ohio paper of October 17, 1905, said, "W. C. Fields, the 'Sherlock Baffles' of *The Ham Tree* company has been offered an engagement at the London Hippodrome. But he won't go. There has been talk of starring him next year in a piece that will give him an opportunity to employ his juggling. The talk has not yet come to anything like a definite arrangement, but Fields has decided that the possibility is worth trying for. He will stay with *The Ham Tree,* meanwhile, waiting for developments."

During the run, Fields felt it vital to impress two things upon the management: (1) that he was outstanding and (2) that he should juggle. In consequence, he was alert and voluble when he collared his old friends of the press. "One of the most amusing bits in *The Ham Tree,*" said the Pittsburgh *Sun* of May 1, 1907, "in which McIntyre and Heath are appearing at the theater this week is the part of Sherlock Baffles which W. C. Fields is portraying. Since *The Ham Tree* has been on the road (and is now in its second season) he has been appearing in the role and his work has been one of the hits of the piece. During one portion of the entertainment he works in his specialty—that of juggling."

From Fields' standpoint, a report forcibly concise and to the point.

For the Chicago *Herald* of January 7, 1906, he consented to do a first-person piece that would appear under the introduction, "Mr. Fields' clever juggling and pantomime are the best feature of a nondescript entertainment called *The Ham Tree,* current at the Colonial."

In the piece itself, Fields strayed somewhat off the subject. It seemed to be a complaining article, with special reference to acts that made use of large, noisy props. In the course of his choler it developed that his trouble could be traced to a family of French acrobats who had once preceded him in Paris and killed his routine entirely. Fields offered no solution for these acts, other than his implied suggestion that they be removed from the theater without delay. Toward the end, in a quieter vein, he went into a few of his own little turns. "My use of extension nippers," he wrote, "came from seeing them employed by the Viennese shopkeepers to lift articles from the window, customers declining to accept any but the identical goods displayed." He could probably have added a few lively, personal notes to the Viennese shopkeeper situation, had he chosen.

The Ham Tree was a success of the period. Of the reviews that greeted it, that of the South Bend (Indiana) *Tribune* was regarded by some of the cast as being the most definitive: "Perhaps the best vaudeville bill ever offered in South Bend was McIntyre and Heath and supporting company in *The Ham Tree* at the Auditorium last evening. *The Ham Tree* is called 'A Musical Novelty,' but in reality it is a series of vaudeville features done up in a flimsy package which for want of any other name may be called 'A Plot.' Every once in a while the package is either forgotten or it is mislaid. No matter which, the audience is entertained and the laughs come thick and fast.

"McIntyre and Heath are clever blackface comedians. They are above the average and never do they have to resort to the tricks and horseplay so common in the variety of comedy which they essay. Generally speaking, their methods are quiet and their efforts are genuinely funny.

Sometimes they laugh at the audience and at other times they laugh with the audience, but whether they laugh with or at, the audience laughs all the time and what more could any entertainers ask or what more could any audience desire? And there you are. Whatever *The Ham Tree* may be, a musical comedy, a musical novelty, or a musical conglomeration of fun, frolic and occasionally a tune, McIntyre and Heath and their support are quite worth seeing. The plot package may be loosely done up and now and then thrown in a corner and forgotten for the time being—but what's the use? One laughs and forgets, and to laugh and forget is something that one can't always do, unless given a lot of encouragement. McIntyre and Heath furnished the encouragement.

"The support was led by W. C. Fields as Sherlock Baffles, a mystery, who reminded one considerably of 'Nervy Nat,' whose antics grace the pages of a well-known humorous weekly. Mr. Fields did some clever juggling when he wasn't otherwise engaged. Frederick K. Bowers sang a number of songs in energetic manner and did his share toward assisting the stars in their fun-making. David Torrence did an 'Earl of Pawtucket' part and tried to imitate, and with some success, the mannerisms of Lawrence D'Orsay. Belle Gold as Desdemona, a colored maid, danced well and sang with enthusiasm. Had the show been labeled 'vaudeville' she would have been down as 'a song-and-dance artist,' and such a classification would not be far from correct. The others, including the chorus, worked hard and pleased, both individually and collectively."

Tex Rickard took Fields around the world one year. Walter went along, and later worked for Rickard as a kind of combination secretary and bodyguard. Besides his trips to Europe, Fields went around the world two different times, juggling, without speaking any lines, before the most widely dissimilar audiences. One week he would perform for the upper-class residents of an English colony, and the following week he would entertain a tribe of naked Waziri. After his first circumnavigation of the globe, a Pittsburgh newspaper said, in listing his waystops, "For years he has been regarded as one of the cleverest jugglers in the business. He appeared in all the first-class vaudeville houses of this

country and then made a tour of the world, during which
he visited Honolulu, Samoa, New Zealand, South Africa,
Australia, Madeira, England, Ireland, Scotland, Wales,
Germany, France, Spain, Italy, Russia and the northern
countries. In most of these countries he appeared before
the crowned heads and he has in his possession many valuable keepsakes given him by nobility before whom he entertained in his once familiar make-up of the tramp."

Though he was reticent about many phases of his early
life, Fields later boasted continually of his travels. He liked
to sit on a movie lot, between scenes, and narrate hair-raising experiences apt to shock young females of the cast. By
his account, he had cultivated romances with women of every known pigment. He enjoyed dwelling in particular on
points of departure from Western standards. "This belle
was a Melanesian," he'd say, with a confiding smile at a
ingénue, "and she had kinky hair that stood up like a briar
bush. She had a wooden soup dish in her nether lip, her
teeth were filed, and through her nose she had a brass ring
that had come off a missionary's hitching post. Aside from
that, she was tattooed all over with pictures of rattlesnakes.
She was one of the prettiest girls in those parts."

If Fields' stories are to be accepted without dilution, he
had children by the majority of the women, married and
single, in the Belgian Congo and in most of the other savage areas of the planet. He spoke freely of legging it through
the brush with tribesmen in pursuit carrying spears. The
implication was clear in his reports that he had evacuated
each community only in time to escape serious damage.
Fields' reminiscences were stimulating, but, as his friends
have pointed out, many of them were probably lies. He
was gratified to find himself, raconteur-wise, in a situation
wherein it was difficult to check up on him. In Fields' favor,
it must be said that his anecdotes centered mainly on troubles rather than triumphs. Every place he went, painful
things happened to him. He established the foundation, in
fact, for a persecution complex of competitive dimensions.
For example, he rarely found a boardinghouse, in the out-
lands, that was not marred by some lethal flaw. He stopped
with one woman in Australia whose establishment, in the
early morning hours, quickened to various, odd jungle cries.
Chilled to the bone, Fields sought out his landlady and

found her in bed with her young son Clark and a leopard.

"I keep a few animals," she said. "The leopard's sick."

Fields thanked her politely, then withdrew to his chamber, encountering on the way, he said afterward, two water buffalo and a Kodiak bear.

Three weeks later he returned to the house and found his hostess in a charming mood. They exchanged notes about the weather, and Fields said, "By the way, how's the leopard?"

"Oh, much better," she replied with a pleased smile. "He flew at Clark this morning and bit him in the shoulder."

Fields sat up overnight in the railroad station.

One of the most distressing facets of his trips was the fact that he seemed to get jailed more often than is common. He had spent much of his childhood in jails, and the habit lingered. In exceptionally relaxed moments, Fields gave out comparative notes on jails, criticizing the cuisine, the cots, and the turnkeys. His remarks about French detention were disparaging in the extreme, though possibly tinctured with bias, while he spoke expansively of the lock-up system in England. His enthusiasm was only moderate about the jails in Australia—he felt that Australians had made no great strides in this field because their jails' most frequent occupants, aborigines, were unused to creature comforts and, provided with the luxury of food and beds, might get a distorted notion of punishment. In the last analysis, Fields, perhaps through municipal pride, thought that Philadelphia's jails stood up with the best. His face would become animated as he recalled the gentility of his keepers, the thick bean soup, and the scrubbed burlap racks. "When you get right down to it, there's nothing like Philadelphia," he would say, with a Rotary Club ring in his voice.

The principal reason for his confinements was gallantry. Fields would steer a girl into an inexpensive saloon, and when some friendly client gave her a harmlesss pinch, he would swing. The proprietors of saloons tend to favor their steady patrons, and Fields came off badly in the arraignments. He was thus jailed in London, and bailed out shortly. A similar case in Australia landed him in jail. "I was defending a dame whose virtue was impugned," went Fields' version as reported in an American newspaper, "and I may have been a little hasty." He was jailed in Germany for throwing what he described as "an overripe bock-wurst" on the floor of a café. They locked him up in London for socking a bobby. "He pushed me into the gutter," said Fields, without further explanation. He had an inflexible feeling for fair play, no doubt because of the unfair drubbings he had collected along the route. It was impossible for him to watch a fight without getting into it. In Paris, a French acrobat of his acquaintance, a man who worked with small, quiet props, was set upon, for reasons unknown to Fields, by three gendarmes, an alignment that struck Fields as thoughtlesss. Without making inquiries, he pitched into the scrap; he knocked out two of the gendarmes and, with the acrobat, assisted the third over the railing of a subway entrance. The winners had scarcely time to congratulate themselves before police reinforcements stampeded over them like cattle. Fields spent a cooling-off period in jail, clanging on his bars with tin cups, bawling for the American ambassador, and building up a profane international understanding with the acrobat, whose apartment was just across the way.

He was beset by other woes. A good many of these appeared to strike him at the Wintergarten, in Berlin. He had successes there, but not for the usual reasons. One time, when he had forwarded his equipment to the Wintergarten from Paris, he arrived to find the top of his billiard table in the theater, as per schedule, and the sides, according to a telegram, in a depot on the Russian border. It was a puzzling situation. Billiards is, or are, an exacting and even a dangerous game on a table without sides. Hastily, Fields engaged a carpenter, who went right to work without having the flimsiest idea what he was building. He and Fields communicated through a sort of emergency esperanto consisting of gutturals, signs, and marks scratched on boards. In the beginning, Fields decided, the man thought he was constructing a coffin for some good-sized but flattish animal, such as a starved goat. Accordingly, the sides emerged from six to eight inches tall, which was too high for an audience to see anything of the balls. As the work progressed, in the rear of the man's shop, which was adjacent to a beer garden, Fields rushed back and forth with a crock. The day wore on, and the carpenter hacked and whittled. At one point he got the sides down to a respectable billiards size, but by the time they finished the work, and ten or twelve crocks of beer, the table bore no resemblance to anything in their previous experience.

That evening he opened at the Wintergarten. He was in a moist humor and, aided by the carpenter's additions, broke new grounds in billiards. At times the orchestra members were compelled to drop their fiddles and take cover. Fields himself, as the act dissolved, was roaring like a bull. It was a new and fresh entertainment for patrons of the Wintergarten. To his astonishment, the comedian was told afterward that the routine had gone over wonderfully. "They iss laughing and laughing," the manager explained, greatly pleased. Of this incident, Fields was once quoted in an interview as saying that "the opening night in Berlin in those days usually set your bookings for the rest of the Continent. All the agents were on hand to watch me and I can say honestly that they had something to watch! Practically nothing went right, but the net result was that the act was so much funnier all of them offered me dates."

Another time at the Wintergarten the management had just installed a beautiful bank of bright lights in the ceiling. Fields had never felt better in his life, he said, but when he tossed up some balls, and looked aloft, all he could see was a kind of white, blinding hell. He tried it again, this time adding a couple of Indian clubs and some hats, with the result that a number of objects came down and banged him on the head. From the time of his birth Fields had been no man to give up easily, on large projects or small, and he dug in, determined to get his hands on the flying props or be carried off on a stretcher. Neither of these eventualities came to pass exactly. He got his hands on several items, mostly by accident, since he still couldn't see anything but a milky blur, and his head on several more, but he never really caught anything. Instead of hissing and booing, or requesting his removal, like a well-bred American or English audience, the Wintergarten patrons took the disaster in fine spirit. The native teutonic mind approves strong entertainment, involving fractures, and the spectators felt that Fields was sacrificing his skull for their diversion. Windy, gratified blasts greeted every ring of wood on bone; the act was getting over well. In the wings, Fields responded to the manager's congratulations with a broadside of profanity that, he decided late in life, he never quite came up to again. He said he matched its length on two or three occasions, but he never equaled its rich imagery or comprehensive zoological allusion.

Once, when he was in Madrid, the Spanish treasury had recently recalled some currency issues and hard coin was the tender of the day. Fields juggled for two weeks, then went to get his money. "Where's your basket?" said the manager. Fields expressed confusion, and the manager said, "I'm paying off in five-peseta pieces. No basket, no salary." With $750 due him, Fields rushed to the nearest grocer's and bought a durable bushel basket. His salary just filled it, the peseta being worth, at the time, around eleven cents. Fields pulled, carried, kicked, and otherwise cajoled the basket back to his room, where he nervously stood guard over it all night. The next day, at his wit's end, he removed it to a bank, where he opened an account, as he told a friend, under the name of Señor Guillermo McKinley, a half-breed from Guatemala. Unless he or an agent of the late President picked it up, it probably rests there yet, accruing pesetas, baffling its handlers—a worn footprint of a long-departed clown.

CHAPTER FOURTEEN

FIELDS FORMED distinct impressions of audiences wherever he went. He made notes on localities, and provided himself with hints about future appearances. He believed that, in order, Washington, Kansas City and St. Louis were the toughest cities on the vaudeville run. "They are the igloos of the theatrical world," he told a reporter. "Even the managers in those communities never know whether to give their patrons Sarah Bernhardt or trained seals." He worked hard in all three places, but his receptions were shifty. Sometimes when he felt that conditions were ripe for a collapse, Washington would greet him with loving zest. In St. Louis, when the carnival spirit was elsewhere high, his patrons looked suicidal. And in Kansas City bitter suffering was often written on every countenance. Over a period of years Fields tried to resolve these paradoxes. The indeterminate trio haunted his dreams. He had a nightmare, he once told his secretary, in which a judge's voice, organlike and funereal, reverberated through a hollow chamber. It said, "The prisoner is sentenced to face a mixed audience of St. Louisians, Washingtonians and Kansas Citians each night for the remainder of his life. Bailiff, lead him to the theater and let the punishment begin."

As he studied the foe, Fields discarded many theories. He took note of the German population in St. Louis, and recalled his workouts at the Wintergarten. But his receptions there, he reflected, had all been gay. He pondered the bleak plains of Kansas, the arid habits of its people, the high voltage of its divinity, and he got no answer. With regard to Washington, he knew, somehow, that the answer was rooted deep in politics. He evolved, at last, a theory, simple and obvious but probably foolproof. Knocked down to its essentials, it was that the people of Washington, accustomed to the incomparable slapstick on Capitol Hill, found lesser comedians a bore. In general, Fields considered that cities, despite the three he had trouble with, provided more fertile ground for stage humor than rural areas. There was an excellent reason for this: city people, at that time, were familiar with more of the world than country folk, and could understand a wider variety of reference. For a while, Fields encountered some embarrassing silences in the small towns with a routine involving subway straps. Conversely, he had many bad moments in New York, during a season when he was using a few lines, by tossing off the word "switchel bucket," which struck him as funny. Of this mishap he said, "I finally learned that the average New Yorker would have to go to the dictionary to find out what a switchel bucket was, even though Calvin Coolidge was someday to present one to the Prince of Wales."

Like most comedians, Fields compiled a list of "locals"

—neighborhood place names that were good for a laugh in cities where he played. He later explained this to a Paramount publicity man, Teet Carle, by saying, "In every big city there is always one surefire laugh, and that lies in hanging some piece of idiocy upon the people of a nearby city or town. I did not mean to imply any disparagement of those towns, but it's a fact that some names just sound funny to people's ears. When I was a boy in Philadelphia, I made that discovery myself. We had a great time at the expense of our neighbor, Mr. Muckle, although he was an estimable gentleman with nothing funny about him except the name." When Fields was appearing in Boston, he always mentioned the settlements of Nahant or Scituate; in Pittsburgh it was East Liberty; in Providence, Woonsocket; Los Angeles, Cucamonga; New York, Canarsie; Chicago, Winnetka; Portland, Kennebunkport; Detroit, Hamtramck; and Philadelphia, Manayunk.

"For reasons I have never understood," he told Carle, "Alexandria, Virginia, is screamingly funny to Washingtonians, while the great city of Oakland never fails to get a chuckle out of San Franciscans. And Bismarck, North Dakota, is funny anywhere in the United States."

During a great part of his life, Fields kept a file of odd names that he ran across in his travels. He used many of them. "Charles Bogle," the pseudonym he preferred, and the one which turned up most frequently among the credits for his pictures, was the name of a bootlegger of his acquaintance. Bogle, a large, affable man, without the quick facility for lawsuits that was to characterize the generation that followed, enjoyed his literary standing. "I used your name on some of those movies of mine, Charlie," Fields said he told him once. "You ever see them?"

"I can't say as I have, Mr. Fields," Bogle replied. "The missus and I don't care for the films. Father Dunlavy says they're immoral."

Fields pressed a couple of passes to *International House* on him, and, it being a quiet night for bootlegging, Bogle relaxed his principles and took his wife to the theater. He was filled with pride. During the credits, when his name appeared, he nudged a neighbor diffidently and murmured, "You'll notice my name, sir? A collaboration with Mr. Fields." Thereafter he became so stuck up about the Bogle works that he was almost ruined for a bootlegger and his wife began to find him intolerable. She complained to Fields that her husband was trying to steal his thunder and begged the comedian to find a new pen name. In an obliging humor, Fields used the more memorable "Mahatma Kane Jeeves" for his next script.

"Chester Snavely" was a name that Fields admired. He used it in two or three of his short comedies. The original owner, as far as he knew, was an undertaker of exceptional accomplishments in a suburb of Philadelphia. As a boy, Fields had blundered across a damp, crepy cortege led by the spotless Snavely, and, curious, had padded along behind. It was a funeral of distinction; Fields never forgot either it or Snavely. In fact, he was so powerfully influenced that he took steps to avoid a similar festivity for himself. The second paragraph of his last will and testament read: "I direct my executors immediately upon the certificate of my death being signed to have my body placed in an inexpensive coffin and taken to a cemetery and cremated, and since I do not wish to cause my friends undue inconvenience or expense I direct my executors not to have any funeral or other ceremony or to permit anyone to view my remains, except as is necessary to furnish satisfactory proof of my death."

In arranging the obsequies, Snavely was only following the custom of the day, and one which has altered little in the passing years. When Fields came upon the scene, having heard a peculiar ululation from his sanctuary in a clump of beeches (where, he said, he was roasting a borrowed chicken), a brief church service had been concluded and the procession was on its way to the grave. Deceased, surrounded by flowers, was in the first carriage, an open one, and behind him were eight other open, filled carriages, a hayrick containing a small party garbed in black, and a buckboard somewhat incongruously loaded with limestone blocks. The latter mystery was solved when it developed that the driver of the buckboard, a farmer, had no connection with the funeral but had been caught behind it on his way home from a lumberyard and was having some difficulty getting around. A group of urchins, indifferently attired, was strung out behind the buckboard, alternately running and walking, whispering, giggling and peering.

Snavely himself, superbly got up in a cutaway, a pair of striped trousers, and a dismal black bowler encircled by a wide band of crepe whose ends trailed off behind him, was walking at the head of this imposing column. His face was arranged in an expression of crushed but competent unction. Fields was impressed by the fact that, although it was midsummer and several of the mourners were clearly sweltering, one or two men having even slipped out of their jackets, Snavely seemed free of perspiration and discomfort. His smooth, bland, elongated face suggested that, in the matter of living, he had struck a nice balance between this world and the next and, though perpetually bereaved, was invulnerable to the annoyances of both. Flanking the procession, at no great distance, were a number of lesser functionaries, part-time employees of the mortuary, whom Snavely had been trying out recently, in a bid for the fashionable trade. They were known as "howlers," and operated as a kind of lachrymose claque, to help bring up the noise in weak or tiring groups. One of these, a youth in his teens, wearing a makeshift costume built around an outsized tuxedo jacket and making passes at his face with a handkerchief, trotted up alongside the leader as Fields hove into earshot near the curb.

"Everything comfortable aft?" asked Snavely.

"I'm having a little trouble with number seven, sir," said the youth.

"Friends or relatives?"

"It's the Wiggins family. They passed a bottle around after church and two of the men fell asleep."

"Well, roust them out. Try ammonia. It's going well, don't you think?"

"I believe it's our best since the Greenwalt job, sir. We won't be coming up to that one soon."

"Well, hardly," said Snavely, with a quick, gelid smile. Then he looked around and muttered, "I'll have to take care of that farmer." He walked back, leaning in and pressing the arms of three or four women on the way, and drew up by the buckboard.

"Your servant, sir," he said, keeping pace with the horse.

"Who's dead?" said the farmer unceremoniously.

"Departed went by the name of Ernest O. Potts," re-

plied Snavely, a little stiffly, and added, "of the Germantown Potts."

At this point the undertaker extended, in a sort of sleight-
of-hand motion, a freshly laundered handkerchief and said,
with feeling, "Will you join us, sir? It will appear better from
the sidelines, so to speak."

"But won't it look a little odd with these blocks?" asked
the farmer, pointing to his load.

"The blocks are of no consequence to Departed. *He*
don't care."

"Well, I don't mind if I do," said the farmer, and, taking
the kerchief, he gave a few warm-up honks.

In his later accounts of this funeral, which shifted from
year to year, Fields supplied a wealth of detail. There are,
however, grounds for the belief that his final version was a
composite, for which he had drawn on all the funerals he
had seen, and perhaps read up in Dickens. When the procession entered a small, populated section (he said) Snavely snapped his fingers several times to summon the howlers. He briefed them quickly, with that easy, prostrated finesse for which he was noted in the area, and they returned to their stations. Then, as the carriages, the hayrick, and the buckboard loaded with limestone blocks
wheeled solemnly toward the rows of gratified onlookers,
the friends and relatives, vigorously exhorted by the howlers, got their teeth into the occasion and raised some la-
mentations that hadn't been matched in those parts for
years. Even Snavely himself, afterward, said he couldn't
recall a more heart-warming exhibition of spot woe in his
entire career as a mortician. It was one of those moments
of response, the pure distillate of excitement, that knits up
the raveled sleeve of the artist. So all-around satisfactory
was the racket that, according to Fields, Snavely circled the
block and had another whack at it, and he wasn't disap-
pointed, either—they buckled down just as hard the second time.

In a way, the cemetery was an anticlimax. At the start
there was a delay while Snavely and two of his helpers put
the pit down another foot, since the gravediggers had apparently thrown up the job in the middle. In this interim
the Wiggins family, having made themselves known to the
farmer (who by now was deep in the spirit of the affair

and was referring to the corpse as "Ernie" and "Good old Potts"), unloaded their bottle and passed it around surreptitiously. By the time the Reverend Sumpter was ready to begin, the farmer had worked himself up to the point where he was taking on worse than anybody.

It was a difficult sermon. The family agreed afterward that the minister had done the best he could with the materials at hand. The truth was that, despite his hearty farewell, Potts had been something of a rip. Reverend Sumpter pounded away at his good points, but at best they had been pretty thin, and in the aggregate, the message took on more or less the tone of an apology. Sumpter said that, although Potts had *not* been active in the church, and in fact was never seen there except on Founder's Day, when he turned up for the free dinner, he had never actually talked *against* it; that, as a good many people knew who abetted him now and then, present company not necessarily excepted, but naming no names, Potts *was* a good deal of a boozer, but he was not a troublesome boozer, and no report had ever come to him (Reverend Sumpter) about departed having knocked his wife or children around to excess; and that, while he was extraordinarily free with his language, to the point where no sensitive person would care to get within half a mile of him, he had seldom cussed anybody out for purely personal reasons, but had stuck fairly close to things like politics and sports right down the line.

They opened the coffin, and Snavely removed a damp cloth from the face, and the mourners came up to have a last look. Not long after that one of the Wiggins boys tripped and fell in the grave, but they got him out in time and lowered Potts to his rest. Then everybody shook hands with the preacher, and thanked him, and they all went home. Fields said he had never seen anything quite so agreeable in the funeral line; he later hung around Snavely's place, and cultivated him, and learned all he could about his business.

"Posthlewhistle and Smunn" were names that Fields used whenever he felt the need for a fictitious law firm. Smunn was a lawyer in Philadelphia, and the majority of the English village of Barrow-in-Furness was named Posthlewhistle, according to Fields. He picked the name "Prettiwillie" off a lumberyard once while riding a train through Michigan; he used it in two of his early movies—*The Old-Fashioned Way* and *The Old Army Game*.

"Every name I used is an actual name I've seen somewhere," he told Norman Taurog, who directed him in *Mrs. Wiggs of the Cabbage Patch*. "If I think they're funny, I remember them. So when an opportunity presents itself, I use them in the pictures."

He used the name "Peppitone" in a short in which he played a dentist. The authentic holder of the name, a dentist in Washington who had installed some fillings for Fields, wrote him a rather sharp letter, saying that the celluloid Peppitone, in his opinion, was an outrageous character, of dubious professional ethics, and that dentistry was a serious business and should be treated with reverence. Although Fields was unmoved, there may have been some basis for the writer's complaint. In the film, Fields, wearing a dingy white jacket and a faraway expression of perplexed ennui, had worked fruitlessly over a client who was so heavily bearded he couldn't find his mouth. Added to that, he had an office full of pale, bandaged people who kept mistaking the noise of a nearby riveting machine for the sound of his drill. Peppitone was probably justified in being sore, but the comedian dismissed him with a snarl. "The bastard overcharged me," Fields said.

Certainly, Fields had a richer chance to collect odd names than most people, since his travels, in the years prior to World War I, were interrupted only by sustained performances. He left a tortuous trail. On May 28, 1907, for example, he was described by the New York *Transcript* as being "the finest act in the first part of the program" at the Jardin de Paris, a roof garden on top of the New York Theatre. Again, the week following April 23, 1908, he was playing the Orpheum in Boston and Hathaway's Theatre in Lowell, Massachusetts. *Variety,* having interviewed him, said, "When W. C. Fields, the juggler, appears on the other side this year he will present a brand-new novelty in the juggling line. Fields has been hard at work for several months constructing a comedy act which will be the first of its kind ever attempted. He will offer an entirely new routine of comedy juggling, featuring a burlesque croquet shot in which the croquet ball is made to go through all the wickets on one shot, the trick being patterned after the pool shot now used in his act."

The old New York *Star* of December 19, 1908, had a story about Fields. It ran in connection with a picture the juggler had drawn of himself. "W. C. Fields, who was recently on a tour of English and Continental music halls," the piece said, "is again making vaudeville audiences laugh in this country. Mr. Fields' comedy is fluent, unforced, and quite unique. No wonder managers pay him big salaries for making their patrons laugh! He does that, all right, and some more besides." Of the caricature (whose caption was "The Great Silly") the *Star* said, "This quaint little portrait does only faint justice to his beauty as he walks out on the stage in a scrubby beard and evening clothes that must have seen better days." On March 2, 1909, he was at Keith's in Philadelphia, where the *Record* said of him, "It would be hard to find anybody better in the juggling line than W. C. Fields. He is an artist in whose work there is no flaw." On the eighteenth of that same month he was up in Boston again, at Keith's, where the *Traveler* felt that "he certainly is a wonder when it comes to working those phony tricks."

Not long after that he went to Europe, and when he returned, the *Traveler* of April 7, 1910 said, "Fields is back in town. The man with the funny legs and the accurate eye is doing his stunts amid uproarious delight at Keith's this week. What, child, you never heard of Fields? Can it be possible? Don't you recall the last time you saw him enter with that dilapidated overcoat and lay it carefully on the lounge, placing a few moth balls in the folds to keep it from harm, and proceed to do a hundred funny things with those three rubber balls?" *Variety* of that year had him listed once as "The International Eccentric Tramp Juggler, obtainable through the Buckner International Agency, Long Acre Building, New York." The next year, *Variety* had him billed, at his own request, as, simply, "The Originator." Throughout his career, Fields was never hampered by false modesty. He took another trip abroad, and *Vanity Fair,* on March 23, 1912, noted, "On the mammoth steamer *Olympic,* due this month, is W. C. Fields, the tramp juggler. Fields is returning to America after successful foreign engagements to fulfill contracts for his appearances over the Orpheum Circuit."

It was soon apparent that Fields' exposures to foreign culture had not slowed him up. The San Francisco *Chronicle,* on August 10, 1912, said, "It isn't often one has a chance to enthuse, let alone rave, over a juggling act, but everybody's doing it. Yesterday afternoon's audience cheered W. C. Fields until the noise of their enthusiasm reached O'Farrell Street and caromed off the fence opposite." And in 1914, in Chicago, the *Herald* observed that Fields had added, "of all things, shillelaghs," to his equipment. Rather than slowing him up, his foreign visits were having a profitable broadening effect.

Among the brilliant qualities that Fields brought to his profession was a faultless memory. A long time before, in the shabby dressing room of an impecunious road company, he had confided his dream of success to a companionable, undernourished player. And to himself he had sworn a mighty, theatrical oath, a defiance, like Macbeth's, of all obstruction earthly or supernatural. Though castles toppled, though pyramids sloped to their foundations, even if destruction sickened, he would, someday, make a thousand dollars a week. The day at length came to pass. It seems possible that no sane man would have seized the opportunity that Fields here regarded as golden. In New York, the Palace offered him his usual $500 a week; uptown, the Alhambra offered him $500 for a late show. It was a regimen that might have killed an ordinary performer, but its symbolism, for Fields, was too significant to deny. Triumphant, he undertook the dual grind, but his contentment proved fleeting. He found that old dreams fulfilled, like old summer resorts revisited, are apt to have lost their flavor. From his brief, rueful enjoyment of the moment, with its nostalgic hark-back to the time of Fulton's burlesque, he looked on to the green pastures. His dissatisfaction had been steadily growing. He was the best-known juggler in the world, but he was athirst for larger glories.

BOOK TWO: *Part One*

CHAPTER FIFTEEN

FIELDS' BIG CHANCE, when it came, was to go down as the most crushing anticlimax in the history of the American stage. The time was 1914, not long after the start of what later would be described, in the interest of avoiding repetition, as World War I. The scene of his good news was Australia, one of his favorite places. As he had done with Ireland, Fields visited Australia to relax after the gracious tension of England. The island continent in the early 1900s was an area of restful informality. The interior was occupied by small, gnarled aborigines, of sanguinary disposition, and the tidewater country supported a mixed society of gold miners, sheep raisers, cattlemen, and adventurer-refugees from the mellower civilizations. "They chew on toothpicks," Fields said. "It puts me at my ease." A dentist had once told him that if he used a toothpick enough he would never lose his teeth. Thereafter, in uncritical localities, he kept a toothpick in his mouth as much as possible. He grew absent-minded about the practice, however, and ran into scattered censure. For example, years later in Hollywood he drifted off to sleep, while nibbling on a toothpick, in a courtroom where he was being sued by an energetic doctor, "a servant of humanity," Fields said, "who had done really brilliant work in isolating fees." The comedian's lawyer, much agitated, shook him awake roughly. "For heaven's sake, Mr. Fields, get rid of that toothpick!" he said.

"What for?" Fields asked.

122

"Because the judge might see it and decide against us," the lawyer told him.

Fields was appalled by the logic in this advice. He never forgot it. He worked up a long, eloquent, feverish tirade about a system of justice in which the merits of a case were forgotten and the decision hinged on a defendant's use of a toothpick. At home, almost any mention of lawyers or doctors, by guests or by the radio, might set him off, and he would go stamping about the place—damning judges, cursing quacks, and in general blasting a world in which a harmless addiction to splinters could cause the heads to roll.

After one spirited performance in Melbourne, Fields strolled back to his hotel and found a cablegram from Charles Dillingham, the New York producer, which said, "Can you come to New York immediately. Have speaking part for you in *Watch Your Step*." Fields sat down on the edge of his bed and reflected on the vagaries of fortune. The message represented the successful conclusion of a campaign he had conducted with unabated vigor since his engagement with McIntyre and Heath. "Other managers couldn't seem to see anything except that label of 'comedy juggler' that had been pinned on me," he explained to an interviewer later. "For *ten years* I fought to get rid of that label. But not a manager would let me have a speaking part. I begged and pleaded like the rawest beginner, but they only laughed at me and told me to stick to the thing I knew how to do. I had to live, so I went on with my vaudeville engagements, wandering around the world, making plenty of money, but getting more and more discouraged about the future."

The glad tidings from Dillingham distracted Fields to the point where he felt the need for a stimulant. He ordered a small bottle of whisky from room service and drank it thoughtfully, after which he put on a false beard, a wig, and a silk hat, and threw a property opera cape around his shoulders. Then he went out in search of entertainment. If his subsequent account was true, he attended a fashionable party, as "Dr. Hugo Sternhammer," a Viennese anthropologist. "I walked along the streets till I saw a lot of vehicles lined up in front of a big house," he told some friends in Chasen's. "I went up to the door and a butler or somebody stuck a silver plate under my nose. I put an old laundry check and a dime on it and went on in. It was a very enjoyable function. I had a long talk with the governor's wife."

"What did you talk about, Bill?" one of his friends asked.

"We talked about the mating habits of the wallaby," Fields said.

He said further that before he left he drank a good deal of champagne and juggled some bric-a-brac for a group in one corner. Throughout the evening he talked in a heavy German accent, drawing suspicious looks from several military men. "I remember telling one woman that the Kaiser was my third cousin," he said. "She gave a little scream and ran like hell." Fields did not recall whether he left the party under his own power or was assisted by the butler. He believed, however, that he was one of the last to leave, and he had a pretty distinct recollection of crying out something like "Veedersehen, alles!" as he went through the door.

He canceled the rest of his Australian, New Zealand and Tasmanian engagements and went about arranging passage home. He found it a difficult undertaking. The German raider *Emden,* sent out by his third cousin, the Kaiser, was harassing shipping in Australian waters. Twice Fields managed to get aboard English freighters that steamed outside the harbor only to turn back at the sight of an ugly black smudge on the horizon. Finally, in Sydney Harbor, he boarded an American tramp and slipped out under cover of a foggy night, to open water and comparative safety. The tramp was bound for San Francisco and made the trip in thirty-nine days, a period Fields spent mostly on deck, juggling, to the delight of the crew. From San Francisco he hurried on to New York, by train, and joined the *Watch Your Step* company in Syracuse, two days before the show's out-of-town opening there. Dillingham wanted him to do his billiard act, with a running patter of jokes. In the two days' time, Fields unearthed one of his old commentaries, a sort of omnibus tribute to snakes, and polished up his billiard shots. He took part in one full rehearsal.

Meanwhile, Gene Buck, an old fan of Fields', who was now Ziegfeld's right-hand man, had decided to come up for the opening. Knocking about backstage before curtain time, he heard a rumor that Fields' act might be dropped, and he sent a note, "See me in New York if anything goes wrong," to his dressing room toward the end of the show.

The day after the opening, Dillingham visited Fields and said, with what must be regarded as sublime heartlessness, "I'm sorry, Bill, but we've got to drop that scene of yours. We haven't room for the billiard table." Just what he meant by "room" Fields never found out, but Dillingham once told a friend that "the billiard act hadn't got over." He believed that it might have been because a noisy act preceded it; an axiom of show business is that a quiet funny act will always fail in a spot following a noisy act.

In any case, Fields found himself in the unparalleled position of having made an expensive, six-week trip halfway around the world to play a one-night stand. The experience added another measure of suspicious toughness to his outlook on humanity. Also, it gave him an even livelier caution about contracts.

Despite the stunning rebuff of his musical-comedy debut, he recovered his composure and his self-confidence quickly. Two days later he appeared in Gene Buck's New York office, his appearance jaunty and his manner slightly bellicose. His pale blond hair was parted in the middle— "like Hoover's," as noted once by Geoffrey T. Hellman in *The New Yorker*—and he was wearing a fake mustache that clipped into his nose. Fields had fashioned the mustache himself, and it gave producers trouble for years. He liked to wear it because it looked offensive, according to Director Eddie Sutherland. "Bill turned up with it on one day in a movie we were making," Sutherland recalled, "and I said, 'What the hell is that dreadful appliance in your nose?' "

Fields replied, with some heat, that it was a mustache, and Sutherland said, "Well, remove it immediately and we'll get on with the picture."

"The mustache stays," said Fields. "What's the matter with it?"

"It's the nastiest-looking thing I ever saw," Sutherland told him. "It's making everybody sick."

Fields insisted on playing one scene with the mustache on, saying that it was "well known in the show world" and that it was widely viewed as "handsome," but Sutherland

and a film cutter later got together and quietly tossed the scene out.

In Buck's office Fields took a chair, without explaining why he had chosen to wear his fake mustache for the interview, and said indignantly, "Did you catch me in that turkey?" (*Watch Your Step* had a successful opening, both in Syracuse and in New York, and played to large audiences for months, but Fields always described it as a flop.)

Buck expressed regret that Fields had got mixed up in such a palpable failure, then said, "I've caught your act many times, Bill. I think it might work out in the *Follies*."

Fields replied, in a condescending voice, that he'd check his commitments, and a few minutes later he began to discuss terms. For a man who had just been booted from a cast after one performance, he was peculiarly high-handed. To land on the legitimate stage, he finally agreed to accept $200 a week, with certain strictures about dressing accommodations, billing and minor expenses and Buck signed him for the *Ziegfeld Follies* of 1915.

In the intervening time, Fields returned to vaudeville, obtaining bookings as before, over the Orpheum Circuit. He commanded higher prices, by advertising himself, verbally and a little prematurely, as a full-fledged *Follies* star. "Wherever he went," said one of his friends of that era, "he spoke familiarly of the legitimate stage and was critical of the best-known musical-comedy figures of the day." In his dressing rooms, during these vaudeville tours, his attitude was florid and majestic; he had quite plainly arrived, but he was tolerant of, and even helpful toward, his struggling colleagues. He leaned on a sort of editorial "we," a reference to himself and his fellow players of the higher spheres. He often laughed indulgently and spoke in the past tense of *Watch Your Step,* which was enjoying an excellent run in New York. To newspapermen everywhere, Fields made sage, proprietary observations about the *Follies* and the state of musical comedy in general. "One gathered that he might make some important changes for the forthcoming season," an acquaintance has observed.

The Duluth *Herald* of April 22, 1915, said, "W. C. Fields is closing his vaudeville work next week to go into the *Follies,* which will open in New York June the first, run through the summer, and tour to the coast and back during the winter." The interview ended with the comment, probably suggested by Fields, since it turned up with remarkable similarity elsewhere during the period, "An attempt to extol W. C. Fields' merit would require the ability to juggle words as adroitly as he does articles."

The *Ziegfeld Follies of 1915,* at the New Amsterdam Theatre, was graced by many names already famous and others about to become famous. As nearly as may be determined, they were regarded as being pretty much of the same common fabric by the new man, who "took the line," one of them said, "that all the rest of us more or less had feet of clay." Fields appeared as "Himself," a simple tribute he had insisted upon when the show was being put together, in Scene Two. He did his billiard act, and the audience stopped the show with an uproar of merriment. "W. C. Fields contributed a screamingly funny exhibition of pool playing," said the New York *Mirror.* Gene Buck's insight in hiring him was borne out handily within half an hour after curtain time on opening night. In Scene Six he appeared as "Adam Fargo" in a skit, "Hallway of the Bunkem Court Apartments," with such lesser luminaries as Ann Pennington as "Sammy, a messenger boy"; Bert Williams, as "Thomas, the hall boy"; and Leon Errol as "Constant Bunn."

The show, nude and rich in the Ziegfeld manner, had many rewarding features for revue lovers. Ed Wynn, also as "Himself," and Fields' principal rival for comedy preeminence, held the stage alone in Scene Seven, and other worth-while offerings included a song, "Marie Odile," by Ina Claire; and a dance, "Flirtation Medley," by Ann Pennington and George White, who was soon to organize a competitive entertainment with his *Scandals.*

Wynn's grapple with Fields for laughs was destined to come to a violent climax and give rise to a celebrated anecdote of the Fields legend. The danger signals were apparent on November 16, 1915, to the critic of the Detroit *News,* who observed, when the show reached his town on its winter tour, "Incidentally, Mr. Fields is losing some laughs in the pool game because Ed Wynn, who is funny, too, is cutting up at the same time." The blowoff took place in Boston, not long afterward. As Fields manipulated his wavy cue, Wynn sneaked beneath the table and the battle was joined. To Fields' dismay, his laughs began to come in the wrong places. He continued to play, collecting off-center guffaws and trying to find out why. "The first thing any comedian does on getting an unscheduled laugh is to verify the state of his buttons; the second is to look around and see if a cat has walked out on the stage," Alva Johnston once wrote. Fields checked both of these possibilities and found no cause for alarm. Then he saw a quick movement under the table and stepped back for an examination. Wynn, all unaware, was "catching flies," as the theatrical phrase goes, or stealing laughs by means of funny facial expressions, gestures, and other antics. Fields returned to the table and continued his act. "I was waiting until I got his head in a particularly good lie," he later said to a friend, dropping into the handy golfing idiom.

The chance came about midway in the scene. Fields, accelerating his action, was piling up laughs, and Wynn, to keep pace, was working like a dog below decks. On all fours, he made the mistake of thrusting his head out about a foot too far. With the juggler's ready eye and coordinated muscle, Fields shifted nimbly into his backswing. His cue whistled through a half-circle and met the objective with the woody "glunk" so dear to the golfer's heart. Wynn keeled over with a hoarse sigh, and Fields resumed at the billiard table, to tremendous applause. As the act progressed, Wynn, struggling toward consciousness, gave vent to an occasional loud groan, and each time the audience howled with joy, the members making such comments to their neighbors as "Wonderful turn" and "Those fellows are certainly getting off some good ones up there." After the show, Fields went to Ziegfeld and offered to incorporate Wynn into the act in that form for the rest of the run. Wynn was said to have turned the opportunity down.

On the whole, Fields got along amicably with his colleagues, even those of whom he was most jealous. He enjoyed arranging pranks to embarrass them. Will Rogers, in dressing-room conversations with Fields and others, often spoke of an old pal of his named Clay McGonigle, from Claremont, Oklahoma. McGonigle had a nickname for Rogers, not entirely printable, over which Rogers frequently chuckled. Before one performance around Thanks-

1. Fields as Micawber in Metro-Goldwyn-Mayer's
DAVID COPPERFIELD

All Photographs, Courtesy of Culver Pictures, Inc.

2. The young man of destiny; twenty years old

3. With Baby Leroy in Paramount's THE OLD FASHIONED WAY

4. In the Broadway musical POPPY

5. Unusual fishing at Toluca Lake

6. Fields in his mid-forties

7. and 8. In Universal's
MY LITTLE CHICKA-
DEE, which co-starred Mae
West.

9. The animal lover, in Universal's THE BANK DICK

10. Temperance dispute—NEVER GIVE A SUCKER AN EVEN BREAK

11. Fields relaxing at home

12. W. C. Fields—"Sucker"

13. The imperishable Micawber—from DAVID COPPERFIELD

giving time, Fields sent a note to Rogers' dressing room, using the nickname and saying, "I'm in town and will be out in front watching the show—your old pard, Clay McGonigle." Rogers was tickled to death; he addressed the majority of his remarks to the absent McGonigle and larded them heavily with personal reminiscence. He kept looking around and waiting for some kind of response—a laugh or a cowpuncher's yip—but none was forthcoming. Nevertheless, he continued to play to McGonigle throughout the evening, to the intense mystification of the audience and the annoyance of the director.

After the show, Rogers dropped into Fields' dressing room and said, "I don't understand it. I didn't hear a peep out of old Clay. I'd better go find him." He dressed hurriedly and hung around the theater door, then spent most of the night combing saloons and railroad stations. He was much chagrined next day, repeating, "I sure can't understand what happened to old Clay." When somebody tipped him off that Fields had sent the note, he said, "I'll get even with that vaudeville ham if it takes me the rest of my life." But as far as anybody knows, he never did.

Fields' relationship with Ziegfeld was one of the oddest in show business. Although the comedian was a member of the *Follies* for seven years, he and the maestro saw eye to eye on practically nothing. The fact is, there was a recognizable air of hostility between them. Ziegfeld had no feeling for funny men; he regarded them as tiresome but necessary time-fillers, placed on the stage so that the girls could change. For his part, Fields, though he granted that pretty girls had their uses, looked upon them dramatically as a harmless backdrop for comedians. "My experiences with this company were many and varied," he once wrote in a series of articles for some newspapers. "Ziegfeld was a weird combination of the great showman and the little child. He really did not like comedians and tolerated them only because of the public. His forte was beautiful girls and costumes with elaborate settings."

The producer and the former juggler had their first falling out over a golf act Fields had put together during his travels. Like the billiard act, it was a parody on the ritual surrounding a basically absurd exercise. In its original version Fields had appeared with an outsize golf bag he'd ordered from an English leatherworker. It was about twice as large as the average golf bag and was equipped with all the professional appliances favored by dedicated, high-score players. It had a prop-up stand, a rolling platform, several secret compartments and sliding panels, wrist guards, club sheathes, complicated rubber tees, ball brushes, and various other indispensable equipment. Inside, he had an extraordinary collection of clubs, including the usual golfing woods and irons, a polo mallet, a buggy whip, a common garden hoe, a mole trap, some surveying instruments, and a shovel, presumably for getting out of bunkers. Fields' clothing for the act was a pointed insult to everybody who had ever appeared on a golf course. It was offensive in almost every detail. Reading from the top down, he had on a heather cap that stuck up like a mushroom, with a button on top; a hideous bow tie; a button-up sweater with striped sleeves which were held back by elastic armbands; limp, voluminous knickers of wild plaid; short socks; three- or four-toned shoes with inch-long spikes. Even so, he was in better shape than his caddy, whom he always selected carefully as being the most grotesque employee available—dwarfed or otherwise malformed if possible. The caddy's ensemble, a compendium of links outrages of every land, was built around a tam-o'-shanter slightly smaller than an umbrella.

Fields' manner as he approached the tee was one of solemn consecration. He marked out a place for the caddy to stand, selected a ball with great care, scrubbed it up, and placed it on one of his patented tees; then he tested the wind. Absently, he reached back and drew out a club, but it turned out to be the hoe, and he gave an agitated start when he saw it. He took the line that he had somehow been victimized by the caddy, whom he beat vigorously about the head and shoulders before proceeding. Then he took a driver and assumed a kind of stance. He sawed away for a few minutes, but each time he started to drive he turned to the caddy and shouted, "Stand clear and keep your eye on the ball!" Before readdressing the ball, Fields changed clubs, and the new one, on the backswing, proved to have a pliable shaft and looped clear around his neck. He fought his way out, flailing the air savagely and uttering threatening cries; then he beat up the caddy again.

The climactic prop of his golf act was a piece of paper that blew across the course and fastened around one of his feet as he prepared at last to drive. Beginning in a tolerant humor, he kicked it loose, but it transferred to his other foot. With a violent wrench, he succeeded in kicking it back to the first foot, and then he picked it off with the head of his golf club, where it stuck snugly. He jabbed the club into the air, whipped it back and forth, and ran around like a man pursued by bees, but the paper clung on. By this time Fields' expression was an interesting study in wrath. His eyes started from his head, his face was red, and his clothing was badly disheveled. He lost his cap, and in retrieving it he managed to put it on his golf club instead of his head; then he spent an anxious period trying to find it. He never did get rid of the paper. kicking, jabbing with his club, bawling at his caddy, and shouting "Fore!" "Fore!" he was snowed under by a threesome of wretched-looking women, who played through in wary disgust. "He must have been drinking," one of them said as they pulled away.

Fields varied this act frequently during his last years in vaudeville; he used a silent version of it for a while in the *Follies*. When he first mentioned it to Ziegfeld, the producer said (as Fields later reported to a man planning to write his life story), "It's a great idea, Bill. I think it will be a hit. There's just one little thing—we have a yacht set, a gorgeous yacht, the most magnificent yacht you've ever seen, and it's all full of beautiful girls. So if you'll just change the golf act to a fishing act, I think we'll be ready to go."

"I thought I'd figured out how to handle Ziegfeld," Fields said. "So I agreed with him. He went ahead with his plans for the yacht, and I went ahead with mine. He kept wanting to see the act, but I'd never show it to him. The only thing I'd say was that it was working out perfectly.

"When the time came, I just walked out on the yacht set and did my golf act, before he could get the girls on. Afterward, Ziegfeld was in tears. It had gone over fine and he couldn't throw it out. But he said, 'We'll compromise, Bill. I'm going to insist on *one* beautiful girl being on that stage while you're doing the act." The next performance, one of those long-legged babies of his came walking across wearing a short fur jacket and leading a Russian wolfhound. I stopped and let my jaw sag. When she reached the center of the stage, I said, '*My, what a beautiful camel!*' Everybody roared and Ziggie threw in the sponge. He was a little sore, but he said, 'O. K., Bill, we'll do it your way. It's the first time I've ever turned one of my lovely girls into a comedian's prop.' "

Fields and Ziegfeld frequently squabbled about money. Besides his long-standing habit of asking for a raise every month or two, Fields had a trick of running up "incidental expenses." Walter Catlett, who was a *Follies* comedian in those days and later went to Hollywood, remembered a scene he and Fields did that caused Ziegfeld a lot of suffering.

"It was a tennis act," Catlett said. "We took turns being straight man. It was a very funny act. Bill later assembled a croquet act that was very much like it. We minced around emphasizing the dainty aspects of the game as it was played at polite upper-class parties of that time. Occasionally we'd have elegant little arguments but allow people to understand that we'd really like to break each other's necks.

"Bill insisted on juggling now and then, though it didn't seem to fit the act. Nobody could argue with him. He'd just pull up when the notion suited him and juggle until he got tired, then we'd go on with the act. He finally conceived the idea of batting all the balls out into the audience when we finished. It was a popular windup, but at the end of the first week Ziegfeld docked Bill's salary thirty-six dollars for tennis balls.

"Bill stormed in and raised the devil, but Ziegfeld was firm. He said, 'Your contract states that you must furnish your own props.' Bill never had much use for him from then on out. They fussed a good deal at the best. To tell you the truth, Bill didn't like Ziegfeld."

Thereafter, when Fields and Ziegfeld met backstage, Fields nodded coldly and studied him with a rather calculating expression. Three months after his salary was docked, he maneuvered the producer into giving him a new contract. Fields hired a lawyer, at considerable expense, and worked out each paragraph with great care. He had bided his time well. One of the clauses in the smallest type read: "The management shall provide all tennis balls used professionally, thought not for personal recreation, by the undersigned."

"Ziegfeld didn't argue," says a man who was there. "He just shook his head sadly and signed. Bill was slumped down in a chair, looking out of a window. That great mind appeared to be occupied elsewhere."

CHAPTER SIXTEEN

EARLY in his *Follies* career, Fields met Billy Grady, an agent, who was to represent him and travel with him off and on for fourteen years. Grady forever retained many vivid impressions of Fields, most of them quite sour. "Bill cheated me continuously throughout our association," he said. "He was the closest man with a dollar I ever met." Despite their endless wrangles over money, Grady stayed on, he thought, because he was fascinated by the bizarre character of his client. "For sheer, unadulterated gall, Bill stood alone. He wasn't happy if he wasn't involved in a scrap of some kind. He thought everybody was trying to skin him, so he tried to skin them first. But he had class— I'll say that. Bill had class. His most larcenous acts were marked by a sort of brilliant dash."

During one period, when he was between contracts, Fields began to get uneasy. He had a mortal fear of unemployment; the threat of it almost drove him crazy. At the time, he and Grady were living in a sizable suite at the Hotel Astor. As he pondered his situation, Fields quickly saw that his salvation lay in accident insurance. He dropped into an insurance office and took out a big policy, with a remunerative clause about unemployment. Then he returned to the Astor, called the company doctor, and went to bed.

"What in the hell are you doing, you old goat?" asked Grady when he came in. (The relationship between the comedian and his agent was distinguished by an uninterrupted and rather abrasive exchange of billingsgate.)

"I've sprained my back," said Fields, regarding Grady steadily with his little frosty blue eyes. "The doctor's coming. Take a seat over in the corner."

The doctor arrived a few minutes later and conducted a search for symptoms.

"Where does it hurt?" he said.

"All over," Fields told him.

"How'd it happen?"

"I was juggling some chairs," Fields said.

The doctor took his temperature again and went over his back with a small rubber hammer. Then he said, "I'll have to come back at five o'clock. I need more equipment."

"When do the payments start?"

"See you around five," the doctor said, and left.

Fields and Grady had been playing handball in their living room for several days, for a dollar a game, and Fields was twelve dollars ahead. As soon as the doctor left, he arose and suggested that they continue. They played steadily until five o'clock, when Fields quit and got back in bed. He just made it. The doctor turned up and took his temperature again. By now, because of the exertion— Grady had been winning—Fields was overheated and sweaty.

"A singular case," the doctor said, reading the thermometer. "Your temperature seems to have gone up."

"Complete disability," Fields agreed, with a noisy rattle in his voice.

Greatly mystified, the doctor went over the patient's back with several additional instruments. He said he was having trouble locating the sprain, an ailment which, like beauty, can exist largely in the eye of the sprainee. "It may be going into something else, such as pneumonia or lockjaw," said the doctor.

He added that he would make a report right away, with the usual recommendations, and he left, with a worried look.

Fields got up again, threw off his robe, and said to Grady, "Now, damn you, let's get back at that handball." He served, and the game resumed.

At this point the doctor threw the door open and yelled,

"*Aha!* I thought so, you faker!" He ducked back as Fields threw a lamp at him, then fled down the stairs.

"Bill was hopping mad for days," Grady said. "He took the attitude that he'd been defrauded. About a week later he said, 'I knew that insurance company was no good the minute I stuck my head in their door.' "

Fields' reaction to things was sometimes hard to figure out, according to Grady. Once when he was making out his income tax—an operation that put him in a blistering humor—Grady came in and looked over the papers. "Why, you can't deduct those things, you crook!" Grady said. "They'll put you in jail. How the hell can I make a living representing an inmate of a federal penitentiary?"

Fields ordered him out of the room and continued to sift the air for deductions. "He was too stingy to hire a lawyer," Grady said. "Besides, he was pretty sure the lawyers were secretly working for the government. I went in my room and sat down, but I was concerned. He was including things like depreciation on vaudeville houses where he'd played, salaries for ball rackers, and donations to churches in the Solomon Islands."

Fields completed his return, filed it with a look of satisfied pride, and continued with his engagements. "A few months later," said Grady, "he got a check from the government for $1100. They said he'd overcharged himself. I thought he'd blow up and crow about it, but he almost went out of his mind. He kept yelling, 'Think! *Think* of all the things I could have taken off in the years past!"

In this period of his *Follies* celebrity Fields took a fondness for big motor cars. "With anything of that sort he was far from stingy," Grady recalled. "He bought the most expensive cars, clothes, food, and so on he could find. It was mainly in his dealings with people that he began to act like a miser. But he wasn't consistent even with that. There were times when he'd sit in a restaurant all night rather than pick up the check. Other times, he wouldn't let anybody buy as much as a cigar. Bill was full of paradoxes." Fields' first car was a seven-passenger, custom-built Cadillac. He had the salesman from whom he bought it investigated by a detective agency. The man's record seemed to be all right, barring a few domestic spats, and Fields paid him in cash, but he insisted on getting a receipt signed in the presence of several witnesses, including a bootblack he brought in from the street. When the garage owner asked if he could drive, he said, with the kind of injured pomp that was making him famous, "I've been driving professionally since I was ten," or several years before automobiles were available. He added that his father had owned one of the first cars in Philadelphia, a purposeless lie. The garage people were relieved that he could drive. They shook hands with him and thanked him for the sale; then he got in the car and went about two hundred yards down the street, where he hit a parked laundry truck. He bawled out the driver, returned to the garage, and had a crushed fender repaired, while he delivered a mendacious account of how the laundryman had backed out of a driveway, at forty miles an hour, and hit him on the opposite side of the street. Although Fields had forked over $5000 cash for the car, he refused to pay a cent for repairs. He took the stand that the garage was liable until he got the automobile home. Before he left the second time, the garage people insisted on teaching him how to drive.

"Bill developed into a wonderful driver," Grady said. "He had, of course, natural co-ordination, and he was strong and athletic besides. He drove fast, took chances, and got into frequent arguments. During my fourteen years as his agent, I never knew him to be wrong. If he went around a curve, jumped up on a parkway and ran into a man's front porch, he'd find some reason why the house shouldn't have been there."

It was not hard for Fields to take on persecution complexes, and he managed a neat one about road hogs. Within six months after he bought the Cadillac he was convinced that 90 per cent of the people driving other cars were after his particular scalp. He rolled down the highway with a malevolent eye fixed on the opposite lane, ready to lock horns at the slightest hostile move. This bias, like most of his personal feelings, seeped into his work. In the movie *If I Had a Million* he worked out a sketch which represented one of his dreams of long standing. The plot directed that a number of persons, including Charles Laughton, Fields, Charles Ruggles, and George Raft, be capriciously given a million dollars by an elderly, cynical miser, who then studied the use each recipient made of the money. Most of the actors were content to abide by the ideas of the script writers; Fields conceived his own distribution of the windfall. Laughton, an obscure clerk for a corporation, walked humbly through several anterooms, to deliver a long pent-up Bronx cheer to his boss; Raft found himself in a position, as a hunted man, in which he couldn't cash his check without being caught; and Ruggles, in an immensely satisfying scene, smashed all the fragile wares in a high-class china shop where he'd worked for twenty-odd years. Fields, with Allison Skipworth, went to a secondhand car lot and bought a collection of wrecks, then asked the proprietor, "Can you furnish me some strong, brave drivers?" When his armored column was complete, he wheeled out onto the highways looking for trouble. "As Bill sat hunched down in that old Ford with his straw hat on, he looked just the way he always looked driving a car—mean as the devil," one of his friends said. It was a sketch that put the comedian in a roseate humor for weeks. In the movie he would sight a stranger getting across the line and hold up one hand, like a cavalry commander. One of his strong, brave drivers would wheel out of column, knock hell out of the offender, and the column would proceed to the next enemy of society. Fields himself hit two or three cars, for various breaches of conduct. His expression, as he rammed them, was demoniac in its glee, and he voiced a high, exultant, rallying cry as the fenders dropped.

During the *Follies,* too, Fields sharpened his taste for liquor. He had become discriminating; he wanted only the choicest brands. Consequently, he bought a third wardrobe trunk, had it fitted out with pigeonholes like a wine cellar, and stocked it with high-test beverages. He took it along wherever he went. Later on he decided he was carrying too many clothes, and he devoted another trunk to liquor. This balance working out about right—two trunks full of booze and one of equipment—he made it his standard traveling impedimenta for years. Even when he and Grady moved between engagements by car, he took one of the dispensaries in the back seat.

Once, when they were driving to Boston in the winter, Fields swerved to miss some children who were coasting, and struck a Ford. The Ford's driver, a farmer, was badly dazed. Fields offered to take care of him while Grady walked to a police station. "Bill had his trunk in the back and had been drinking a little," Grady said, "but I hadn't had a drink all evening. I found a sergeant named O'Malley at the station and we fell into a pleasant discussion about the Church. I figured we were going to get off scot-free. The sergeant was sympathetic when he heard about the crash. He said those things were sometimes unavoidable. I was about ready to leave when Fields and the farmer burst in through the door. They were both lit up to the sky. Bill had spent half an hour getting him drunk. When he saw me, he yelled, 'What are you doing, you Irish bum?' The sergeant thought he meant him and threw all three of us in jail. It cost us fifty dollars apiece. Bill made me pay the farmer's fine out of my own pocket. He said I'd handled it undiplomatically."

Grady was driving the car through the South one night while Fields sat in the back seat on the trunk. The comedian was drinking what he described as "martinis;" he had a bottle of gin in one hand and a bottle of vermouth in the other, and he took alternate pulls, favoring the gin. At an intersection in a country town they saw a man with a satchel making signals under a street lamp. Grady said, "Fellow wants a ride."

"Pick him up," cried Fields. "Where's your sense of charity?"

Grady slowed down, called out, "Hop in the back," and waited till the man got aboard. As they drove off, Fields extended the gin bottle to him, but the man refused, with a look of offended piety. About five miles down the road the stranger took some tracts out of his coat pocket and said, "Brothers, I'm a minister of the gospel."

Fields blew a mouthful of gin on the floor and the man went on, "You're sinning in this automobile and though I don't ordinarily do no free preaching, I'm going to preach a free sermon right here." He examined the tracts and added, "To tell you the truth, I'm a-going to give you Number Four."

"What's Number Four?" said Fields.

"Called the 'Evils of Alcohol,'" said the minister.

Fields leaned forward and said to Grady, "Pull up beside the first ditch you see."

The minister's narrative had reached a point where a

roustabout had pawned his small daughter's shoes to raise money for a drink when Grady slammed on the brakes. *"Aus! Aus!"* Fields began to cry, harking back to his German period, and he kicked the minister into the ditch. Then he opened his trunk, removed an unopened bottle of gin, and tossed it down beside him. "There's my Number Three," he yelled. "Called 'How to Keep Warm in a Ditch.'"

Grady drove on. Fields told him afterward that he'd suspected the minister might be a Methodist. He'd had a lot of trouble with Methodists, he said, but he refused to describe it in detail.

Fields loved to motor through the South. He admired the Southern customs and traditions. He had a story, which shifted from month to month, about a terrible fight he got into with a crossing watchman. "I was on my way to Homosassa, Florida," he would say, dwelling lovingly on the name. ("That was probably a lie right there," Grady said. "He just liked the name Homosassa. He managed to ring it in every time he mentioned Florida.") Fields said he was en route to Homosassa on a fishing expedition and, on a back road, came on a blocked railroad crossing—a spur line grown up with weeds. There was a shack about twenty yards down the track. He stopped, and a watchman strolled up leisurely.

"You expecting a train?" Fields asked.

"Why, no," said the watchman, knocking the tops off some weeds with a stick. "I can't rightly say that I am."

"Not expecting one, hey?" said Fields.

"No. We only get a train along here on Tuesdays and Thursdays."

"Unless I'm mistaken," said Fields, "this is Wednesday. Why the hell have you got the gate down?"

"Well, they've been known to turn up early," said the watchman.

"Open that damned gate," roared Fields.

"My suggestion would be to try it on the main road. Used to be, they didn't put the gate down only on Tuesdays and Thursdays, but I hain't been up that way in three or four year."

Fields said he gave the man an average cursing and got out to do battle. The fellow was tougher than he looked. With his face fixed in a mournful, resigned expression, he hit Fields alongside the head with his stick every time Fields swung. "It's my bounden duty to pertect railroad prop'ty," he'd say, and, using his stick skillfully, duck a haymaker.

"I finally had to trip him up and brain him with a rock," Fields said later. "Then I tore down the crossing gate and went on to Homosassa. It was a nerve-racking experience for me." In other accounts, he said that he'd also destroyed the watchman's shack before he left and that he'd "put to rout" a large section gang that had come to the man's aid.

Fields prided himself on his knowledge of Southern history. He always tied it up with his own experiences. He could explain the entire South by means of a few personal observations. One time at his Hollywood home he got into a brisk argument with a college professor, a "doctor" of history, who was outlining the technical reasons why Sherman had got through to the sea, with statistics on such things as logistics, supply, ordnance, lines of communication, and so on. Fields rejected the explanation, substituting a theory of his own. It hinged on deliberation. "They move in slow motion down there," he said. "I studied Sherman's march—read a lot of books about it—and the reason he made it was because Southern troops didn't get up till around noon, and most of them had breakfast in bed." Later on it developed that Fields was still smarting from a near-escape he'd once had from a Southern railroad accident. Driving through Georgia with Grady and a girl, he skidded on a railroad track and came to rest crossways on the rails. The car refused to start. They worked at it apprehensively for five minutes or so and a cracker came along in a wagon.

"A train ever pass along here?" Fields asked.

The man pulled out an Ingersoll watch, studied it, shook it, looked at the sun, wound his watch, and said, "The six-fifteen's due right now."

"Well, get a rope!" Fields yelled. "Pull me out of here."

The man climbed down from his wagon and tied his horse to a sapling, after which he got an old curtain out of the wagon and put it over the horse's back to keep off the flies. Then he found a piece of rope. He ambled over to the car, sat down on the front bumper, and, while he untied a knot in the end of the rope, asked pleasantly, "Yawl from the Nawth?"

Fields, who was in back of the car, futilely shoving, screamed at him to quit talking and hurry, and the man tied the rope on. Then he untied his horse, put the curtain back in the bed, led the horse over, and fixed the other end of the rope to the wagon.

The horse leaned half-heartedly into the traces, but the car still stuck fast. They heard a train whistle far down the tracks.

"She's coming!" Fields screamed. "We'll have to lighten the load." He and Grady started tossing out objects like press booklets, hampers, rugs, the girl, borrowed watermelons, and even liquor.

By now the cracker was down with an ear to a rail. "Yes, sir," he said, straightening up, "she sure is coming."

The train, an antediluvian shambles, came clanking around a curve at about fifteen miles an hour and stopped. The engineer and fireman got out deliberately. They introduced themselves, chatted a few minutes, and shoved the car back onto the road.

As the engine labored off down the tracks, the cracker permitted himself an observation. "I figured they wasn't any use gittin' worked up," he said. "We might as well wait till we got some he'p."

Nearly everywhere he went in the South, Fields ran into alligators. He had a fixation on the subject. Often, he said, he came dangerously close to being eaten. To hear him tell it, the entire South was overrun by alligators, most of which had a personal grudge against him. Grady believed that Fields actually did encounter one alligator in the South, at a time when he was driving through with Grady and a lady passenger. The day was warm and the lady wanted a drink. Fields pulled up beside a rotting farmhouse and made inquiries.

"You'll have to go down to the spring," said the farmer, rousing himself from a nap on the front porch and pointing to the path through the woods.

Fields took a thermos bottle and stepped down to the spring, "about a two-day trip by pack train," he said later, with his usual hyperbole. "I figured they'd have to get me out with bloodhounds."

He eventually found the spring, a rivulet of fresh water

that trickled into a rusty, sunken kettle and then into a slough. But as he leaned over to dip in the thermos, an alligator coughed and slid off a log on the bank near by.

"We heard a dreadful cry and Bill came running out of the woods, white as a sheet," Grady said. "The thermos was missing and he was yelling, 'Start up the motor! Start up the motor!' It took a long time to get him quieted down."

It was not uncommon for Fields to be bullied by animals other than dogs. His trouble with a swan, later on in Hollywood, was notorious. He had rented a large establishment on Toluca Lake, a body of water inhabited by a peevish, noisy, outsized white swan, which took an instant dislike to Fields. Mary Brian, Bing Crosby, and Richard Arlen, movie people who had houses on the lake have recalled many interesting sights of the comedian fitted out for combat. For several days after he moved in, the swan would catch him near the shore and chase him back to his house. Then Fields got a cane with a curved handle and took to hiding in the reeds near the water. He would produce noises that he fancied were recognizable as authentic swan talk, and, when the bird came in to investigate, he'd rush out and try to get the cane around its neck.

"Mr. Fields was sure enough scared of that swan," felt one of his former servants. "Almost every time they met, he wound up runnin'."

After three or four futile brushes with the cane, he decided on heavier ordnance, and he switched to a golf club, selecting a number-four iron. The bird showed considerable respect for the iron, and Fields went on the offensive. He bought a canoe and chased the swan all over the lake every day. But no matter how hard he paddled, the bird managed to stay out in front. It was hot work, and Fields, on one occasion, lay back to rest and get his strength up. He dozed off, and the swan circled around, like Nelson at Trafalgar, and fell on him from the rear.

The comedian returned home in a homicidal humor. He stormed around the house trying to enlist sympathy for his cause. "The goddamned bird broke all the rules of civilized warfare," he kept saying. He got a revolver and loaded it up, but one of his household talked him into sticking to the golf club.

Grady could not be too profuse in his praise of Fields' driving. One time during prohibition the comedian heard that a friend on Long Island had just received two cases of contraband Irish whisky. He and Grady drove out immediately. They and the friend spent the night making sure the government would be unable to recover part of the whisky, at least, and Fields and Grady left for home around dawn. Owing to their host's generosity, they took five or six quarts along with them, externally. Both Fields and Grady later remembered that it was snowing when they left, and they settled down for an exhausting drive. En route they took frequent pulls at the whisky and remarked at the surprising length of Long Island. Their heads were pretty fuzzy during the trip. They put in at filling stations now and then, gassed up, and sought information about the route. However, in response to a question like "How far's the Queensboro Bridge?" the attendants would only laugh, or stare stupidly. Also, as time wore on, the travelers got the cloudy impression that many people they talked to were essaying dialects, for some reason. "I don't recollect no place name of Manhasset," a man might tell them, and they would applaud, then career on down the road, drinking his health. Their heads finally cleared, and Grady found himself looking out of a window at a palm tree. They seemed to be in a hotel room. He dressed quickly and, while Fields slept on, exhausted by the Long Island roads, went down in search of a newspaper. The first intelligence he gleaned, when he got one, was that Ocala, Florida, was expecting no more than a moderate rainfall for the time of year, and that things looked good for a big citrus crop.

He went back to the hotel room and shook up Fields.

"The paper here says we're in Ocala, Florida," he reported.

"I always said those Long Island roads were poorly marked," Fields replied.

They lingered on for a week and went on several picnics. They left after Fields had been fined two hundred and seven dollars for removing two hundred and seven dogwood blossoms from the municipal park.

CHAPTER SEVENTEEN

FIELDS WAS in every edition of the Follies from 1915 through 1921. It is interesting to note that never once in that time could he have been described accurately as the principal comedian on the bill. To begin with, Ziegfeld was always wary of letting one name outshine the rest of his show. His attitude was like that of a football coach who prefers not to have a team built around a star. Besides, Fields had a great deal of high-voltage competition for humorous honors in the *Follies*. In the 1916 and 1917 versions, Fanny Brice was probably the most popular member of the cast, and in the latter year Will Rogers, Eddie Cantor and Bert Williams also conspired to detract from Fields' quest for singularity. "The inimitable Mr. Williams impersonates a Grand Central redcap," said the New York *Times* after the 1917 opening, "and Mr. Cantor plays the role of a porter's son coming home from college. Here surely was an opportunity for a scene of real humor between the illiterate father, dubious as to the value of a college education, and a member of the haughtily superior second generation. But the authors missed their chance competely and made the character of the son an unwholesome and objectionable type too frequently portrayed on the local stage."

Although these remarks gave extended space to his rivals, Fields was, on the whole, pleased with their general tone. He was somewhat less pleased by the next paragraph of the *Times* review, which said, in listing other players, "—Will Rogers, whose wit never flags, and William C. Fields, whose tennis game suffers only by its similarity with his billiard and croquet stunts." Fields always preferred the straightaway rave, the unqualified endorsement, suitable for promotional use.

Ziegfeld, with his distrust of comedians, favored subdued laughter rather than hearty laughter, if he had to have laughter at all. This preference was one of the main bones of contention between him and Fields. The truth was that Fields himself leaned to restraint, except when he worked for Ziegfeld. Knowing how the producer shrank from emphatic merriment, Fields strove for belly laughs. By the *Follies* of 1920 he was ready with several noisy skits, including a car act he had stolen from Harry Tate, the Englishman. "Chief expression of the quieter comedy," said one of the reviewers of the 1920 edition, "is found in the excellent lyrics of Irving Berlin, and for the boisterous there is the automobile episode, in which W. C. Fields is the leading figure. The latter is hardly more than an amplified version of the British Tate's 'Motoring' and a sketch of the same sort once done by Conroy and Le Maire, but it's the sort of comedy which rings true every time. Those who have a liking for Miss Ray Dooley, as a howling infant in another scene with Mr. Winninger, are entitled to be amused by her."

The 1921 *Follies* next year was a historic show. Victor Herbert and Rudolf Friml wrote music for it, Fanny Brice sang "My Man," and "There is the dry and personal humor of Raymond Hitchcock," as the *World* noted, "who opened the show with the satirical 'Statue of Liberty' scene. Among the guests," the *World* said, counting the stars on both sides of the footlights, were "Mr. and Mrs. Vincent Astor, Mr. and Mrs. Donald Wagstaff, Ambassador to Germany James W. Gerard and Mrs. Gerard, Mr. and Mrs. William Randolph Hearst, Mr. and Mrs. Herbert Bayard Swope, Mr. and Mrs. Julius Fleischmann, and Mr. and Mrs. John Ringling."

Fields appeared in quite a few scenes, or as many as he could manage after spirited arguments with Ziegfeld. "His main scene this year," *Variety* thought, "is a subway train. Supported by Misses Brice and Dooley, and Hitchy, he got some laughs. This skit will work up. It is the kind that only many performances and a few accidents can round out. Fields sidled along all through the show, appearing wherever a spot was possible, unctuous, amusing, always the high-grade jester, always helping the book laughs, always feeding as well as partaking. He proved a tower of strength in the laugh department. He did no juggling at any time."

The *Telegram* took note of his successful efforts to annoy Ziegfeld, slightly amplifying *Variety's* account of the subway scene. "The *Follies* is gay as ever," it said, "with only an occasional descent into the rough comedy of earlier days. A scene in the subway with a family party starting out on vacation affords the broadest fun of the piece. The raucous sound of the approaching train is a sound all New Yorkers know. In this scene it always heralds a bit of boisterous burlesque as the family party tries vainly to enter the car."

Years later Fields was to tell a friend that "the 1921 *Follies* was my happiest year with Ziegfeld and the best revue I ever saw in my life." All the critics found his comedy particularly satisfying, but several of them still considered Miss Brice the funniest performer in the show. An out-of-town reviewer said, "Fanny handed me the laugh of the season, with her burlesque of Ethel Barrymore as Camille. There she lay on her tuberculous bedstead, with Raymond Hitchcock as Armand. 'I've been a bad woman,' sighed K'meel, 'but such good company.' In her delirium, she failed to recognize Hitchie as Armand. 'The face is familiar,' she said, 'but I can't place the body.' "

Fields was fond of Miss Brice, but there were times when he found her notoriety tiresome. "The woman's a publicity hog," he once told Sam Hardy, an acquaintance in the *Follies* who was to become one of his best friends in after life.

Outside of burlesque and peep shows, the 1921 *Follies* was probably as naked a public spectacle as America has ever enjoyed. Every other set was a kind of Rubens mob scene, featuring the female pelt in its most intimate contours. All the reviewers mentioned the tall, ripe maidens with especial relish; the consensus was that Ziegfield, for the 1921 number, had risen up in a distinguished spasm of sexuality. The man for *Variety,* still a little shaken, said, "Mitti the Parisian furore of international nudity was the trick sensation. Ziegfeld did not fool the customers. She was even nuder than had been described. She wore more on her hair than on all the rest of her. And what infinitesimal cobweb she wore was perforated, cut out, ventilated."

Fields' lady friends in this period were mainly theatrical workers, and Grady occasionally found his choices inexplicable. One night during a *Follies* performance Fields drew Grady aside and asked him to go sit with a girl he'd stashed in a private room at Billy Haas' restaurant. He said, "Be careful what you say, watch your manners. This girl is educated, cultured, refined. I want to make an impression on her." Grady scrubbed up a little, changed his tie, and went to Haas', where he found Fields' girl in the private room, smoking a cigar, with her feet on the table. "I was disgusted," he said. "I went back and demanded, 'What the devil do you mean asking me to meet that sideshow freak?' 'The girl's eccentric,' Bill said, 'but she's got class. Did you notice those fifty-cent cigars she was smoking?' "

Grady claimed that even in the *Follies,* with its opportunities for rapid turnover, Fields stuck pretty much to one girl at a time. "Bill changed women every seven years, as some people get rid of the itch," he said. During one seven-year period the comedian lived with Bessie Poole, a Ziegfeld girl. He was supposed to have had a son by her, and to have cared for the son later through weekly payments to Miss Poole. After Fields' death, a Los Angeles attorney appeared in court there with "assurances," according to the Los Angeles *Times,* "that the late W. C. Fields, the film comic, left a heretofore undisclosed son who may yet make a claim to the actor's $800,000 estate." Fields and Miss Poole occupied a comfortable apartment for a while in New York and rented a summer place at Onset, Massachusetts, near the home of Victor Moore, of whom they saw a good deal. Friends have reported that Fields was open-handed with Miss Poole, presenting her, in addition to her sustenance, with many expensive gifts. A relative of Fields believed, however, that the gifts, which included a Flint automobile and diamond jewelry, were handed over with the stipulation that if she died, they should all come bouncing back to the comedian. Miss Poole died several years after their seven-year siege, and the gifts duly bounced back, the relative stated.

An important member of Fields' staff during the *Follies*

years was William Blanche, better known as "Shorty," a dwarf he used as stooge. He originally hired Shorty to plague Ziegfeld, who was a superstitious man and, like sailors, considered people with malformities a menace to good luck. Fields closed a deal with Shorty as soon as he heard about this quirk of the producer's. In the beginning, Blanche was Fields' dresser, but the arrangement proved unsatisfactory. The dwarf was far from bright, and he seldom understood an order. As Fields sat making up for his scenes, Blanche stood by with a vacant expression, handing over things like bathtowels, doilies, pictures, and suitcase straps. Once, before a performance around Christmas, Fields declared that he was hungry and said to Blanche, "Go out and get me a turkey leg." The dwarf nodded, cried, "Right, boss," and hurried away. Several hours passed; the show was drawing to a close when he returned, looking crestfallen. He waited in the dressing room till Fields came offstage. "Where the hell have you been?" the comedian roared. "I've been starving here for three hours."

"I'm sorry, boss," said Shorty. "I checked every delicatessen, grocery, and restaurant on this side of town, and they said they hadn't seen a turkey egg for several years."

Fields hit him a glancing blow and fired him on the spot. He fired Blanche at least twice a week. The action got to be part of his routine, like putting on make-up, and looking for flycatchers. He fired Blanche once in Chicago on the rather flimsy ground that the dischargee was "dangerously unobservant." Fields was in a hotel room and sent Shorty out after liquor. It was a brisk winter day, enlivened by high winds and snow flurries. When Blanche came back into the room, covered with snow, Fields was seated at a dressing table.

"Snowing again?" he asked, without turning around.

"I don't know," Blanche said. "I didn't notice."

Fields turned around and saw the snow, then blew up.

"You're fired!" he yelled. "A burglar could come in here and steal everything I've got and you'd look right through him."

Blanche packed a bag and went out, following the well-established ritual, but Fields saw him on the street two days later.

"Why the hell haven't you left town?" demanded the comedian.

"I ordered two suits a week ago and they aren't ready yet," said Blanche.

"You can come back to work," Fields said, "but I'm going to dock your salary for walking out on me."

Blanche was such a rotten valet that Fields put him in the act. "It's selfish of me to hog your incompetence," he told him. "I want to share you with the public." Blanche, dressed up for the golf act, probably influenced a good many into giving up the game. "How do you want me to look, boss?" he asked when he started. "Use your Number Two expression," Fields told him in the presence of two or three other actors, thus launching a conversational trend. In the beginning, for the golf act, Fields got Shorty a pair of squeaky shoes and had him walk across the green at a critical time. This proved to be such a hit that Fields gave it up, convinced that Blanche was trying to dominate the act.

The dwarf had no teeth, and Fields bought him a set of false ones, during a period when the two were especially harmonious. Blanche could never establish permanent claim to them, however, because Fields kept taking them back. Every time the dwarf displeased him, he got him down on the floor and repossessed the teeth. As a rule, Fields carried Blanche's teeth in a vest pocket and would dangle them invitingly when he wanted something difficult done. Once when Shorty had been balky he took him to dinner at a famous chophouse. He ordered two sirloin steaks, removed the dwarf's teeth, and then ate slowly, while Blanche, nearly weeping, nuzzled the pitiless fibers.

"O.K., I'll do it, boss," he said finally. "Hand over the teeth."

Fields had wanted him to shadow a girl on a night when the temperature was five below zero.

During the *Follies,* Fields kept all three of his wardrobe trunks, including the ones with liquor, in his dressing room. He was careless of his clothes, but he guarded his booze like a man keeping a harem. One of the main reasons he hired Blanche, he told somebody later, was to acquire a guard for his liquor. Although the dwarf was not much of a drinker, leaning almost entirely to short beers, Fields suspected him of raiding the stocks. Often Fields would eye Shorty appraisingly, then yell "Attention!" and remove a piece of chalk he carried in another vest pocket. He would draw a line on the floor, command Shorty to walk it, and step along beside him, alert for faltering as the dwarf trod the punitive streak.

Blanche kept keys to Fields' liquor chests, but the fact gave him little comfort. Fields checked both the number of bottles and the levels of the liquids every night. It was a rite often enjoyed by other members of the company, who dropped in to watch.

"All set?" Fields would cry, as he sat in a chair in one corner.

"Ready, boss," Blanche would say.

"Top shelf."

"Three full gin, one three quarter, two full vermouth, one about half, small bottle bitters."

"O.K.," Fields would reply. "Hand over to check levels."

Spotting a case of suspected shrinkage, he would bring out the chalk and say, "Stand by to walk the line—you've been guzzling again."

One time when Ziegfeld's superstition was running high, he substituted Ray Dooley, afterward the wife of actor-producer Eddie Dowling, for Shorty in the golf act. By mischance it had been one of the dwarf's worst days. Miss Dooley, in Shorty's clothes, was waiting in the wings when Fields came out. Seeing what he took to be his nemesis at a propitious, unobserving angle, he tiptoed up and gave Miss Dooley a kick that lifted her slightly off the floor. Then he grabbed her around the neck and shook her a few times, or until her tam-o'-shanter came off and revealed her curls. He was terribly chagrined; he followed her around all day, apologizing. He tried to apologize in an undertone during their act, but she began to giggle. Later, he made several offers to let her kick him, and each time assumed the stance, but she refused.

At first glance, Fields' treatment of Shorty seemed harsh, but a streak of sentiment underlay the blows, kicks and curses. To begin with, he gave the dwarf a much better job than he could have got elsewhere. Blanche traveled in fairly good circumstances with Fields; he lived a stimulating life, giving rise frequently to his unsensitive joke—"Mr.

Fields scared me out of a year's growth;" and he was paid a decent salary. Fields docked him, verbally, several times a day, for one infraction or another, but he never actually got around to reducing the cash. Too, as Fields himself afterward pointed out, he came through nobly on the dwarf's one abiding desire. Often, Blanche remarked wistfully that he'd like to have a dress suit. He died while still in the comedian's employ, and Fields bought him a nice tuxedo to be buried in.

Fields made and saved a great deal of money in his *Follies* years. His salary rose from $200 a week to several thousand, in a period when income taxes were negligible. "I believe Bill was putting away at least $1000 a week right along," Bill Grady said. "He would never allow me or anybody else to handle his money a minute longer than was necessary. I used to collect his salary, bring it to him, and say, 'I'm headed for the bank, Bill. You want me to deposit your check?' He'd make some excuse, acting very furtive and mysterious. He had a pretty good idea that I was going to rob him." Once in a while, in a badgering humor, Grady would ask Fields questions like, "How'd you figure out your savings program, Bill?" or "Can you give me some advice on investments?" Fields would look around uneasily, and perhaps whistle, or pretend to be reading.

His behavior about money, to the end of his days, was highly interesting, and paradoxical in the extreme. Though very guarded about his earnings, he sometimes carried tremendous sums on his person. These times, his acutest students believe, coincided with his feeling that his fame was about to collapse. Certainly he suffered harkbacks to the starvation periods of his youth. William Le Baron, the Paramount official, once visited a Fields show in Chicago, hoping to sign him for a movie, and stepped into his dressing room while the comedian was onstage. "The door was open to a public corridor," Le Baron said later, "and one of his suits was thrown carelessly over a chair. In plain view, protruding from a pocket, was a sheaf of bills several inches thick. I looked closer; most of them were hundreds." Another time, in Hollywood, Gene Fowler visited Fields' house and found the proprietor at work in his upstairs study. He was dressed in a bathrobe and said he was composing a movie script about an idiot widow who kept a boa constrictor farm. In one pocket of his robe there was visible a roll of bills that was eye-catching even in Hollywood.

"What's that in your pocket, Bill?" asked Fowler.

Fields inspected the pocket, presumably just then aware that it was filled.

"Appears to be bank notes," he said.

"Looks like a lot of money," said Fowler, who was curious and determined to get at the truth.

"It's four thousand dollars," said Fields, with a stiffening in his manner.

"What's it for, Bill?"

"It's getaway money," said Fields, and his tone suggested that the subject was closed.

The *Follies* people knew him as a careful man who was given to sudden, inexplicable bursts of generosity. But after each one a reaction usually set in. One time Fields and Will Rogers and Chic Sale attended a big Lambs Club Gambol and went to an expensive restaurant later. Fields footed the bills. Then they got in his Cadillac and headed toward Long Island, where some friends were living. Fields rolled out on a smooth road and accelerated his much-prized car to sixty miles an hour. He was basking in the admiration of his distinguished colleagues when a colored boy whisked by on a motorcycle.

"Don't let that boy get around you, Bill. It's bad luck," cried Rogers.

"Have no fears, my friend," Fields said in a pompous voice, and he kicked the car up to sixty-five, skidded around a curve, and turned over three or four times in a ditch. It was a bad accident. Passing motorists called an ambulance, and Rogers, with a broken leg, was taken to a hospital. Fields and Sale were luckily unhurt, but the latter had smeared grease on the snow-white uppers of his new high-button shoes. He kept complaining about the damage to his shoes, and his companion was worried. Fields apparently gave little thought to the Cadillac, which was wrecked, but he inspected the shoes, and dabbed at them with a cloth.

Finally, in the hospital, as they waited for reports on

Rogers, Fields marched up to Sale and said, "See here, do you hold me responsible for those shoes?"

"It hadn't even entered my mind," said Sale, looking down ruefully.

"Well, I'm going to take care of this," said Fields, "and I want you to forget about it."

"Nonsense," said Sale.

"I mean it," said Fields. "I'm going to have my cobbler rip those greasy parts off and put you on a brand-new set of uppers."

CHAPTER EIGHTEEN

FIELDS SPENT a year in George White's *Scandals* after the *Follies* and then decided that he was ready for a starring role. At first he sent out feelers, through Grady, through friends, and through other channels less direct, to see how the news might burst upon Broadway. His message was, in essence, that Fields was willing. Like the carter in Dickens' story, he stood alerted, but he shrank from an open statement. Although in years past he had begged for a dramatic part, he had grown too big for favors.

His system worked admirably. Philip Goodman, a producer, was preparing to cast a musical comedy by Dorothy Donnelly called *Poppy*. He saw quickly that it had a part almost miraculously suited to Fields. This insight of Goodman's was not basically complimentary, since the role was that of Eustace McGargle, a preposterous fraud, whose livelihood was gained by milking the citizenry at small country fairs. When Fields got the offer from Goodman, he overlooked the tribute to his character, and said, on the telephone, "I'll give the piece a reading." Goodman had explained the part briefly, and Fields began to experiment with the elegant syllables of the high-sounding name. "I think it was Eustace McGargle that attracted him more than anything else," one of his friends of the period felt, "for the money was less than he could get from Ziegfeld."

The show went into production, and Fields, after joining the cast, took to prancing and capering in the most expert style. He was autocratic about rehearsals, shuffling the players about onstage and giving many valuable hints to the director, an unfortunate victim of progress who was so cowed by the princely air of his comedian that he bowed out before the opening. This was an important period in Fields' life, one which had great effect upon his later manner. He found all his instincts attuned to the grandiose humbug of his part; thereafter he seldom strayed far from his character in *Poppy*. The truth is (as one of his closest friends noted) that the nomadic peculations of Eustace McGargle would have agreed with Fields perfectly. All his life he was distressed that he could not live by misdemeanors and small felonies alone.

Bob Howard, who was to be his trainer years afterward in Hollywood, thought that Fields was essentially a confidence man. "When things were going smoothly, Bill was unhappy," he once said. "He had to have somebody or something to pit his wits against." To Howard, Fields made frequent mysterious mentions of his past with the shell game. He indicated, with winks and faraway mutterings, that he had taken a great deal of money from farmers by making the little balls roll. He told Howard, "I could be stranded in any town in the United States with ten cents and within an hour make twenty dollars with the shell game." He loved to invent tales about how he had gypped people. "Most of it was imaginary," Howard said, "but he had a few authentic dodges he worked now and then, and they put him in a fine humor." One of his favorites was to receive a script from his studio, then find all manner of fault with it. He would call his bosses and say, "This script's full of holes, but I'll tell you what I'll do——I'll straighten it out for fifteen thousand dollars." After that he would make a few important-looking marks on the pages and send them back. "It really made very little difference one way or the other, for when he got on the set he said exactly what he pleased."

Poppy opened at the New Apollo Theatre in New York on the third of September, 1923. Miss Donnelly's original draft of the play had not called for any juggling, but the final, or Donnelly-Fields version, required McGargle to juggle quite a lot. Nobody could ever explain why it was that Fields, though he clamored for straight comedy parts, insisted on juggling as soon as he got them. The show itself was a success, but Fields was a sensation. The night of September 3, 1923, ended for all time his appearances as a co-comedian or as a comedian in a subordinate role. He was "made," in the theatrical vernacular. In the space of a few hours the stigma of juggler was forever erased and the title of comedian took its place. Fields was to remember the opening of *Poppy* as one of the great nights of his life.

Heywood Broun's review is of interest for several reasons. *"Poppy* is our idea of a good musical comedy," wrote the late columnist-politician-unionist-liberal-Catholic in the New York *World*. "Dorothy Donnelly has provided the new piece at the Apollo with a coherent, amusing, and often genuinely dramatic book. Indeed, it would be quite possible to forego music and build a first-rate comedy around the story which she has fashioned of a strolling swindler and his daughter.

"Still, it is better that the musical-comedy method was chosen, for otherwise W. C. Fields might not have been hit upon as the person to play the sharper. Mr. Fields is so good a juggler that recognition of his ability as an actor was delayed until last night. Not only does he handle lines just as deftly as cigar boxes, but he creates an authentic and appealing character. At the moment we can't remember anybody who ever made us laugh more. It is first-rate clowning, but that is only the beginning of the job which Fields has done. In addition to his familiar but nonetheless hilarious stunts he gives us a real and complete portrait of as merry a rascal as the stage has seen in years.

"Poppy marks the debut of Miss Madge Kennedy in musical comedy, and it is a charming performance, although we have here nothing which is not along pretty well-established lines. As an adventure, Miss Kennedy's dash into songs and dancing and such like is good fun, but we trust

this does not indicate a permanent vocation. Musical comedy is almost certain to be wasteful of a player who is one of the two or three best light-comedy actresses in America and the best *farceuse* of them all. We like her enormously in *Poppy,* but when she goes home at the end of the evening there remain in her equipment of charms and excellences at least a hundred and twenty-one things which she has had no opportunity to use.

"The music of *Poppy,* which was written by Steven Jones and Arthur Samuels, is agreeable, but with one exception not difficult to forget. However, there is an outstanding song hit which we imagine it will be quite impossible to ignore within a month or so. The song is called 'Mary' and it has that ingratiating persistence which will make it insinuate itself deeper and deeper into the sounds of our daily life. Two months from today we feel sure we shall hate it, but last night it was a rousing tune. There is also a good although less infectious number called 'Alibi Baby' and both songs fall to Miss Luella Gear. Now Miss Gear doesn't seem to sing very much, but she has a way with her and she, too, belongs very definitely among the hits of the show.

"We were also amused by Jimmy Barry, Robert Woolsey, and Emma Janvier. Alan Edwards is the young man who marries the girl in the last act, and for once the conventional happy ending didn't seem a tragedy for the heroine.

"The first-night audience was enthusiastic about *Poppy* and it should have been."

Fields enjoyed Broun's review; he clipped it out and saved it, but he was especially soothed by the remarks in the *Tribune,* which found fault with much of the proceedings. "*Poppy* was rather a dull show last night except when W. C. Fields, the tramp juggler, was operating, which was a good deal of the time," the paper's critic felt. "Its infirmities included another sappy Cinderella story, two or three humdrum hick comedians, and a lot of nondescript tunes, all of them appropriate for late dancing. But its tiresome elements were insufficient to overcome Mr. Fields' infectious good humor; and the entertainment is to be set down as laughable though tedious."

Fields considered that the *Tribune* man, in his lead paragraph, had struck just about the right note of critical inquiry. Some days later, however, comparing Broun's rhapsody with the *Tribune's* peevish complaint he began to wonder about the validity of critics in general. It was typical of Fields that, although the critics had been unanimously kind to him, he still could find flaws in their deportment. "Why the hell should these fellows think for the public?" he demanded of a colleague. "They can't even agree among themselves."

The *Tribune* review continued with details of the comedian's performance, saying, "Mr. Fields represented an unctuous faker, ransacking the Connecticut country fairs of a hundred years ago, accompanied by his lovely and honest daughter. While she (Miss Madge Kennedy) did songs and dancing, her father supplied the yokels with magic herbs and balsams. Also, he allowed them to speculate with him in the shell game and other devices, greatly to the distress of his virtuous offspring. The eloquence of the old-time mountebank is a rich and comic language, much funnier than that of today's promoter of oil stocks; and Miss Dorothy Donnelly, the librettist, has furnished Mr. Fields with many of its most priceless phrases. Incidental to the proceedings, Mr. Fields indulged in some of his humorous juggling, in one part of which he employed mucilege to aid his dexterous manipulations! It was in his smiling counterfeit of the ancient vagabond, however, that he was most deft and most amusing. We suspect him to be the funniest man in town since Will Rogers went away."

Fields was distressed to note that by this point in his account the *Tribune* man was beginning to go to pieces, though toward the end, in the comedian's opinion, the writer rallied slightly, concluding with, "*Poppy* is a sweet mess out of the everlasting musical-comedy honey pots, and savored considerably by Mr. Fields' luxurious clowning and by Miss Kennedy's eager and very good acting. You can go to it, if you have nothing else to do, without being too much ashamed of yourself."

The other papers were equally impressed by Fields, the *Herald* calling him "as adroit and astonishing as ever at his tricks and more comical far than ever. We had seen him do every one of the vaudeville stunts before, but had never before come upon him when it had occurred to someone that he was also an enormously amusing comedian who might be entrusted safely with a role in a play."

One of Fields' happiest scenes in the play—somewhat similar to a skit he was to do later in the movie *Mississippi* with Bing Crosby—revolved around a poker game in which he condescended to take a hand. During rehearsals Fields had insisted on the scene, helping to put it together, he said, "from experience." As he developed the sketch, he gave out that he had participated in some of the most earth-shaking poker sessions in American gambling history and that he had unmercifully trimmed the cleverest sharpers in the game.

"Where did you do most of this, Mr. Fields?" one of the young actors asked him.

"Hither and yon," Fields said, using a stock answer he was favoring in that period.

The truth is that he practically never gambled on anything. He felt that there was an ugly element of chance in gambling which made it possible for somebody other than himself to win. In his wealthiest phase he shied away from the relaxing dedication to dice, cards and horses that was favored by many of his successful friends. However, it was never difficult for him to persuade producers, whether in the theater or in movies, to allow him fictional gambling scenes. There was something so blatantly felonious about the sight of Fields in a poker game that its humor was assured from the start. The unlikely possibility that his companions at the table could look at him and feel at ease shook the imagination. His whole manner suggested fakery in its most flagrant form; he was the apotheosis of the quack. Two or three of his friends felt that the spirit of Fields was preserved by one of the stills from *My Little Chickadee*. It shows him, as Cuthbert J. Twillie, a crooked oil man, in a Western poker game with several desperadoes. Most of them are eying him appraisingly, as if trying to make up their minds what to do about him. Fields himself is rigged out in a cutaway, striped trousers, and a high gray felt hat with a broad black band; he is wearing formal white gloves, which are turned back delicately, and he has a wilted lily in his buttonhole. His hands, graceful and expresssive, are carefully shielding his cards from any possible snooping by the man on his left, while his own furtive, suspicious gaze is plainly directed into the hand of the player on his right. His attitude is so frankly dishonest that the other players seem to sense the inevitability of their financial downfall. Their stunned faces pay homage to a situation, and a character, which defy all the known rules regarding cheats.

Of his poker game in *Poppy,* the *Herald* said admiringly, "The stud game in which he manages to deal himself four fours and to win a thousand-dollar pot without having undergone the burdensome necessity of putting up any money himself is the most hilarious minor episode of the new season."

The Robert Woolsey mentioned in Broun's review was a young comedian who, a few years later, would come to be known as one of the most popular players in the movies. With Burt Wheeler and Dorothy Lee, Woolsey was to have a vogue in musical comedies somewhat comparable to that of Eddie Cantor and Danny Kaye. At the time of *Poppy,* though, he was struggling in the best tradition of impecunious juveniles everywhere. The *Herald* review tendered him a classic left-handed compliment, saying that "Miss Gear was helped enormously through the 'Mary' matter by Robert Woolsey, one of those complacent, sledge-hammer comics whom, up to then, a good many of us had rather intended to kill."

Despite the *Herald,* Woolsey was to go ahead and ride a crest of Hollywood fame at a time when Fields, his superior comedian of the *Poppy* cast, was having movie troubles of the direst kind.

Poppy ran for more than a year and Fields got to be a big man around town. He was sought out by celebrities and socialites, nearly all of whom made him nervous. He had a not-uncommon personality quirk: persons in the upper social brackets made him ill at ease. He was never at his best, for a while, with people who were in any way exalted. He was diffident, and a little tense, until he got to know them well, and then, having their number, he would re-establish his usual condescension in an excessive degree, convinced of his undoubted superiority to them all.

William Le Baron, who was to employ Fields for Paramount soon after *Poppy,* recalled a party the comedian gave at a house he'd taken for the summer in Bayside, Long Island. Hot summers bothered Fields; the sun plagued his nose, causing it to turn red and expand. When he went to bed at night, he had to rub Allen's Footease on it, and this struck him as a nuisance. His house at Bayside, which was to give him the benefit of cooling ocean breezes and eliminate the Footease, was discovered by a group of couples from the Westbury horse set. Happily, they demanded that their famous parishioner entertain them. Fields' stable lore was pretty well limited to a rear view of the ice horse he had followed in his youth, and he was further awed by the formidable lineage of the well-meaning but saddle-weary clique that had flushed him. "The fact is," said Le Baron, "they were very nice people and approached Bill in no spirit of slumming. They liked and enjoyed him both on the stage and in person."

Fields began to organize a formal dinner, though stricken with icy waves of social terror. At length, in a pitiable condition, he called Le Baron and said, "I'm in a hell of a mess. I don't know anything about dinner parties. You've got to come over here and give me a hand." Le Baron agreed to lend both his counsel and his presence, and he repaired forthwith to the battle front. Fields was wild and perspiring, but he was proceeding with great fanfare. He had put on some extra servants, including a spot butler of mien almost crushingly aristocratic. He towered over his employer, and his craggy features looked down upon a world that was patently inadequate to his background and proclivities. His name was Fillmore, but Fields, when Le Baron arrived, was addressing him as "Mr. Fillmore," and making a slight, involuntary gesture as of pulling his forelock. Toward the end of the party, by which time the comedian had recovered his composure, he was calling the butler "son" and "Bud," and ordering him about like a poodle. Fields later said he learned that Fillmore had come by his patrician attitude honestly; he was the son of a very successful waiter and had worked for a space as doorman at a fashionable hotel.

Fields had bought a large quantity of European wines and ordered foods of the most exotic order. He had inspected a handy booklet called *The Gourmet's Guide,* which he bought in a stationery store, and had arranged a digestive line-up that set him back several hundred dollars. Even Fillmore looked a little impressed when he surveyed the larder. The comedian had also done a bangup job on his person: he had arrayed himself in evening clothes of faultless good taste and was brushed, pruned, barbered, dry-cleaned and pressed to a magnificent degree. Notwithstanding his progress, he was rigid with tension when Le Baron arrived, some hour or so ahead of the first guests. "How's everything look, how's everything look?" Fields kept babbling, and Le Baron advised him to sit down and relax.

"I don't know what to say to these people," Fields said.

"Why don't you just try being natural?" Le Baron replied.

His advice went all unheeded, for Fields greeted his guests, when they began to turn up, with a sedate, upper-class restraint that was only slightly less painful than Fillmore's. He was very stiff and proper, and he had settled on a sort of broad-a singsong as being the precise accent of the aristocracy. Fillmore served drinks—small, unostentatious ones—and the group filed funereally in to dinner. Le Baron kept trying to jolly Fields up, but during the hors d'oeuvres, the fish and the partridge, Fields' demeanor bore a strong resemblance to that of an elderly, bilious floorwalker. His guests probed gently for humor, but he gave them genteel observations on the weather and a discourse on a novel he'd been reading by a man named Meredith.

"I think it was about simultaneous with the filet," said Le Baron, "that Bill looked around and saw, to his surprise, that his guests were people just like himself. I think it came as a terrible shock."

The comedian let his muscles sag a trifle, advanced one elbow to the table, and told a scrubbed-up lie about a widow he'd known in New Guinea. The response was so brisk that he began to beam, and snapped his fingers at the butler. "Fill up the wineglasses, Filbert," he said. "Keep it coming." A man near the far end of the table responded with an amusing incident he had witnessed in a Pullman, and Fields rose to his feet. Walking around the room (thereafter for the rest of his life he was to be more or less in transit at dinner parties) he launched a series of uproariously funny exaggerations about his travels, dropping his broad a in the process. Everybody loosened up, and the conversation departed from the enervating poli-

tesse of the first few courses. The night was humid, and
Fields asked permission to loosen his collar. His suggestion prompted another man to remove his shirt, then a
young matron observed that her feet hurt, and she took off
her shoes. The evening wore on, relaxed, rich in anecdote,
an occasion of memorable grace and warmth. Midnight
found Fields, minus his tie, collar and shirt, sitting with his
feet propped up on the table, an empty champagne bottle
balanced on his head, deep in an analysis of show people.

"It was really quite a worth-while business," said Le
Baron, "of a kind that was rare with Bill before or afterward. He was not really a gregarious man. He didn't seek
people out; they sought him."

For weeks after his party, Fields raved about what a
fine time he'd had, and how much he enjoyed his guests.
But their subsequent invitations found him as elusive as
ever; he made excuses, as was his instinct always.

CHAPTER NINETEEN

THE DEBUT in motion pictures of the man who was to
become that industry's most famous comedian took place
on Long Island in 1925. D. W. Griffith, a nickelodeon pioneer who was noted principally for "spectacles," many of
them stark, had been assigned by Paramount to do a film
version of *Poppy*, starring Carol Dempster, a winsome cinema ingénue of the period. It was the custom of movies then,
as now, to strive for popularity on the basis of their
"stars," with the result that, through the years, the public
has been treated to such masterworks of casting as Wallace Beery as Long John Silver, Robert Walker as Jo-
hannes Brahms, Shirley Temple as Henry the Eighth,

George Arliss as John L. Sullivan, and Martha Raye as Camille. Paramount, meditating on *Poppy,* regretfully discarded Fatty Arbuckle and "Freckles" Barry, and turned to Fields as a last resort. It was an inevitable choice; Fields had made the part and could play it in his sleep. Paramount rather hoped that he would, for it was the company's plan to trim Eustace McGargle to the bone so that Miss Dempster could shine the more brilliantly for her following— a mixture of shopgirls and male equivalents of bobby soxers.

The plan ganged badly agley, as the poet Burns had suggested that it might. Fields appeared at Paramount's Long Island studio wearing his clip-in mustache and his most overbearing manner. His first act was to pre-empt the star's dressing room. When Miss Dempster had been revived with ammonia, a conference was held about the script. The problem of lines was, of course, non-existent, since the movie was silent, but Fields was told that many scenes that had been much favored by the legitimate audiences would be deleted. In their stead, Miss Dempster would substitute things such as a Slavonic folk dance, a scene in which her mother died, at a snail's pace, and several passages featuring wooing, ranging from sweet to hot. Fields retired to his dressing room, seated himself in a comfortable rocker, and indicated that the movie was at a standstill, which was correct. The bosses shouted in vain. Eventually, rather than scrap the project, they more or less allowed him a free hand, forging the first link of a chain of similar compromises with which Hollywood would become all too familiar during the following years.

"In the windup," William Le Baron recalled, "they tried desperately even to keep Miss Dempster's part on an equal footing with Bill's. But it was no use—he walked off with the picture, and made everybody half mad in the process. He was just suited; that kind of thing was right in his department. When he left the set at the end he looked watchful but triumphant. He'd got the upper hand and he couldn't have been happier."

The film version of *Poppy,* whose title was changed to *Sally of the Sawdust,* as being more commonplace and unwieldy, showed to satisfied audiences everywhere. The studio heads congratulated themselves on having had the foresight to encourage initiative in their comedian. A year later, Le Baron, who had taken no official hand in *Sally of the Sawdust,* signed Fields for several additional pictues. Le Baron had come to Paramount only recently, having previously written plays, edited *Collier's Weekly,* and then managed, briefly, William Randolph Hearst's *Cosmopolitan* motion-picture enterprises on Long Island. He signed with Hearst believing he was to edit the *Cosmopolitan* magazine, but when he reported for work Hearst sent him out to the studio. "I don't know anything about pictures," Le Baron told him. "Neither do the people that are making them," replied Hearst. Hoping to be fired quickly, Le Baron converted Frank Borzage, a leading man Hearst had imported from Hollywood, into a director and turned out a spectacularly quick film treatment of a book he'd liked, Fannie Hurst's *Humoresque*. The picture bore the hallmarks of an ignoramus, was hailed as a classic, and was widely showered with gold medals. Le Baron decided that the medium had possibilities. To bone up, he attended several movies, since he had previously seen only a handful, all of which put him to sleep.

Le Baron and Fields made a felicitous team of employer-employee. Le Baron thought Fields was hilariously funny, both personally and professionally, and was content to put up with a great deal of bullying, minor fraud, and humbug. Fields, for his part, trusted Le Baron, insofar as he trusted any human being, and was amenable to limited counsel and direction. Among Le Baron's first acts, upon acquiring the stormy petrel of the *Follies,* was to assign a director with whom Fields might work in some semblance of peace. Looking around, he decided that a new man named Gregory La Cava and Fields had many points in common. La Cava had come to Paramount as a gag writer from the New York *Sunday Herald,* for which he had done a cartoon strip with Milt Gross. He was interested in animated cartoons, and trained most of Disney's first artists. His first directing job for Le Baron was on an automobile racing picture starring Richard Dix. The original director on the project had withdrawn, saying that he knew nothing whatever about racing. "What do *you* know about racing?" Le Baron asked La Cava. "Everything," replied La Cava quietly. It later developed that he'd never seen an automobile race in his life, nor had he known anybody who had seen one, but he turned out some memorable scenes with Richard Dix. Certainly Dix will never forget them, for he came within a hair of being killed on several occasions. It was La Cava's hope to get the feeling of motion into his racing picture, and to that end he threw in everything he could think of—wrecks, fires, explosions, death, smoke, dust, and all-around destruction. "Throughout the picture," said Le Baron, "the air was clogged with flying humans and automotive parts."

La Cava had a certain subdued but reckless humor that Le Baron believed would be attractive to Fields. The producer's bringing them together provided one of the enduring friendships of Fields' life, but it struck fire from the beginning and continued to be rackety to the end. The first picture they worked on together was *So's Your Old Man*. After the first day's shooting, Le Baron came onto the set and drew La Cava aside.

"How do you like him?"

"He's a terribly mean man," said La Cava.

Later in the day, Le Baron cornered Fields and said, "What do you think of La Cava?"

"He's a dago son of a bitch," replied Fields, with his usual loose grouping of people and events.

After two weeks Le Baron consulted La Cava again. "How do you like him now, Greg?" he asked hopefully.

"I hate his guts," said La Cava, "but he's the greatest comedian that ever lived."

As before, Le Baron queried Fields later on, saying, "How are you and La Cava making out, Bill?"

"I can't stand the bastard," said Fields, "but he's the best director in the business."

The sets that Fields and La Cava worked on were always popular. Employees from the neighboring sets liked to drop in and visit. The actor and the director were generally locked in a jangling row. "It was almost impossible to drive a new idea down Bill's throat," La Cava said recently. *So's Your Old Man* was supposed to be a wistful, tender, rather touching story about a princess who visited Fields' home town. Fields cared little or nothing for the mood of the piece. The fourth morning of work, La Cava got on the scene, found Fields there early, the cameras set up and grinding, and dirt and other debris rising from one corner of the lot.

"What in the hell's going on here?" he cried, running up, terribly agitated.

"Mr. Fields said this would be an excellent time to work in his golf act," said one of the cameramen, pointing to the disturbance in the corner.

"Why, you can't see anything but dirt flying," said La Cava. He told them to knock off grinding.

By now Fields had stopped swinging and was looking on with contemptuous suspicion.

"You know that golf act won't fit into this thing, Bill," said La Cava, approaching warily.

"Why not?" demanded the comedian.

"It's not that kind of a story. What about the princess?"

"We can use her as a caddy," suggested Fields.

After three or four very strenuous hours, La Cava talked Fields out of playing golf in the middle of the plot, and the shooting resumed.

A few days later Fields came onto the set bristling with importance. He had a "wonderful gag" he'd worked out the previous night, when he had insomnia. He and La Cava sat down, and Fields explained.

"Well, there's a big bunch of cattails," he began, but La Cava interrupted by saying, "We've shot all over the lot. Any audience will know there aren't any cattails growing around here by now."

"This can be across the street, at a neighbor's," Fields went on. "Hell, those things grow up overnight, anyway. Well, I'm out in the middle of them with a big scythe and I'm cutting down cattails, and all of a sudden a Manx cat runs out, see?"

La Cava regarded him speculatively for a moment, then he said, "Where's it funny?"

"Why, it's a Manx cat," said Fields. "I cut the bastard's tail off. Don't you get it?"

"I get it all right," said La Cava, "and it's repulsive. Half of the audience will think you actually did cut the cat's tail off."

"Well, we're going to do this scene," said Fields. "I've made up my mind. I like it."

La Cava said he'd have to talk to the producer first.

When he returned from the supposed talk, he told Fields that, since the costs of the picture were running dangerously high, the producer wanted the cattail episode done at the end, as an extra scene. "They say we'll have to do it separately, Bill," La Cava said. "It'll be better that way—we'll be able to give it the careful treatment it deserves."

When *So's Your Old Man* was finished, La Cava didn't mention the cattails, and neither did his comedian. It was presumed that he had forgotten it. But Fields never really forgot anything. A few months later, when he was working on another picture, its director came to La Cava, much perturbed, and said, "Say, I'm having trouble with Bill Fields over a scene involving a Manx cat. He's got some laborers sticking a lot of cattails in the ground, and he's sitting on a box sharpening up a scythe. What do you think I ought to do?"

"Tell him you're running over the budget and that you'll work the scene in as an extra at the end," advised La Cava. "That's what I did."

For several years La Cava kept hearing reports that Fields was trying to work his cattail gag into a movie. For once, all of the comedian's attempts were unsuccessful; despite the brilliant conception of the scene, no director seemed willing to subordinate a plot to it.

La Cava and Fields made *So's Your Old Man* in 1926 and *Running Wild* in 1927. Both pictures were done for Paramount and released through Famous Players Lasky. Fields remained steadily intractable throughout. One day on the set he found that the script (to which he had previously agreed) called for him to wrestle with a bear. A trainer had just arrived towing a rather scaly-looking but substantial black bear on the end of a chain.

"What's this?" Fields cried, drawing up in indignant apprehension.

"Man's got the bear you're to wrestle with," said La Cava.

"The hell with it," Fields cried. "I won't do it."

The trainer was to get forty dollars a day for the use of his animal and he was anxious not to lose the job.

"Is a gentle bear," he cried, in a slight accent. "Bear never hurt no mans. See here, one can hit the bear. One hits the bear in the nose," and he reached over and rapped the bear soundly.

The bear shook its head with an annoyed expression and uncorked a left hook that stretched the trainer flat on his back.

"Take that damned bear away from here!" Fields roared. "I don't even like his smell."

The trainer, pretty groggy, was rising to one knee, muttering something that sounded like, "I'll get him next round," but Fields kept yelling to remove the bear, which, standing a little to one side, had the appearance of waiting in a neutral corner.

The trainer's head soon cleared and he apologized profusely, saying that the bear was always a little jumpy during an opening. "No harm in this bear," he emphasized. "He's just a big kid."

Fields remained adamant, and the trainer suggested an alternative: he would put on an old bearskin he had at home and do the wrestling himself. Fields agreed, with a snarl. A few minutes after they had begun to wrestle, the trainer, working methodically, eager to make up for the bear's poor showing, applied a flying mare to his opponent and brought him crashing to the pavement. Fields arose weakly; he seemed to be trying to say something. La Cava bent an ear to his lips and listened intently.

The director straightened up in a second, his face animated. "Mr. Fields says to take the bearskin home and bring back the bear," he told the trainer. The bear was returned to the set, and the scene was shot as originally planned.

La Cava studied Fields for years and stored up interesting theories about him. He believed, as several others did, that Fields' personal and professional later life was dedicated to repaying society for the hurts of his childhood. "Nearly everything Bill tried to get into his movies was something that lashed out at the world," he said. "The peculiar thing is that although he was being pretty mean there wasn't any real sting in it. It was only funny. Bill never really wanted to hurt anybody. He just felt an obligation."

Years after their Long Island phase, when both Fields and La Cava were living in big houses in Hollywood, La Cava would drive Fields into a frenzy by analyzing his gifts.

"You're not a natural comedian, Bill," he'd say. "You're a counter puncher. You're the greatest straight man that ever lived. It's a mistake for you ever to do the leading. When you start to bawl out and ham around and trip over things, you're pushing. I hate to see it, Bill."

"What do you know about comedy, you dago bastard?" Fields would growl, and go out on the lawn and sulk.

La Cava once told Fields, "Bill, I'm making a picture down at Paramount that I want you to study. It's a comedy, and we're using some new techniques."

Fields laughed scornfully, re-emphasized his classification of La Cava by race and ancestry, and said, "I'll be down in the front row—with a basket of last month's eggs."

The picture was *My Man Godfrey,* with Carole Lombard and William Powell, which won La Cava the New York critics' award for best direction in 1934. Fields went to see it, but refused to deliver an opinion on it for several days. La Cava, who loved to badger him, kept mentioning the movie in a deprecating way whenever they met. "I thought the thing was funny, at first," he said, "but I see what you mean now. I had another look at it a few nights ago, and it's awful. It's strained."

"The picture is amusing in spots," said Fields, in a stiffish tone.

"Well, we should have slapsticked it up some," said La Cava.

"You'd have ruined it," Fields said, a reminiscent look coming into his eye. "The fact is, you dago son of a bitch," he went on, "the thing was as funny as hell."

Over several drinks, and in a boisterous good humor, La Cava explained to Fields the new techniques which had helped keep his cast and crew in top comic condition. On the first day of shooting, La Cava announced that he was planning to follow no set script, but would just shoot whatever came to mind at the moment. Also, he said, it might be fun to maintain a sort of party atmosphere on the set. Accordingly, he arrived each day with many bottled drinks, canapés, and other equipment usually reserved for the cocktail hour. The morning was generally given over to warming up to a festive mood, with anecdotes, frequent visits to the refectory table, and, on occasion, song. Then somebody, perhaps spotting a camera or other piece of technical apparatus, might remember the movie, and the conversation would take a professional turn.

"We might as well fix up a scene, fellows," La Cava would cry, and call for suggestions. His writers would get busy, and others would come forward with ideas—Miss Lombard, or Mr. Powell, or perhaps Eugene Pallette or Mischa Auer, who were in the cast. Again, it might be a prop boy, or a watchman. Once something was worked up, they would shoot it leisurely, attempting, meanwhile, to maintain the party spirit, and then start drawing corks for the next scene.

The picture was by no means made possible by liquor, but La Cava believes that his keen analysis of the causes and cures of scenario tension was much appreciated by the company.

Fields spent a lot of time with La Cava and Gene Fowler in Hollywood, though neither of the latter, by that stage, would have anything to do with him professionally. Once in a while, when they were together, Fields would become animated over the possibility of his starring in a picture which La Cava would direct and Fowler would write. Both La Cava and Fowler would laugh loudly. "We don't want any truck with such a mean, cantankerous old man," they'd tell him. "I wouldn't direct you if you were the last actor alive," La Cava would add, and Fowler would chip in with, "Bill, if I ever get an urge to write for you, I'll know it's time to go back to the newspapers."

Fowler nearly slipped up on this resolve one time. Fields had indicated that he was wildly enthusiastic over Fowler's new book, *Salute to Yesterday*. He sent a telegram to Fowler, who had made a trip to New York in connection with the book's publication, which read as follows: "Had to go to four shops to buy eleven copies of *Salute to Yesterday*. This gives you some idea of how it is selling here. I am half through the book. It is the meatiest and fruitiest tale I have ever read. Dickens or Twain never drew finer or funnier characters. Two belly laughs in every line. I hope it is my good fortune to play Captain Trolley. Your loving uncle—Bill Fields."

"I'm going to play it, Gene," he told Fowler a couple of weeks later. "It'll make a wonderful picture."

Following his instinct and his often-repeated vow, Fowler declined, with thanks, and tried to change the subject, but Fields persisted.

"I finally got the impression that he really wanted the book," Fowler says, "and naturally I could use the money. So we arranged a meeting."

When they got together, at Fields' home, they settled a few details, and Fowler said, "Now about the money, Bill. I think we ought to work out a fair percentage split."

Fields began to take on a vacant, faraway look; he muttered indistinctly about some new hollyhocks he had in the side yard. Then he arose and wandered away from the disturbing table. Since the meeting seemed unlikely to return to its announced topic, Fowler went home.

A few days later Fields called up and said, "About that book of yours—the one you were trying to sell me for a movie."

Fowler began an indignant protest, but Fields broke in.

"The only way I work," he said emphatically, "is *cash on the barrelhead!*"

"Why, you miserable old devil!" Fowler cried. "I don't give a damn whether you——"

"Cash on the barrelhead," yelled Fields, drowning him out. "Cash on the barrelhead."

He hung up before he heard Fowler's next comment, which, all things considered, was probably just as well.

CHAPTER TWENTY

BILLY GRADY quit Fields, after representing him for fourteen years, because of a dispute involving Earl Carroll's *Vanities*. The comedian's early pictures on Long Island—*Sally of the Sawdust, So's Your Old Man, Running Wild,* and *The Old Army Game,* were artistically successful but made little money. He was starred in *The Old Army Game,* a Fieldsian kind of story about a sharpshooting fraud who lived principally by the shell game, and became well liked by movie-goers. To Fields, stardom meant big money, whether the box office flourished or not. He argued that he deserved at least as much as Rudolph Valentino and Wallace Reid were making, and probably more. Paramount, with some justification, contended that he should be paid in accordance with the popularity of his pictures. It was a hopeless deadlock; while Fields was unable to wangle the fantastic sums he demanded, Paramount's combined lung power was insufficient to convert Fields. "As none of our hopes materialized during that period, I returned to the stage," he wrote Jim Tully later. Another time after that, helping a Paramount publicity man prepare a sketch of his life, he gave additional details, not quite accurate, on his first film venture. "All my life," he said, "I had earned my living by entertaining people. I figured I had a vague idea what people liked, and what they would laugh at. I knew what I could do best, and what I couldn't do.

"So when I signed my first contract to make pictures, the studio heads told me my worries were over. I could go out and play golf. Meanwhile, they had experts who would write comedy and funny lines, other experts who would figure out things for me to wear, and things for me to do. More experts would tell me how to do them. I could just loaf until they wanted me, and then I could come into the studio and follow instructions.

"I did. And when my contract was up, it was not only not renewed, but nobody else would have me. So I went back to the stage."

When he left the movies he instructed Grady to see what was doing, then withdrew into dignified but uneasy vigilance.

"Bill never liked to talk to the other principal in a financial deal," Grady said. "He was so belligerent the negotiations always fell down that way, anyhow. His system was to keep somebody running back and forth with angry messages."

Fields had been approached some months before by Carroll. On a golf course at Long Island, a boy had run out from the clubhouse to notify Fields that Carroll wanted him on the phone.

"Tell him to go to hell!" said the comedian, and he chopped viciously at his ball, which was in a sand trap.

"But he said he wanted you to appear in the *Vanities!*" exclaimed the boy.

"Tell him to take the *Vanities* and stick——" (Fields offered here an improbable solution for disposing of the *Vanities*—one which Carroll, showman though he was, would doubtless have rejected even had it been feasible.)

Nothing came of this exchange, but Grady and Carroll held a conference when Fields quit the movies. "He wants you pretty bad, Bill," Grady told his client after the conference.

"Oh, he does, does he?" snarled Fields, who was immediately put into a combative humor because Carroll thought well of him.

"Yes," said Grady simply, having gone over this road several times before.

"Well, he'll damn well pay for me," said Fields. He got a pencil and a piece of paper and figured out a list of penalties for Carroll's rash urge.

"Tell him," he said at length, "that I'll work for $6500 a week, plus substantial bonuses and percentage clauses."

Grady sat reflective a minute, then arose and said, "All right, I'll do it, but it's the most outrageous demand I've ever struck in all my years in show business.

Eying him carefully, Fields lit a cigar.

Grady called on Carroll, presented the surrender terms, and came back in about an hour. "Believe it or not," he reported, "Carroll said he would do it."

"Said he would, did he?" Fields gritted savagely.

"Don't ask me why."

"Well, you trot right back and tell him I've changed my mind," said the comedian. "There's another condition—he'll have to drop his name off the marquee and make it read 'W. C. Fields in the *Vanities*.'"

Grady left without comment. Somewhat later in the day he looked into Carroll's office and delivered the shift in terms. "Frankly," he added, "it's disgraceful behavior. If I were you, I'd tell him where to go."

By an unlucky chance, Grady had underestimated the producer's compulsion to employ Fields. Shortly after the agent left his office, Carroll telephoned Fields, agreed to the new condition, and relayed Grady's conversation word for word.

The meeting of Grady and Fields that evening was highly spirited. Among other things, the comedian said, "Your ten per cent's cut off during this run, and I hope we keep going till around the turn of the century."

In what he came to believe was a rather distinguished speech of severance, comparable to Washington's Farewell to his Troops, Grady ended one of the authentically polychromatic relationships of show business. His remarks were liberally sprinkled with four-letter nouns, for emphasis, and he recalled, at one point, ducking a shoe. When Fields began to see that his trusted (as it were) agent and companion was serious, he modified the punishment.

"Never mind the 10 per cent, never mind," he said. You won't miss it—I'll include you in my will."

Grady has explained that this system came to be a standard Fields panacea for evading financial obligations. With girls, he often waved generously when they began to eye the diamonds and furs, and said, "Don't bother your pretty head about material things, my dear—I'll see that you're taken care of in my will." He got to the point where he resolved anybody's questions about money by hinting of lavish bequests. Certainly his will at the time of his death proved to be a remarkable document, but it was hardly the cornucopia advertised by its creator.

Fields' will began to run through his thoughts as King Charles' head got into Mr. Dick's *Memorial*, in *David Copperfield*. His allusions to it provided another of the great Fields paradoxes, for in a single breath he would proclaim his poverty and hint of vast riches for those who, by their single-minded devotion to the master, might be mentioned. It was a kind of treasure chart, with the promise of pots of gold at the end of the Fields rainbow. Once in a while, as he felt his power, he would make expansive declarations to his intimate friends.

Grady, who remained a companion of Fields, though

their professional ties were broken, once appeared in his will, and so did La Cava and Fowler. While walking in his Hollywood grounds one day, Fields decided that the three men were among the princes of humanity; he was emotionally affected by their loyalty, their support, their comradely ways. He repaired to his study, summoned a young graduate lawyer with whom he had struck up a deal, providing that the man relieve Fields of certain legal responsibilities for the sum of eight dollars per day (eight hours), and announced an important change in the will. "I want those boys to share in this thing," he told the lawyer. "There aren't three finer men in America." He then added hastily that the will was entirely speculative; the sums mentioned had not yet been made. "To tell you the truth," he said, "I haven't got a dime to my name."

Notwithstanding, he and the lawyer altered the will to include substantial bequests to Grady, La Cava, and Fowler, all of whom were living close by and were lucratively employed by the movies.

Some time afterward, when they all got together, Fields movingly announced his charities; then he shook hands all around. The beneficiaries thanked him politely and changed the subject as fast as possible. In the weeks that followed, Fields referred with satisfaction to the bequests and got a lot of enjoyment out of his kindness. Then he finished a movie and sat around for two or three months, growing fidgety. His old hallucinations were revived by the idleness. His face settled into suspicious lines; he began to conceive intimations of a monster conspiracy. Presently he got in touch with a cheap detective agency and gave certain furtive, whispered instructions after a somewhat louder harangue about the pay.

"He had us investigated," Fowler said. "He found out that, at the time, we were all making more than he was. He was furious, and called us on the telephone to bawl us out. He took the attitude that we were plotting to defraud him."

The beneficiaries told him substantially the same thing.

"You ugly old skinflint, who wants in your will?" said La Cava. "Go along and don't bother me."

"By the way," said Fowler, "I forgot to tell you that I'm thinking about including *you* in *my* will."

Grady, who was then casting director for Metro-Gold-wyn-Mayer, said he was having a terribly busy morning and would have to switch him to a Mr. Tomkins, in charge of B musicals. "He may be able to get you a couple of days' extra work in January," Grady said.

Fields lost no time in sending for his lawyer. Holding the clock on him, he was able to remove the odious bequests in a little less than half a day, bringing the fee, which Fields paid to the penny, to $3.94.

"I got out of that thing very neatly," he later told his cook.

In the *Vanities,* Fields' manner was assured, poised. Both his celebrity and his confidence had ripened. He did variations on his old routines, and, as in the *Follies,* appeared in several skits with other players. To his colleagues, by now, he seemed helpfully mellowed, even patriarchal, though he was considerably younger than many of them, including some of the juveniles. "It was a kind of aura that did it," a fellow actor has since said. "His occupancy of the number-one dressing room was carried out with a kingly flourish which may never again be seen on the American stage." His deportment was in the rococo style of Caruso at Milan, Bernhardt at the Comédie Française. The novice members of the cast tiptoed by his quarters, curtsied and saluted when they met him, and often applauded from the wings.

Although many people, audience and actors alike, had all but forgotten that Carroll was mixed up in the *Vanities,* the comedian's name having supplanted that of the producer in nearly all the important promotion, Fields was not inflexibly austere. He granted Carroll interviews, permitted him a decent but not exceptional return on his investment, and allowed him to come and go unmolested backstage.

It was in the *Vanities* that Fields acquired some reputation for being quick with the ad-libbed line. This was the beginning of a departure that was to become a nuisance in Hollywood. In the *Follies* and in the *Scandals* he had been largely content to abide by the agreed-upon script, with such exceptions as his mistaking the Russian wolfhound for a camel in the golfing scene. But with the added luster of cinema stardom he felt an obligation to improvise. Thereafter, he said pretty much what he pleased. "A lot of it was funny, but a good deal was pure balderdash," recalled a singer of the period. On occasion, Fields' nimble mind saved an embarrassing situation. During one of his scenes in the *Vanities* a backdrop collapsed somewhere offstage with an ear-splitting crash. Fields lifted his nose inquisitively and remarked, "Mice." The audience howled, and the ad lib became the foundation for a whole new structure of jokes.

Another time, onstage by himself, he leaned against a huge piece of scenery, which swayed limply, then fell forward with a dusty thwack at his feet. "They don't build these houses the way they used to," Fields roared, and the audience, convulsed, was sure that the incident had been contrived.

Because he never appeared as a night-club comedian, or worked in similar places where the ad lib receives special publicity, Fields was slow in developing a name for fast thinking. But many people who knew him were long impressed with his wit. Mr. and Mrs. James Thurber were preparing to enter the Mocambo once in Hollywood when Fields came out with a dazzling blonde. The girl threw her arms around his neck and gave him a loud smack.

"Is this a private party or can anybody get in on it?" Mrs. Thurber asked the comedian.

"My lips are sealed, Mrs. T., my lips are sealed," he replied.

Because of his lingering frustration about movies, Fields decided to move to Hollywood in 1931. He had no contract, but at fifty-one, he was a multiple success in the entertainment world, he had saved a great deal of money for a runaway who spent his young years sleeping in boxes and barrels, and he had faith in his ability. Contrary to nearly all the published reports, Fields survived the crash of the stock market in good order. His survival was, in fact, assured, since he owned no stocks or bonds. There is even room for the belief that he welcomed the market's collapse with a certain selfish glee. In essence, he viewed it as an excellent method for making people think he was penniless. Always thereafter in interviews he took pains to mention the devastating sag in his fortune occasioned by the fiasco of 1929. "I was wiped out," he would say, and look bitter and gloomy.

The most reliable private sources do agree, however, that Fields was subsequently nipped by the deceitful advice of a New York bank official. It is a shocking story, and unquestionably true. The banker came to Fields during the thickest pressure of the Wall Street break and said, "I'm going to let you in on some of our preferred stock—it's a giveaway at this price." Despite his prudence about investments, Fields had always an eye for a bargain, particularly if it carried a slight stigma of slyness, and he bought twenty-five thousand dollars' worth of the stock. At noon the next day, newspapers were ablaze with accounts of the bank's failure. The stock carried the clause for double jeopardy, as bank stock often did, and Fields was obliged to pay over an additional $25,000. His loss—$50,000 in a few days—did little to make him feel more trustful of bankers, brokers, or other financial advisers. He never speculated in any form again.

Besides the heavy penalties for his incautious plunge, he lost an additional sum on deposit in the rump-sprung institution. But he had impressive accounts elsewhere, and he gathered many of them up before he left for the Coast. Fields rolled out of New York in a new Lincoln, carrying, in his jacket pockets, three hundred and fifty thousand dollars in thousand-dollar bills. "What will you do if you get robbed, Mr. Fields?" a reporter asked him, and he replied, "What do the banks do?" His implication, the man assumed, was that the banks would steal more, but this went unexplained in his story.

After three decades of big-city theater, Fields was finished with the stage and with New York. He never went back. With the steely resolution that had enabled him to leave home at eleven and not return, he left the medium in which he had found security and headed for an opportunity of dubious worth. The years of his gaudiest triumphs, of his national notoriety, lay ahead, but he was starting, in advanced middle age, from professional scratch. It was a situation that pleased him; he was only happy when the barriers were exceptionally high. He had no ties, no home, no family that claimed his attention. A change of personal scene, for Fields, involved no more emotional risk than shifting the furniture of a stage. Nevertheless, as he crossed into New Jersey he felt already a faint breath of nostalgia. "When I got over the river," he told a friend later, "I twisted around for a last look at the skyline. I had an idea somehow that I wouldn't see it again. But I felt young, and I knew I was good, and it was a wonderfully sunny day. So I drove on toward a very uncertain future, about the same as I had in the past."

BOOK TWO: *Part Two*

CHAPTER TWENTY-ONE

AFTER A TRIP filled with pleasant dalliance, Fields entered Hollywood in the shiniest possible condition. He had heard disturbing stories about the desert before he left New York, and his car was equipped with strong precautions against thirst. He found the desert oppressive, as announced, and he took no chances. Every few miles he stopped and, by tapping the refreshment section of his luggage, mixed a drink. On the outskirts of the movie capital he eased into a filling station and had his car washed. He had heard, he said later, that it was very important, on the West Coast, "to put on face." Toward the end of the desert, his worries on that score were reduced to a minimum, for what with the sun, and its antidote, he put on a good deal, with particular reference to his nose, whose radiant sheen was matched only by that of his freshly scrubbed car.

According to his later account, he pulled up in front of the most gorgeous hotel he could find, climbed down, tossed his car keys to a uniformed lackey, whom he scrutinized carefully, in order to remember his face, and descended upon the lobby. He made "quite a procession," as he described it. Several bellhops struggled along behind with his luggage, all of it picturesque, including one valise which seemed to be leaking and others plastered with promotional labels on the order of "W. C. Fields, Greatest Juggler on Earth." He was wearing his cutaway and morning trousers, into which he had slipped in the lavatory of the filling station, and he was carrying a gold-headed cane. His step was jaunty; as he trod the flowered carpet he lifted a frayed and dented silk hat to the various startled persons in the lobby, one of whom, an elderly lady in a wheel chair, sniffed suspiciously and broke into a rolling sprint for the side exit.

At the desk, Fields rapped with his cane and asked for "the bridal suite."

The manager, recoiling slightly, causing Fields to start and clutch his hat, informed him that the bridal suite was usually reserved for gentlemen with brides.

"I'll pick up one in town," the comedian told him.

After a lengthy nasal harangue, during which Fields spoke familiarly and even patronizingly of all the crowned heads of celluloid, he obtained a medium-sized room. His next move was to consult a local real estate dealer. He wanted a house, a pretty large house, he said, where he could relax without molestation after his daily grind at the studios. The house, a mansion at Toluca Lake, materialized shortly, but the daily grind at the studios held off for eighteen months.

In that period—one of the most anxious of his life—Fields tried every device he could hit upon to get back into the movies. For the first time in years he humbled himself completely. "I even went to one studio," he said, "and made them a proposition. I offered to write, star in, and direct a two-reel short for no money whatsoever. If the comedy got over, the studio was to give me a contract. They turned me down cold."

The word had gone around Hollywood that Fields' pictures, though funny, were not money-earners, and the men who made the decisions, while artistic and cultured to a fault, preferred to play it safe with Gable and Nelson Eddy. In the tycoons' defense, it must be said that Fields' reputation for truculence, unmatched in entertainment history, except possibly by John Wilkes Booth, was an effective danger signal. There were two or three studio officials, small men, who were frightened of him physically. "He beat Ed Wynn over the head with a billiard cue," one of them told an awed group in a Beverly Hills restaurant.

During this period of his travail, Fields occupied himself in playing golf, getting acquainted, talking loudly against the movie people, and running his large establishment. His old friends Le Baron and La Cava were in Hollywood, Le Baron now working for RKO and La Cava directing at Paramount; Fields saw a good deal of them, of Grady, who was with Metro-Goldwyn-Mayer, and of Gene Fowler and Mack Sennett. Once or twice a week he drove down to Dave Chasen's restaurant and, at a table always reserved for him on those nights, bragged spaciously about the movie offers he was rejecting. He and Sennett played golf at the Lakeside course; every time they played, Fields would say at some point, "You know, Mack, I ought to be working at that studio of yours." Sennett, who had been considering this possibility for some while, usually nodded thoughtfully. One day he replied, "That's not a bad idea, Bill."

"I'll do anything," Fields said, "write, produce, direct, anything."

Sennett thought it curious that Fields had failed to mention acting, but he said, "Why don't you drop out some day next week, Bill? We'll talk it over."

Fields shook his hand warmly, crying, "Why, that's wonderful, Mack. As I said, I'll do anything. I don't care about the money—I just want to get back to work."

On Wednesday of the following week, the comedian, in his immaculate Lincoln, pulled up at Sennett's Keystone Studios. He was carefully groomed, carrying his cane, and "seemed," Sennett said, "to have regained all his old pomp." He was crackling with authority as he warped around several outbuildings and into Sennett's office. He didn't bother to remove his hat. "I had the impression that he could only stay a minute," Sennet remembered.

They held a conference, which Fields dominated.

"You'll act, of course," said Sennett at one point, and Fields, giving him a keen look, replied, "I hadn't counted on it—*act?*" and he mused for a moment, a little troubled in his mind.

"Well, if I act," he said finally, "we'd better have a talk about the money."

His ensuing behavior was singular for a man whose principal motive was getting back to work. "Right off, he demanded $5000 a week," said Sennett, "and he asked several questions about my solvency. Then he said he would prefer to write his own contract. I had an idea that Bill and I could make some successful comedies, so I told him to go ahead."

Two days later Fields returned with a document that is believed to have been without parallel in show business. He had stuck to his guns about the $5000, Sennett noted with relief, but he had added a number of clauses that opened new vistas for contracts of that kind. Chief among them was the intelligence that, of his weekly $5000, he must be paid $2500 on Monday morning and the other $2500 on Wednesday.

"I inspected the papers," related Sennett, "and said, 'It looks like a first-rate piece of work, Bill.'"

"It will hold water," said Fields mysteriously.

They signed the historic articles and prepared for production. And now began a series of arguments that occupied a good portion of each working day as long as the two were together. It was the old trouble about who knew what was funny. To keep the ball rolling, Sennett fixed a system whereby he might retain a slight hand in the studio's management and keep Fields propitiated besides. "It was very simple," he says. "All I had to do was make Bill feel that he thought of everything, and he co-operated perfectly."

Sennett would develop a gag, mention it to Fields, hear it damned and blasted, and drop it meekly for about a week. Then he would say, "You know, Bill, I've been thinking over that business of yours about the washtub and the goat, and I believe it would work out fine."

"I thought you'd see the light on that one," Fields would reply, and add, "I did it in the *Follies*."

He had a stock answer any time he was pushed. "I'm afraid that's for some other boy," he'd say, then he would pick up a newspaper and retire to a rocker he kept in his dressing room.

Despite the arguments, Sennett and his new comedian remained friendly and turned out a string of brilliant comedies. Fields liked the atmosphere of informal gaiety around the Keystone Studios, which were unique in Hollywood. Sennett, amused by the formidable bastions surrounding the major lots, had no fences, no walls, no watchmen, no barriers of any kind to keep out the public. He even did without the vital Hollywood secretary, whose principal function, as she did sentry-go in the outer office, was to provide a spurious air of jammed-up importance while her mentor, huddled inside, nervously studied his option and swilled Bromo-Seltzer. People wishing to observe a Keystone comedy in the making could wander in and out at their leisure; if by inadvertence they got in front of a camera, Sennett seldom bothered to reshoot. "Most everybody's funny, one way or another," he told an author.

Fields also approved the absence of prohibitive signs on the Keystone walls. The big studios were, and are, generously decorated with semi-hysterical warnings such as "Quiet!" "Not Responsible for Stolen Overcoats" "No Spitting on Thursdays" and "Watch Out!" Sennett took a line, much appreciated by his employees, that clear-headed adults could pretty well be trusted not to destroy their livelihood, and he suspected further that in the case of most Americans, signs only remind them of potential pleasures and are in general an incitement to mischief.

In the course of their harangues, Sennett and Fields used to tick off their triumphs, to build sound cases. They spent hours discussing theories of comic technique, getting nowhere. "I might remind you," Fields would say, "that in addition to being the biggest name in international vaudeville, I have starred in the *Follies,* the *Scandals,* the *Vanities,* and in musical plays." As rebuttal, Sennett would mention, with diffidence, that he had discovered and started both Bing Crosby and Charlie Chaplin in movies—Crosby when he was singing, after his Paul Whiteman period, at the Ambassador Theatre in Los Angeles, and Chaplin when he was an obscure performer in vaudeville. "You'll forgive me for adding," he'd say, "that Frank Capra and Leo McCarey, the comedy directors, both broke in with me. You've heard of the Keystone cops? Ford Sterling, Chester Conklin, Ben Turpin?"

At about this point in the dialogue, Fields would disgust Sennett by saying, "You don't know anything about comedy, you dumb Irishman. You'd never have got to first base if you hadn't dressed up a bunch of big-titted floosies in tights and called them bathing beauties."

The injustice of these remarks made Sennett stamp with anger. The aggressively moral tone of his establishment was a byword in movie circles. He was so sensitive on the subject that he had his bathing beauties guarded by police matrons, as a boarding school is governed by its heads. "Why, damn you," he'd yell at Fields, "I invite those girls' mothers to come down to the lot almost every day!"

"Floosies," Fields would mutter, hoping to bring on some sort of cardiac disturbance.

"I made four [the number was actually seven] comedies for the Irishman," he once wrote for a newspaper, "and had forty more or less friendly fights. Neither of us could agree on the nature of comedy. One of the comedies paid for itself three days after release."

Sennett was interested in Fields' early life, and Fields was amused by Sennett's. The fact that the producer, whose father was a Northhampton (Massachusetts) contractor, had got into films by studying to be an opera singer seemed of telltale significance to Fields, who spoke with sarcastic relish of the humor he'd seen on the operatic stage. The producer would urge that the sin of his near-musical career had been expiated by the novelty of his switch to the screen. One day in a restaurant near Carnegie Hall, young Sennett had chanced to ask a successful baritone how much he was making, and when the man, with some gloom, replied, "Seventy-five a week, clear," the boy's faith in the melodic plot was shaken. He obtained work as a three-dollar-a-day extra at the Biograph Studio on Fourteenth Street, soon gravitating to the funny movies—an ordeal, since practically everything they were doing struck him as funny. In a month he changed over to assistant director and received a salary boost to $80 a week, which went immediately to his head. He began to heave petty cash around like the Aga Khan. He bought a checkered vest and took to playing the ponies. For a beginner, his luck was remarkably steady—he never won a dime—and before long he found himself in hock for a hundred dollars to a group of gamblers. For weeks his life consisted of trying to duck them on the streets.

Eventually, by hiding in a doorway, they trapped him,

and as he slunk furtively by they pranced out, in the manner of cinema gangsters, and cried "Ha!"

"Oh, good afternoon, fellows," said Sennett, paling. "Well, I've got to be going."

"O.K., squirt," replied one of them, digging in his hip pocket for what turned out to be a handkerchief. "How about that C-note?" (In later years Sennett was not positive about the exact phrase—it may have been "Yard" or "Century".)

"Say, fellows," he said, brightening up, "I've got a wonderful idea how you might get back that hundred—I've been thinking about it a lot."

"Spill it, punk," said one of them.

"Well," Sennett went on, "the way I got it figured, you give me $2500 to start a studio with and you'll get back your money just as soon as the profits start coming in. Among the very first receipts."

The gamblers gave him the $2500, and the Keystone Studios were in business.

"You still don't know anything about comedy," Fields would observe after the above recital.

Sennett insisted that slapstick, to be artistically funny, must be carefully prepared for. "It has a cause-and-effect motivation," he would tell Fields. "You can't just spring it unexpectedly, it has to built up."

Fields: "Pfffffft."

"—on a rising tide of laughter you can make something absurd at the climax seem excusable. Introduce it at the beginning and it will seem awful and embarrassing. You can take tremendous liberties with it *only* if you built it up. Right?"

"I think I'll work my golf act into this two-reeler about the dentist," Fields would agree.

Sennett would pick up a property poker and eye him wistfully.

One of the comedies they made was called *The Chemist,* a title Sennett clinched after a bloody engagement touched off by Fields' insistence on calling it, simply *W. C. Fields in a Drugstore*. After the smoke had cleared away from the title fight, they combined their genius and produced a work for which the comedian, in particular, is fondly remembered by the Fields cult.

Wearing a depressing white jacket, he appeared as the baffled but helpful proprietor of a small, shabby drugstore. As he stepped around his shop, carrying a feather duster and whisking gracefully at things like dollar alarm clocks, hot-water bottles, trusses and bonbons, various customers arrived. The first man said he was "just looking." Fields, behind the counter, kept pace with him, pointing out some of the more attractive offerings, ranging from dandruff cure to corn plasters, and finally pulled out a performing monkey on a stick.

"Amusing little beggar?" he said, with a false ingratiating laugh, and the man went to the rear of the store, used the telephone, and left.

The next prospect, a woman of affluence, opened an expensive purse, and Fields rubbed his hands eagerly. She wanted a stamp.

"Just one?" he inquired, smiling his comradely smile, and she said, "One will be plenty." He removed a sheet of stamps about two feet square and prepared to pinch one off the upper right hand corner.

"Could I have the one in the middle, please?" she asked.

"Of course, of course," he cried, with an understanding laugh, and he spent several minutes removing the stamp that appeared to be in the dead center. She handed over two cents and went out, to brave, happy cries of "Come in and see us again, won't you?"

Fields' next customer, also a woman, approached with a painful show of timidity. She simpered and stood on one foot after the other. It was plain that her purchase was involved with some intimate requirement of her sex, and the proprietor looked tactfully professional.

She looked up at last and said, "Do you have a female attendant?"

"Why, yes," he replied. "I'll call her right away." He hurried up a flight of stairs in the back, summoned his wife, who was busy with her housework, and hurried back. "She'll be down in half a mo," he assured the flustered caller, and resumed his dusting—humming, examining his merchandise, often with galvanic starts of surprise, and throwing the woman little darting looks, winks, and smiles.

His wife went through an elaborate program of removing her domestic garb, replaced it with a starched uniform, and came downstairs. The customer tiptoed up and whispered in her ear, then, upon receiving some advice in an undertone, withdrew to the rear and used the ladies' room.

From beginning to end, the sketch was a study in frustration, of the general sort that Fields felt qualified, by long experience, to demonstrate with feeling.

"When we finished it," said Sennett, "I had the notion that he had settled several old scores known only to himself."

With Sennett, Fields also resolved mysterious grievances against barbers and dentists and others of the legions that plagued him. Perhaps the best known of the two-reelers they made was *The Fatal Glass of Beer*. The comedian was in top form; he had his way about many details of the plot, which was uniquely meager. In general, it consisted of Fields sitting on a campstool in a far Northern shack, dressed in a coonskin coat, a fur cap and mittens, and singing a tuneless song about his unlikely downfall, while accompanying himself on a zither. Periodically he would arise, walk to the door, fling it open, and cry, "It ain't a fit night out for man or beast!" upon which an invisible extra would pelt him in the face with a double handful of snow. He varied this shrewd observation on the weather with miscellaneous declarations of policy. "The time has come," he said at one point, "to take the bull by the tail and face the situation." It was a noble and uplifting study of Northern life, and while it didn't settle anything, it was uproariously funny. His meteorological note, though not exactly original, caught on and swept over the land. It was a popular *mot* of the impoverished thirties and is still a lively part of the language.

Chester Conklin, then a Keystone cop and featured comedian, and who continued to play comedy parts for Paramount, has recalled Fields' predilection for wearing the clip-in mustache. They appeared in one film together. "We were on the set one day," he said, "and they brought Mae Worth out—she was one of the great bareback riders of that time, with Ringling Brothers. The publicity boys wanted some pictures of the three of us. Bill refused to take off his mustache, and I remember Miss Worth looking at it with dismay. He'd had a few during the morning and was enjoying life. He kept telling her the mustache was real. 'All the men in my family were bearded,' he said, 'and most of the women.' Then he went into details about an aunt of his—she had some impossible name he'd made up, I disremember what it was—who had a red beard down to her waist. 'She wore it tucked into her vest,' he told Miss Worth. Later on, between stills, I heard him explaining that he'd got his red nose by bruising it on a cocktail glass in his extreme youth. I think she was a little shocked."

In posing for the pictures, Fields cut up so energetically that Miss Worth never got quite into them. One of the clearest shows Fields, again wearing his cutaway and silk hat, and with the mustache clipped in, holding Conklin in a fierce travesty of an acrobatic stance. Miss Worth nearly made it; about three quarters of her right arm is on view, pushing against Fields' elbow and holding a black handbag.

Conklin, a St. Louis baker who got sick of making pies and became a comedian, after which he had pies thrown at him daily for years, believed that Fields always wanted to steal a gag from him. "Ches," Fields would say, "I've been thinking about that skit of yours with the taxi meter. I may switch it around a little and use it."

"How do you plan to switch it, Bill?" Conklin would ask, and the reply was always, "Only slightly, Ches, only slightly."

"He was just sounding me out," Conklin said. "Bill was a wonderful comedian—he never stopped gathering material."

Conklin remembered his taxi-meter gag chiefly as an illustration of how easy it is to get typed in pictures. As a taxi driver, he was taking a fare on a longish haul, overland, and got caught in an overflowing river. The cab, with the easy extravagance of those days, submerged for quite a space and Conklin, without the cab but carrying the meter, finally walked out on the opposite bank. His agitated efforts to locate his fare, as the meter continued to tick, met with amused approval by movie audiences everywhere. From then on into middle age he was cast predominately as a taxi driver, whether the part was funny or not.

Fields enjoyed loafing around the sets where the Keystone cops were at work; his attempts to loaf near the bathing beauties were discouraged by the police matron. He was interested in the fact that Conklin often feigned cross eyes, for comedy purposes, and that Ben Turpin's eyes actually were crossed. The abnormality struck him as an intriguing comic device. To help directors handle Turpin, whose high spirits sometimes made him intractable (actually, he saw eye to eye with very few directors), Fields suggested a simple but effective device. Turpin, an ardent Catholic, depended on his angular vision for his livelihood, and when he cut up, a director would say (thanks to Fields), "Ben, if you don't behave yourself, I'm going to pray to St. Joseph to straighten out your eyes." Terrified, Turpin would play the scene with pious obedience.

Excitement appeared to follow Fields around the sets. In one scene he was supposed to spring across a courtyard a couple of jumps ahead of some lions. Sennett had contracted with an animal man for the use of three elderly, toothless lions, but when the beasts arrived they appeared to be in very youthful condition; and large, strong teeth, or dentures, formed a memorable part of their features. Fields, of course, demurred at what he regarded as certain suicide in one of its most disagreeable forms, and the action was halted while they hashed things out.

"It's only a short run, Bill," said Sennett, "and you'll hop through this door on the right while the lions take the one on the left. Even if they *should* turn ugly, they can't possibly get you."

"They aren't friendly," said Fields. "Those aren't friendly lions. I can tell. They've been starved down and they'll eat anything."

By some means that Sennett forgot, he was persuaded to make the dash. As soon as he entered the courtyard, at a clip which provoked admiration from men half his age, the trainer shoved the lions forward and gave them a boosting kick. They took out after Fields as if he were the last remaining game at the old water hole. Looking around, he read what he interpreted as intimations of dinner in their faces and stepped up his tempo. But when he neared his exit, he heard an anguished yell from behind it, "Who the hell locked this door?" The comedian gave voice to a blood-curdling cry and charged through the locked door with a splintering crash. The lions, crestfallen and mumbling, brought up at the wreckage, then went through their own door, as planned.

Some time later, Fields was supposed to ride a bicycle gently into the rear end of a backing truck and fall down. Both he and the truck were going too fast; they collided sharply and Fields fell with great force to the ground. Bystanders noticed that his head was tilted at a grotesque angle. After the impact, the truck continued to roll and Johnny Sinclair, then a stunt man and later a comedy writer, leaped underneath and snatched the comedian out just before the back wheels reached him. Holding his head in his hands, Fields was hurried into a car and rushed to a hospital. The doctors made a quick diagnosis—he had a broken neck.

"How long have I got?" he asked an examining surgeon.

"If you co-operate, many years, I expect," replied the surgeon. "It's only a single vertebra."

The surgeon and the whole hospital soon had occasion to regret his casual advice, for Fields, viewing the injury as trivial, refused to co-operate in any way whatever. He removed the brace from his neck. Whenever a nurse tried to refit it, he would wave her away, crying, "Never mind— it's only a flesh wound." He moved his head about with perfect freedom, though it clicked audibly, and he had a bar set up in his room. The hospital staff were distraught; their attempts to reason with the patient resulted only in disconnected narratives about other, more horrible injuries he had suffered and fixed with something he identified as "Doctor Buckhalter's Kidney Reviver." Within a week or so, Fields took to walking the corridors. When the hospital people spotted him, they got him into a wheel chair, almost by main strength. But it was energy wasted. Toward the close of the very next day after several visitors had arrived bringing martinis, he wheeled his chair into the hall and down a long flight of stairs. When they found him and checked up, it was discovered that he had also broken his coccyx.

"Damnation," he kept crying afterward, "I came into this institution broken at one end and now I'm broken at both."

The hospital employees, from the chief of staff down to

the last bedpan carrier, were much relieved when he went home.

Though Fields and Sennett scrapped on the set, they saw a lot of each other socially. Fields would invite Sennett to Toluca Lake to dine on Virginia ham, to which the producer was partial, and Sennett would coax Fields out on his yacht. The comedian disliked boats, despite the many voyages he had made during his vaudeville years. On any but the blandest days he became violently seasick, and he took it personally. One time when there had been no suggestion of a breeze for more than a week, Sennett persuaded him to ride out to Catalina, a haul that, for rough water, compares favorably with the English Channel. Before boarding the yacht, Fields tested the air repeatedly with a moistened finger: a dead calm prevailed. The meaning of the calm was resolved about six miles from shore, where one of the briskest squalls for months swooped down and caught them. The yacht was tossed about like a bubble, and Fields' anguished howls, as he lay strapped to a bunk, were easily the most positive of the storm noises.

Through what Sennett believed was exceptional seamanship, the yacht reached the island, and Fields debarked without speaking to anybody. After some difficulty, the anxious host found him registered at a small hotel.

"Well, what do you say we get going, Bill?" said Sennett.

"I'm staying here," replied Fields.

"Why, the sea's almost flat again."

Fields said, "I'll be here in the hotel until it's *entirely* flat."

"It'll never get that way," said Sennett. "The Pacific always has a little swell, you know."

"Then I'll settle here," said the comedian. "I'll buy a house."

Sennett had several comedies in the works and needed to get back, but for three days he was obliged to transact his business by telephone, while his passenger remained steadfast. For the most part Fields stuck close to the hotel, only coming out now and then to walk down to the shore and view the water wrathfully. The ocean finally looked glassy for a couple of hours, and he consented to return, but he complained all the way.

CHAPTER TWENTY-TWO

THE ANOMALIES of Fields' character were a study to Mack Sennett, as they were to his other friends. Despite all his bluster, he was hypersensitive, and hated to hurt anybody's feelings. He disliked refusing people things; if possible, he did it through a third person.

One evening Sennett motored to Fields' Toluca Lake residence, where he hoped to discuss some comedy ideas. The comedian's servants, acting mysterious and secretive, said he had gone out. "He's taking a long trip," added one of them. "He may not be back until next year."

Thoroughly confused, Sennett retreated toward his car, but on the way he heard a rustling in some bushes and stepped over to investigate. He found Fields crouching low in a clump of azaleas.

"What the devil are you doing in there?" cried the producer.

"Shhhhh!" cautioned Fields. "Get your voice down."

"You sick?" said Sennett. "What's the matter with you, Bill?"

"Not so loud," said Fields. "I just got word that Earl Carroll was sending his brother up here to try and borrow $8000 to start a restaurant with."

"Well, why don't you just say no?" was Sennett's logical inquiry.

Fields replied that he'd rather "wait it out."

"I'll duck him," he said. "You'll see."

Half persuaded to call a psychiatrist, Sennett left, to Fields' hoarse entreaties of "Tiptoe! Tiptoe!" and put the matter out of his mind. The next day about noon the comedian appeared at the studio wearing dark glasses and a beard so patently false that he would have been arrested on suspicion by any alert policeman.

"How's it going?" asked Sennett, recalling the bushes and the loan.

"I've got him," said Fields. "I rolled right by him near Sepulveda and Sunset. He didn't know me from Adam."

Sennett wanted to know how long the masquerade was likely to continue, and Fields said, "Till the bastard gives up."

"He was obviously having a very fine time," said Sennett. "Later on I heard that Carroll finally caught him at home but that Bill got in bed and sent word down that he was 'just beginning a long illness.' "

Fields' separation from the Keystone Studios was accomplished only after the most elaborate and indirect preliminaries. In his two years with Sennett he had achieved an important transition in his popular reputation. Instead of being a funny actor in a funny movie, he had become an individual, an institution unto himself. Whereas a fan of his earlier movie period would have said, "Did you see *So's Your Old Man* with that fellow Fields?" he might now say, "Did you see W. C. Fields' latest comedy?" The former juggler was being talked about, and the big studios began to listen.

"I could feel a slight chill coming into the air," says Sennett, "and I realized he'd had a better offer. But knowing Bill, I didn't imagine he could come right out with it, so I just sat back and watched."

Fields' manner shifted. Nothing quite suited him; he was able to find fault with nearly everything on the set—the script, the dressing accommodations, the brashness of the employees (including Sennett), and even the geographical location of the studio. He acquired a heavy martyrdom, a peevish melancholy that suggested the follies of sacrificing his colossal gifts on the altar of Keystone insufficiency.

Sennett, enjoying himself, let him sulk for a while, then he said, "Bill, I've been thinking over that contract of ours. I'm not going to hold you to it. We're just a small outfit, and I don't want to stand in the way of progress. You've outgrown us."

Fields looked both shocked and distressed, but his spirit

perked right up. He finished the current two-reeler with cheery dispatch, then bought an enormous ham and invited Sennett to dinner. They continued friends.

For Paramount, which had made him the better offer, he now began the string of pictures that was to build him into a national phenomenon. The studio itself thought that Fields "started on the backtrack in a picture called *If I Had a Million,* which dealt with what ten different people did when they suddenly inherited a million dollars." Paramount's publicity department still speaks lovingly of the "roadhog sequence" in that film. By his next one—*International House,* with Peggy Hopkins Joyce—he was firmly established in command. Eddie Sutherland directed him. They had innumerable quarrels, chiefly over ideas of Fields that went far astray from the plot. *International House* had a sort of plot, about intrigue in China, but it was filled, in addition, with Fields' observations on life. At one point he and Sutherland and Rudy Vallee, who was also in the cast, had a warm wrangle over a commentary Fields had worked out on crooners.

It was Vallee's thought, and a viewpoint not difficult to understand, that no commentary on crooners was necessary. Sutherland agreed, with genuine fervor. But Fields was immovable, and the director persuaded Vallee that the scene was harmless.

"I wasn't really convinced myself," says Sutherland, "but we had to get on with the picture."

So, granted a free hand, Fields walked into a room where a television set was turned on, saw Vallee singing on the screen, and without hesitation pulled out a revolver and shot him, the crooner falling dead instantly. It was the first television joke of a kind that is still going strong.

All his life Fields saw depths of humor in the Chinese that many others missed; he was pleased that *International House* had a Chinese locale. It was his custom, in the Hollywood days, to address one of his girl friends as "the Chinaman" and to clothe her in a Chinese costume. She always viewed his motives as obscure, but the sight of her padding along in satin slippers and a split black skirt awoke in him some immensely satisfying inner hilarity. He romped through the Chinese sets of *International House* as though he were involved in an authentic Cook's tour of the country. In an elaborate Shanghai restaurant, occidental in tone, he studied the menu at a dinner party and told the waiter, with traveled familiarity, that he'd have "a bird's nest and a couple of hundred-year-old eggs boiled in perfume." The waiter nodded, as if he had made a wise choice, and duly noted the order on his pad. In this movie, fired upon by ruffians, Fields leaned out of a window and delivered a sarcasm that became, for a few years, a popular blanket denunciation.

"Can't hit a moving target, hey?" he said; then, outside the house and beleaguered by enemies approaching from opposite directions, he spread the barrels of a double-barreled shotgun and felled them with a single, epic blast.

On the strength of *International House,* which appeared in 1932, Paramount signed him to a long-term contract, but his signature was obtained only after vexatious snags had developed. For the last parliamentary session, Fields appeared with a heavy list of hand-drawn objections. He would refuse to sign a contract, he said, unless he were given carte blanche in the preparation, direction, and production of his movies. As before with Paramount, his negotiations seemed to have reached an impasse; however, after hours of argument and recrimination, from which he withdrew frequently to meditate and refuel, a compromise was reached. He was to be given immense liberties in the presentation of his work, though he was not yet in complete charge of the studio.

Fields' friend and former employer, William Le Baron, had returned to Paramount from RKO and Fields, because of the company's natural reluctance to decentralize its powers, forever afterward referred to him as "Santa Claus with a stiletto." The comedian was able to work for Le Baron, though, as he worked for nobody previously or later, and he turned out a series of films which contain some of the most worth while of America's humor. Altogether, Fields made, for Paramount, counting his movies on Long Island, *Sally of the Sawdust, So's Your Old Man, The Old Army Game, That Royal Girl, The Potters, Running Wild, Two Flaming Youths, Tillie and Gus, Fools for Luck, Her Majesty, Love, Million-Dollar Legs, If I Had a Million, International House, Six of a Kind, You're Telling Me, The Old-*

Fashioned Way, Mrs. Wiggs of the Cabbage Patch, It's a Gift, Mississippi, and *Man on the Flying Trapeze.*

His roles were widely different, but his demeanor—revolving around the pricked balloon of pomposity—became part of the national scene. His nasal mutter was imitated by laymen, his favorite endearments, such as "My dove," "My little chickadee," and "My glowworm," which first appeared in *If I Had a Million* (being addressed to the un-dove-like Alison Skipworth), were repeated ad nauseum, and his mannerisms and snouty appearance were burlesqued by many a mime of the vaudeville stage.

Fields' favorite exclamations—"Godfrey Daniel," "Mother of Pearl," "Drat!" and others—always had a peculiar standing at the Hays office. Just as many comedians have been able, on the legitimate stage, to utter the fiercest oaths and make them sound innocent, Fields could voice tea-party pleasantries and make them sound profane. An audience, seeing the wicked leer and sensing the unfathomable mischief behind his frosty, belligerent stare, realized that, whatever he might say, he meant considerable more, so that "Godfrey Daniel" always came out "Goddamn," not only to the Hayes office but to the general public. In spite of this, the essential fraudulence of his established character removed the sting from all hints of the grossest immorality.

The censors were obliged to keep an especially alert eye on Fields' educational efforts for children, both in the script and on the set. There can be no question that Fields disliked children, in a persecuted, un-angry sort of way. His encounters with the infant thespian, Baby LeRoy, with whom he played in several films, were well known to Hollywood. He considered that the child was deliberately trying to wreck his career, and he stalked him remorselessly. "When he stole entire scenes from Baby LeRoy in *Tillie and Gus* a year and a half ago, his greatness was acknowledged," a reporter said of Fields in 1935. The comedian realized that, whatever else might be going on in a scene, people would watch the antics of a baby. His competitive treatment of LeRoy was, therefore, exactly the same as he would have accorded an adult. Between takes he sat in a corner, eyed the child, and muttered vague, injured threats.

In one Fields-LeRoy picture directed by Norman Taurog, action was suspended so that the infant could have his orange juice. When the others busied themselves with scripts, Fields approached the child's nurse and said, "Why don't you take a breather? I'll give the little nipper his juice." She nodded gratefully, and left the set.

With a solicitous nursery air, Fields shook the bottle and removed its nipple, then he drew a flask from his pocket and strengthened the citrus with a generous noggin of gin.

Baby LeRoy, a popular, warm-hearted youngster, showed his appreciation by gulping down the dynamite with a minimum of the caterwauling that distinguishes the orange-juice hour in so many homes. But when the shooting was ready to recommence, he was in a state of inoperative bliss.

Taurog and others, including the returned nurse, inspected the tot with real concern. "I don't believe he's just sleepy," said the nurse. "He had a good night's rest."

"Jiggle him some more," suggested Taurog. "We're running a little behind schedule."

Several assistants broke into cries of "Hold it!" "Stand by with Number Seven!" and "Make-up—LeRoy's lost his color!"

"Walk him around, walk him around," was Fields' hoarse and baffling comment from a secluded corner.

The child was more or less restored to consciousness, but in the scene that followed, Taurog complained of his lack of animation. Despite the most urgent measures to revive him he remained glassy-eyed and in a partial coma. For some inexplicable reason Fields seemed jubilant.

"He's no trouper," he kept yelling. "The kid's no trouper. Send him home."

Several years later, when Baby LeRoy was grown to boyhood, Fields heard he was re-entering films. "The kid's no trouper," the comedian told several people. "He'll never make a comeback." LeRoy did come back, however, and continued to perform successfully.

Fields always thought that one of the most agreeable events in his movie career took place in *The Old-Fashioned Way,* during a scene with the troublesome LeRoy. In the course of a boarding-house meal, the infant dropped Fields' watch in the molasses, turned over his soup, and hit him in the face with a spoonful of cream. After dinner, by chance, Fields found himself in a room alone with his tormentor, who was in the all-fours stance on the carpet. Tiptoeing up softly, his face filled with benevolence, he took a full leg swing and kicked the happy youngster about six feet. The comedian threw himself into this scene, as he tried to do with all his pictures, and wrapped up some splendid footage for Paramount.

But his conscience must have bothered him, for the next day he appeared on the set with presents for Baby LeRoy. It taxes the historian's ingenuity to explain the many paradoxes of Fields. While he was authentically jealous of the child, he made sheepish and comradely gestures on the sly. One time when Baby LeRoy's option was due, Fields needlessly wrote a part for him into one of his pictures, to emphasize the child's importance to the studio. In his home the comedian once had a photograph, prominently displayed, of himself and the child star riding kiddie cars. And yet, asked in interviews how he liked children, or child actors, he always replied with a sincere growl, "Fried," or "Parboiled," or something equally unaffectionate.

In *The Old-Fashioned Way* one of Fields' most curious total irrelevancies occurred. He was cast as the impecunious manager of a problem-ridden vaudeville troupe, a part upon which he brought to bear a lot of dubious personal experience. At one point, traveling in a coach with his hungry band, he received a telegram canceling an engagement somewhat farther up the line. The sender's identity was of no consequence to the story, but Fields, as he read the message in high-flown tones to his charges, was unable to resist an ad-libbed flourish at the end. He finished the wire, studied a fictitious signature, and with his upper lip lifted in careful enunciation, said "Sneed Hearn."

An assistant director later asked him out of curiosity what had prompted him to tack on the name, and he said, "It just seemed like a good idea at the time."

It was an incident similar to his irrelevant comment a few years later during a radio program. In the middle of a script he remarked conversationally, "I wear red woolen underwear winter and summer"—a gratuitous lie, since he never owned a suit of woolen underwear in his life. A member of the production staff expressed interest in the statement and he said, "Oh, I don't know—people are always telling me things like that as if they were letting me in on something."

The business of scene-stealing represented total war to Fields. He had no scruples about tricking his closest friends. His behavior was much like that of an amiable but efficient prize fighter; during the rounds he was occupied in trying to fracture his opponents' skulls; at the bell he was ready to embrace and exchange amenities. Fields had real affection for Bing Crosby, his neighbor and occasional companion. In turn, Crosby had an idolatrous, filial attitude toward Fields, whom he always called "Uncle Bill." They were both gratified when they were cast together in the picture *Mississippi,* which Eddie Sutherland directed. Fields was never in better form. His accounts to his gambler friends of "cutting a swath" through a living wall of Indians; his manipulation of the river boat's wheel, absently tilting his cigar as each spoke came by; his poker games —these were sequences that pleased him, and he capered along in his most larcenous style.

Crosby played the scenes with his usual quiet, high competence, satisfied to let the director worry about where the emphasis was falling. He sang and he made love to Joan Bennett, though he was consistently interrupted by the overpowering rasp of the film's comedian, who jumped the gun on nearly every cue and covered the sets like a Great Dane. In a calm way, Crosby has always been a hard man to steal scenes from (he could scarcely have survived a string of co-starring pictures with Bob Hope otherwise); in *Mississippi,* he gave the impression of abetting the thefts, but in doing so he radiated such disarming geniality that the felon was caught red-handed.

In Fields he met a scoundrel of exceptional powers. With all Crosby's natural charm he seemed inadequate to the comedian's artistic assaults on the limelight. Midway through *Mississippi,* Eddie Sutherland drew Crosby aside and said, "See here, Bing, I'm worried about this thing. Bill Fields is walking off with it. The old devil's stealing every scene."

"Well, say, boy," said Crosby, "that's good for the picture, isn't it?"

Sutherland shrugged, and they continued the work.

When *Mississippi* was released, Fields went to see it, in one of his cockiest humors. He was happy to note that, as predicted, the ferocity of the comedian was the dominant chord in the over-all production. Toward the end, however, he got the uneasy notion that somehow none of this was detracting from Crosby. In the lobby afterward (he told a friend) he heard a girl say to her companion, "Wasn't he wonderful?"

Fields coughed modestly, and she added, "I could listen to him sing forever."

Thereafter, Fields implied to several people that Crosby was an underhanded sort of fellow, who churlishly relied on the illegitimate device of singing. The complainant's tone suggested that the practice ought to be stopped.

Eddie Sutherland feels that the peak of Fields' perversity was reached during *Poppy,* a second cinema version of the stage play, which they made together in 1935. For years Fields had been trying to introduce his old wheezes, such as his golf and pool acts and his croquet sketch, into movies. Knowing this, Sutherland, an affable, co-operative man, was happy to tell him, after an arduous scene, "Bill, I've got some good news for you."

Fields looked as if he doubted it.

"I've figured out a way how we can work the pool game into *Poppy*. It took a lot of reshuffling, but I think I've got it."

"Well, I won't do it," said Fields, "so that's that."

Sutherland, staggered, said, "Well, why won't you?"

"Because it doesn't fit into the plot," said Fields. "Directors are always trying to get me to do something like that—and it throws everything off balance."

Sutherland had a cooling drink and sat down in a deck chair for a while. He had been dangerously ill with pneumonia only recently and was not yet strong. After a while his pulse and temperature returned to normal and he approached Fields again. "Bill," he said, "I've already told Arthur Hornblow, Jr., we'd do this scene."

"Well, untell him," said Fields. "Producers are all bums anyhow."

Sutherland called a recess, dropped into Hornblow's office, and explained his star's latest recalcitrance.

"I'll go out and talk to him," said Hornblow.

On the set, the producer, trying to be diplomatic, explained that he and Sutherland had already made arrangements for the scene and that they would be especially obliged if Fields would do it, not only for them but for the public, which hadn't seen it recently.

"I'll bet there are kids in this land who have *never* seen you do that turn, Bill," he concluded.

Fields' face was clouded by surprise. "Naturally I'll do my pool act in this picture," he said. "It would be ridiculous not to."

Hornblow shook hands around and withdrew to his eyrie.

Sutherland, who was feeling his pneumonia coming back, sat down again. "Bill," he said at last, "you haven't any intention of doing that pool scene, have you?"

Fields was whistling, but he broke off to remark, "Not the slightest."

"Then what in the name of heaven prompted you to tell Hornblow you had?"

The comedian's answer left a good deal to be explained, a not-unusual occurrence in his movie career.

"Aw, the hell with the old buzzard," he said, and left to get a drink.

CHAPTER TWENTY-THREE

OF FIELDS' several peculiarities, his drinking aroused the widest interest and misinformation. By the middle of his movie period his need for alcohol had crystallized into a habit pattern from which he deviated only slightly until the end of his life. On the radio, in interviews, often in the movies, he was pictured as a frequent drunk, a rip who enjoyed wild excesses and spent a lot of time under tables. It would be difficult to imagine a more erroneous conception.

Fields drank steadily, but he abhorred drunks. Drunken visitors in his home seldom came back a second time. The signs of drunkenness—thick speech, unsteady gait, rowdiness, overemotional confidences—filled him with unease and disgust. Of one of the best-known figures of the American stage, after a party at Fields' house, Fields said to his secretary, "Never let that fellow come through these doors again." The comedian once sulked for weeks at John Barrymore, of whom he was particularly fond, because the great lover, in elevating his feet to relax, scratched up Fields' favorite sofa. "All that Romeo stuff's gone to his head," Fields told his secretary as he telephoned some inexpensive upholsterers.

In his later years, he started a day off with two double martinis before breakfast. He arose about nine o'clock, took a shower, came downstairs, and drank the martinis slowly, on a porch or terrace if the day was fine. His breakfast was modest, by the most austere standards. A small glass of pineapple juice generally sufficed, but if he was especially ravenous, he added a piece of toast and another martini to the menu. The liquor had no apparent effect save to sharpen, ever so slightly, his usual morning good humor and enhance his appreciation of the California weather, which he loved. After breakfast, before going to work, whether he was employed at the studios or occupied with scripts at home, he walked over his grounds for an hour. He inspected his flowers, an exercise that became a guiding passion in his life. Fields was one of the great nature men of his generation. His cultivation of flowers and his pride at exhibiting them to guests were not affected; he was happiest, some of his friends believed, when he was submerged in horticulture and removed from the strain of society. He had a tendency, however, to personalize his flowers, which occasionally plagued him as people did. He once called up Gregory La Cava, who devoted many hours, in the California manner, to watering plants, and said, "I want you to come right over here—I've got some Jack roses that are blooming as big as cabbages."

"Oh, nonsense," La Cava replied. "There isn't any such thing. I'm busy."

Fields insisted, with angry trumpetings, and La Cava left

his house at Malibu Beach and drove over, a trip of several miles. The day was warm, the traffic brisk, and it was some time before he arrived. Fields growled at the delay, but ushered him swiftly down a lane toward the waiting exhibit. The roses had apparently made their bow for the morning; when their sponsor arrived with his guest they had re-treated into small, tight buds. Fields was enraged. He ran up and down the lane, lashing at the offenders with a cane, and crying, "Bloom! Bloom, damn you! Bloom for my friend!"

When Fields went to the studios, he took an oversized cocktail shaker full of martinis. From the day in New York when he bought his first Cadillac, he kept expensive cars (at one time in Hollywood he had three Lincolns, two Cadillacs, and a smaller station wagon) and he was always driven to work by a chauffeur. The comedian arrived in some state at his places of employment. Often he and the chauffeur would make several trips from the car to his dressing room, carrying refreshments, clothes and other gear. Fields kept up a pretense, which the studio was will-ing to endorse, that his giant cocktail shaker was filled with pineapple juice. A joke which went around Hollywood arose from this flimsy deception. One afternoon some wags gained access to the shaker, when he was absent from the set, and poured in a quantity of authentic pineapple juice. When he returned, a few minutes later, he took a hearty draft of the liquid and roared, "Somebody's been putting pineapple juice in my pineapple juice!"

During the day's shooting he consulted the shaker with regularity. He was never drunk, never noticeably affected, but around 4 P.M. he hit a low spot. "He had a little dodge he always worked," said Eddie Sutherland. "He would act confused about the story and call a conference. We'd put all the chairs around in a circle, and he would regale the actors, writers, directors, and technicians with stories about his work and his travels. Then, when somebody else took up the cudgel, he'd drift off to sleep." Fields' caved-in con-dition lasted no longer than half an hour, after which he was good for a couple of hours' work before knocking off.

The other actors and employees lunched in the studios' commissaries, which serve good food at reasonable prices, but Fields always took his noonday meal in his dressing room. Even after his skimpy breakfast, he ate very little. His staple lunch was crabmeat salad washed down by two or three martinis. As a rule, he took a little nap during the lunch hour, too. Though martinis formed the skeleton of his liquid diet, he drank other things from time to time. At different stages he rested on Irish whisky, scotch, bourbon, rye, gin and grapefruit juice, red wine, sherry, rum and Coca Cola, and beer. Invariably he had a good reason for shifting his tippling habits. Rye whisky kept him awake; scotch began to taste like medicine; bourbon led to drunkenness; red wine made him hot; sherry was rough on his stomach; rum went to his nose. His affections sometimes wavered, but his true married love was martinis. Members of his household staff estimated that his average daily consumption of gin ran to about two quarts. He bought nothing but the best of all kinds of liquor, and kept hundreds of bottles stored in an upstairs room, to which only he had the key. During the recent war, when liquor was scarce, he conceived delusions of liquor thefts, and changed the lock guarding the scared chamber once or twice a month. Quite often he went in with a top-secret inventory, compiled by himself, and carefully counted his stocks. The indication was always that things were in order, but Fields never felt certain. He would go downstairs and study his servants' faces, searching for clues to abstractions.

Fields had several jocose utterances on the subject of his drinking. "I exercise extreme self-control," he liked to say in Hollywood. "I never drink anything stronger than gin before breakfast." In his early middle age he had said substantially the same thing, but substituting beer for gin in the sentence. His standards and his appetites had altered in the few years. On the general subject of his light eating, and of his steady drinking, he sometimes said, "I don't believe in dining on an empty stomach." The comedian had a trick, late in the evening, of balancing a full martini glass on his head, as he had done with the beer bottle at his mother-in-law's. If the glass trembled, he said, "There, I've had a sufficiency." His skill and his self-command were such that the glass seldom shook, and he rewarded himself by lightening its load.

For a man who hated drunks, Fields was in an untenable

position. His own strongly publicized drinking prompted many of his visitors to overindulgence, so as not to be considered sissified. They were perplexed when their sporting efforts seemed to depress their host. Fields would have preferred that they remain entirely sober, for several reasons. Primarily, he disliked them drunk; also he was reluctant to dissipate his stocks. Except for a handful of intimates, he did not encourage callers, but they turned up just the same. "It's not my friends but my friends' friends that annoy me," he once told a servant. The beforehand knowledge that strangers were likely to arrive made him ill at ease. He paced around the house, and drank more than usual. He always suspected that they would somehow prove troublesome; in addition, he could be pretty sure that they would swill his liquor, cut up noisily, and tell him jokes, at which he would be expected to laugh immoderately. Everybody told Fields jokes. Just as people meeting a writer know all about books and writing, people meeting a comedian treat him as a straight man. A neighbor of Fields, a very slight acquaintance, once appeared at his house and begged that he accompany him to call on a woman "who has been dying to meet you." Fields grumbled, thought up numerous excuses, all of which were brushed aside, and finally went along, in a sour frame of mind. They arrived at a large house, on the porch and front lawn of which was a group of people.

"What is it, a party?" Fields asked uneasily.

"Oh no, she's quite alone," said his guide. "We'll go in a side entrance." He took the comedian into a room decked with flowers and up to an opened coffin, where he said to the occupant, "Mrs. Burton, may I present W. C. Fields? Mr. Fields, Mrs. Burton."

The comedian was horrified and angry. Looking the acquaintance sternly in the eye, he said, "I consider this a disgraceful breach of good taste. You are no longer welcome on my property."

Fields made up his mind to swear off now and then. He swore off once when he was in a sanitarium, taking a rest cure. His room was on the second floor, a pleasant room that looked out on trim, landscaped grounds. About a dozen feet from his window a couple of languid palms rustled and bent in the light ocean breeze. He was happy, and comfortable, and resting up well, and he had a little pull from a gin bottle every so often to add that important fillip which makes bliss complete, and nails it down, so to speak. Unbeknown to Fields, it was the Halloween season, and the management had voted in favor of decoration. A large corps of Japanese, hired for the job, was in the process of ascending the trees, carrying jack o' lanterns. Fields awoke from a refreshing nap, looked out at his palms, threw his gin bottle at the nearest one, and began to bawl for a nurse. "The trees are full of monkeys with balloons," he shouted, agitating the adjacent sufferers. He got dressed and left as rapidly as possible. When he reached home he decided that, even though it was wrong of the sanitarium to put monkeys with balloons in the trees, he would knock off the gin for a while. He laid in some good sherry and drank several bottles a day for a week or so. His stomach ached pretty steadily during that period, and he finally returned to the gin. But he watched his trees carefully for two or three months.

After one severe illness, in 1936, Fields quit drinking entirely for nearly a year. He began to smoke cigarettes instead, "for relaxing purposes," as he told his household. Alcohol was never a stimulant with him; for years he used it as a sedative. His old saying, "Happiness means quiet nerves," was directly involved with his drinking. The comedian's nerves were never of much account, being chaffed, lacerated, sensitized, and in general badly worn by adversity and work. Physicians now say that some persons are born with defective nervous systems, as others are born with weak hearts, frail lungs, or infirm heads. Fields, though springing from sturdy, placid stock, got off to a restive start. Along the way he had extraordinary troubles, and a ghostly army of fears and worries began to camp on his trail. In his young manhood he discovered that peace of mind, of a rather inferior order, came in bottles, and he addressed himself to the remedy. Throughout his life it was the only one that ever worked. Despite the cigarettes, his year of temperance was a raging failure. He felt weak, rundown, tense, sleepless, and pursued. He had previously smoked cigars, though listlessly and without relish. The addiction to tobacco struck him as a dull habit; besides, he could never hold cigars without wanting to juggle. In his time on the vaudeville stage, cigars had formed an important party of his flying paraphernalia. So that later, after he lit one, his mind would wander, his hands would begin to twitch, and the cigar would presently describe a half-flip and come to rest on his index finger, where it might burn a hole.

Cigarettes gave him even less comfort than cigars, being just as inadequate to his need for artificial repose and too small to juggle. He never inhaled the smoke; eventually he found some comic device whereby he could amuse himself, and others, with a cigarette. He would stick one between his nose and upper lip, or put one in an ear, and pretend to smoke it with some *outré* and slightly sinister enjoyment. Strangers at a party were likely to nudge one another and point at the curious man with the lighted cigarette in his ear. In one of his last movies, *The Bank Dick,* he was seen sitting on a park bench surrounded by admiring youngsters. The close-up camera explained their interest: the great man was going through his old manual of arms with a cigarette, and saying, at the end, "Nothing to it, really. I'll teach you when you grow up. I never smoked a thing before I was nine."

Alcohol whetted Fields' sense of humor. Nearly everything struck him as funny, in addition to being absurd and reprehensible, but his appreciation was keener when his nerves were quiet. "His timing was better when he was drinking," Mack Sennett thought. "Often when he hadn't had a drink he seemed indecisive, other times he was sharp, sure, positive. He was terrified of speaking lines too fast, which he sometimes did if he was sober. He had a saying, 'If you're talking and get nervous, don't go fast—slow down.'" Toward the end of his year on soft drinks, Fields decided that the game was scarcely worth the candle, and he began to freshen up with an occasional nip. Several doctors in his employ at fantastic sums—one of them was on a retainer of $100 a day—tried to keep booze out of his reach. The comedian made a sport out of circumventing them. "We'll play golf," said one of the doctors. "That'll tone you up and keep your mind off the strong waters." Fields nodded glumly, got out his commodious golf bag, and made a show of docileness. But during the morning, before each date, he would secrete a dozen or so miniature bottles of whisky at various places in the bag.

When they reached the first tee, the doctor would say, "Now, this is the life! All sober? Smell your breath."

He would check the patient's sobriety, which was, at that point, unimpeachable, and get things under way. At the start Fields was in a cloudy, uncommunicative mood. This was corrected as soon as the doctor whaled into the rough or got behind a tree. The patient himself seemed to stray into many unflattering spots. During the early holes, for example, he seldom missed a sand trap and he spent an unusual amount of time in the woods.

The doctor was pleased to observe that both Fields' spirit and his skill improved steadily as they progressed. By and large the game had somewhat the reverse effect on the doctor, whom the invalid inveigled into making foolhardy bets.

After the fifth or sixth hole, by which point the patient appeared to have worked the stiffness out of his muscles, they were betting on individual shots as well as on the holes themselves. The pattern of wins and losses was pretty constant and even similar, the doctor once reflected, to a shell-game sequence he had seen Fields do in the movies. The comedian would fumble two or three seemingly easy tries, then double up on an impossible approach, sink it by a sort of juggling accident, and collect a handful of bills with cries of "Well, what do you know about that, Doc, old boy?" and "By gad, this golf's doing the trick!"—meanwhile taking deep breaths, beating on his breast, directing practice swings at dandelions, and lifting his cap to amused onlookers.

By the end of each day's treatment, Fields had usually recovered his medical fee and made enough over to take care of the next day's whisky.

Unless he was being preached at, Fields had qualms about drinking in front of the clergy. He was an honest agnostic, often saying, "I'll go without knuckling under—they won't find me cringing for religion"—but he was respectful around unobtrusive religious persons, of whatever faith. Gregory La Cava, who grew up a Catholic, was once visited by two young priests from his boyhood parish. They expressed an awed regard for Fields, and after lunch their host took them to the comedian's house, with misgivings. When the party arrived, Fields was in a sulphurous humor; he'd hidden a Mason jar full of martinis and was unable to find it. He came to the door, cursing, and threw it open with a ceremonial cry of "What the hell do you——" then stopped, embarrassed. "Oh, excuse me, Fathers," he said, and added, "Come in, come in, Greg." For a few minutes his manner was stiff, as it often was with strangers, but the priests were so appreciative, and so entertained by everything he said, that he thawed out and, making a circuitous approach to his upstairs wine closet (to confound spies), he came down with one of his best bottles of whisky.

"I hope your orders won't prevent you gentlemen from having a friendly snort," he said. "The afternoon's drawing on and there's a chill in the air." He was delighted when the priests, disclaiming total abstinence as part of their vows, praised his whisky like connoisseurs. Fields unbent as his household had not seen him do for months. Even La Cava, an intimate, was surprised at the range and warmth of his conversation.

Toward dinnertime, Fields arose and said, "All of you will dine with me at Chasen's—I insist on it." He ordered out his best car—at that point a $7000 Lincoln with a silver-plated engine—and they repaired to his favorite restaurant. Their arrival caused a sensation. Habitués of the place, who knew him as irreligious and often blasphemous, sat with mouths agape as the procession made its way through the crowded rooms. Fields seemed proud of his guests; he stopped at several tables and introduced them to celebrities. "Father Foley and Father O'Connor are visiting me for a while," he said at one table. La Cava, bringing up the rear, looked sad and resigned.

Perhaps the most shocked of the diners was Billy Grady, Fields' old agent and companion, a devout Catholic, who immediately construed the priests as fakes and the parade as one of Fields' inexplicable urges for comedy. He was infuriated. As the party filed to an upstairs room, he followed along and as soon as they were seated he burst in.

Looking at Fields, and pointing a shaking finger, he said, "You sacrilegious old devil, what do you mean pulling this kind of thing in here? You're going straight to hell!" To the priests, he said, "If you punks are from Central

Casting I'll see that you never get any more work in this town."

"Forgive him, Fathers," cried Fields in a loud voice, "he knoweth not what he do."

After a sort of all-around curse, Grady left, and the priests waved Fields' apology aside. They were having a wonderful time; they had come to see Hollywood, and they were getting a rare, secular close-up of film high life at its best. The diners turned their attention to Chasen's excellent food and drink, their spirits high, their minds at peace.

Below decks, Grady was far from easy. A disturbing notion had begun to set in. Had he by chance committed a harebrained act of lèse clergy? Had he, acting with typical lay impulsiveness, denounced two authentic messengers of the Lord? He went back upstairs and looked in timidly. But his old pard, the skinflint, was involved in such an earnest wassail, and seemed so comradely with the befrocked pair, that his anger revived, and he hurled several more "sacrileges" and "fakers" at them before retiring. Fields' pious intonation pursued him down the stairs. Grady passed a restless evening. By midnight he was drenched in a perspiration of remorse.

He visited them once more, to thrust in his head and say, "You fellows *are* from Central Casting, aren't you?" The priests bent their heads, Fields made a sign to ward off the devil, and the visitor withdrew with celerity.

When the party left, around one o'clock, Grady accompanied them to the door. His face was a study in conflicting emotions. "I *still* don't believe it," he said, as Fields drew delicately aside to let the priests pass. The comedian's booming "Forgive him, Fathers!" rang through the restaurant as the door swung shut. For weeks, Grady tried to pry the truth out of Fields, with no success whatever. He received identical advice—"If I were in your shoes, I'd get to my prayers"—on the occasion of each try.

Although Fields made public sport of his drinking, he was sometimes touchy if other people mentioned it. Toward the end of his life he took umbrage at Eddie Cline, who had directed him, because of statements Cline made about him to a writer. Fields was so incensed that he prepared a big ad for the *Hollywood Reporter,* a movie trade paper. It went:

Eddie Cline, the director, in his interview with W. Ward Marsh of the Cleveland Plain Dealer *on April 9, 1945, seems to be doing his darnedest to ruin me in the motion-picture business. I quote excerpts from the interview: "Fields hasn't been able to get off the hard stuff," Cline is supposed to have said. "That's why he doesn't appear any more. Understand, I love him, he's a great guy, but he will overindulge." He further states that I couldn't remember my lines.*

SELF-DEFENSE—I have always finished my pictures, or should I say their pictures, in far less time than was allotted to me. I ad lib most of my dialogue. If I did remember my lines, it would be too bad for me.

At M-G-M in David Copperfield *my part was scheduled for ten days; I did it in nine days.*

At Universal my part was allotted ten days; I finished in a day and a half.

At Mack Sennett's I was given two weeks to write and perform in a two-reeler. I finished the picture in a day and a half.

I have worked for such top-flight directors as George Cukor, David Wark Griffith, Paul Jones, Gregory La Cava, Leo McCarey, Norman McLeod, and Eddie Sutherland (alphabetically listed).

On the legitimate stage I worked for such master showmen as Earl Carroll, Flo Ziegfeld (for whom I worked for nine successive years, never missing a performance), George White, etc., etc.

In radio I worked for Chase & Sanborn and Lucky Strike Cigarettes and I quit both engagements of my own volition.

I have never been late or missed a performance either on screen, stage, or radio in some forty-odd years. It is true that I occasionally take a little rum and Coca-Cola or a martini medicinally, but I am very proud of my record. I refer you to the above first-line directors for verification of the veracity of this statement.

I don't mean this venomously. I love the guy. But I have been looking for an excuse to take a full-page ad in the Reporter *for some time, and here it is. Defendant rests.*

W. C. FIELDS

Comedian at Large Without Portfolio

CHAPTER TWENTY-FOUR

FIELDS LIKED houses. He was forever telling real estate men he was "in the market for something good," with the result that they rode him all over Southern California for years, showing him places. The comedian never bought a house, never had any intention of buying one, but he loved to look. The places he rented were all elaborate and expensive; Fields had a horror of cramped quarters, dating from the time when he lived in caves and barrels, and he left any neighborhood where an influx of population seemed imminent.

His establishment at Toluca Lake, which probably would have been commodious enough for Death Valley Scotty or Peter the Hermit, finally gave him claustrophobia. "It's getting crowded in here," he told his staff, as he prepared to search out another roost. The immediate reason for his discomfort was a rumor that a well-known film singer had bought a lot and was "thinking about" building some three miles from Fields' front gate. Besides this evidence of congestion he was annoyed by gulls. The big birds had a trick of coming in from the ocean and fishing in the lake, now and then harpooning a worthless specimen about three inches long. The comedian resented these incursions bitterly. He himself never fished, as one of his household pointed out to him, but he said he'd be damned if he would provide free delicatessen for all the feathered drifters on the Coast. The further fact that he did not own the lake, or the fish therein, had no effect on his attitude. He bought a gun, a worn army revolver, for $4.50 in a pawnshop, and crouched for days behind a stump, trying to get a pot shot at the intruders.

"You shoot that gun around here and they'll lock you up," Gregory La Cava advised him, after witnessing his ambush with disgust.

"They'll have to catch me first," said Fields, squinting meanly through some reeds.

He enjoyed playing the country squire, or, rather, he enjoyed the theory of this manner of life, since his household was often in a state of turbulence. At Toluca Lake, Fields had a butler named "Rod," a colored cook named "Dell," a laundress, various maids who appeared and then vanished with lightning rapidity, a chauffeur, an occasional trainer, Bob Howard—a great authority on Fields—and a secretary, Magda Michael, who, as nearly as was humanly possible, put order into his last years. For the purpose of summoning his staff, the comedian carried a Halloween horn, upon which he would sound a blast when he needed domestic aid. The horn was mostly for out of doors; he disliked yelling to the house from distant spots on the grounds. In the ambush, for example, he would send out a resonant, jarring call, which would cause the birds on the lake to flap their wings and complain, and then, when Rod or one of the others approached, he would say, "Bring me a shaker of martinis."

"Here in the bushes, sir?" the butler would inquire.

"Yes, here in the bushes," Fields would reply testily. "Watch yourself, now. Duck down. Don't let them see you. I catch one of these buzzards fishing and I'll——"

The butler would pace quickly away, keeping a cautious eye on the gun.

Fields' servants came and went, spurred into transit by his peculiar ways. Dell, the cook, outlasted several regimes. During one period he discovered that another butler he had was a former private detective; from then on he was convinced that his staff was spying on him. His panacea for this was to try to play them against one another, to divert attention from himself. He would draw his cook aside and say, "I know there's nothing in this, but that damned butler told me you were stealing canned goods. You'd better keep an eye on him." Later on, to the butler, he would say, "Mind you, I'm on your side, but the cook's been carrying tales about you and the upstairs maid." His house was in perfect running order, Fields considered, when his servants had quit speaking to one another and were in a condition bordering on collapse.

After Toluca Lake he rented a house and seven acres at Encino, a sort of ranch house with an orange grove. It was a beautiful place and had a big tile pool, which Fields never used, and a tennis court, which he used a great deal. When he was home, he played almost every day with Sam Hardy, a giant of a man, an actor friend of Fields from the *Follies* days. Also much in evidence at Encino was a stooge of Fields, a vastly shorter fellow named Tammany Young, who appeared in pictures with him and looked after his martini glass off the set. For some reason, Fields always had a fancy for people out of the common run physically. At one time on the West Coast he employed a stooge with a head about the size of a number-two grapefruit. "With that head he'll own Hollywood," Fields told several friends.

He and Sam Hardy played tennis by the hour. Hardy played stripped to the waist, but Fields, whose skin was sensitive to the sun, wore a shirt, a sleeveless sweater, and a linen cap. His nose was generously larded with Allen's Footease. After considerable work in the comedian's garage they fitted out a coaster wagon with two decks and used it as a kind of rolling bar, on which were carried ice buckets, mixes, a dozen or so bottles, and both cocktail and highball glasses. Fields often played tennis with a racket in one hand and a martini glass in the other. He was a competent player, accurate, powerful, and ruthless, though disinclined to chase a ball that looked out of reach. He had a vicious chop shot that landed just over the net, with reverse English, and bounced back on his side, much as he had made tennis balls behave when he was juggling. His years of precision work and split-second timing had given him an uncanny eye; like Dempsey and a few other sports champions, he could read the printing on a revolving phonograph disk. His drives at the base line raised lime often enough to keep Sam Hardy, like Fields' doctor, hard pressed for cash.

In one way, Fields had more peace of mind at Toluca Lake than at Encino. During much of his residence at the first place he was unemployed; in addition, he had established the myth of his disaster in the stock market. By Encino he was making big money again and his thoughts had turned to kidnaping. He began to be a little touched on the subject. Often he would quiz his staff as to whether they had heard eerie noises during the night. Usually he carried one of his two blackjacks, either an ordinary one that he had bought or a streamlined one a policeman had given him for "evening wear."

Fields was positive that villains were frequently a-prowl downstairs in the small hours of the morning. His device for frightening them off made sleep impossible for everybody near by. He carried on loud conversations with fictitious bodyguards, punctuating his remarks with grisly laughter provoked by thoughts of the carnage to follow. "All right, you ready, Joe, Bull, Muggsy?" he'd yell around 2 A.M. "Let's go down and get 'em, then. Take it a little easy—I know you boys are former prize fighters and gunmen but I'd rather you didn't shoot to kill. Try to get them in the spinal cord or the pelvis. Ha ha ha ha ha—this ought to be good!" His servants would curse and toss in their beds.

The Encino residence was rented for only a year, from a family that was taking a trip. So great was Fields' fondness for the house that, when they returned, he tried to double the rent and keep it. But they preferred to move back in, and he engaged a mansion at Bel-Air, a fashionable section near Beverly Hills. Among the first things he did in the new house was to get a carpenter and an ironmonger and put heavy bars on both the outside and the inside of the upstairs doors. The owner called one day on business and was clearly peeved at the new decorations. "But it seems so *unnecessary*," he kept saying. Fields gave him a mysterious look, to indicate that there was more here than met the eye, and tried to reassure him. "I'm going to leave them for you," he said, "and I'm not going to charge you a dime."

At Bel-Air, more than at any of his other residences, Fields lived a social life. He was deep in the movie swim, and he gave occasional parties, with the most lavish attention to food and wines. Several of his soirees were complicated by domestic trouble. He had one butler at Bel-Air, a small, wizened man, whom Fields suspected of being an international poisoner. It was the comedian's unflattering custom to inspect fancy dishes handled by this butler, and to have somebody, such as a maid or the chauffeur, come in and taste them. If the guinea pigs didn't fall over and die, the master went ahead and dined. The butler being a thin-skinned fellow, all this led to bad feeling. In rebuttal, Fields refused to pay his salary. One evening during a dinner for sixteen people, the butler came in and demanded to be paid. Fields continued imperturbably to eat, though a number of his guests gave positive indication of tension. The man finally became so vociferous that Fields blew up and telephoned the police. At the same time, Gene Fowler, one of the guests, called some of his friends on the homicide squad.

At first glance, what with the abundance of official help, it would seem that the problem might soon have been solved. But when the patrolmen and the homicide agents arrived they got into a rackety jurisdictional row, and the matter of Fields and his butler was more or less shelved. Throughout most of the uproar Fields continued to eat, having had nothing but martinis since breakfast. Around midnight he gave the butler a check and fired him. Three days later, the man having refused to leave, Fields chased him off the grounds with a revolver. He fired several shots and thought he winged him as the butler vaulted over a neighbor's wall, though no report was ever made. The fellow got clean away. About two months after this, Fields went to dinner at the home of producer Pandro Berman and the talk turned to butlers. "I've got a gem," said Berman. "A wonderful stroke of luck, really. He runs this house like a well-oiled machine." A few minutes later the small, wizened man whom Fields had fired came in and set a plate of unidentifiable hors d'oeuvres in front of the comedian. Fields refused to eat them. "This guy will poison you," he yelled at Berman. "You'll see." He left the table and sat in the living room during dinner; afterward, on his way home, he stopped at a roadside stand and ate four hot dogs.

Fields had more than the average run of butler trouble. Another man he hired, a strapping bruiser known around the house as "The chimpanzee," raised dissension from the beginning. Fields was afraid of the chimpanzee, who belonged to a *Turnverein* and spent all his spare time developing his muscles. He hung a couple of big rings in the garage and worked out on them daily. One time after his boss had detected impudence in his manner, the chimpanzee went out to the garage, jumped up to his rings, and took a gigantic swing, with exceptionally bad results. At the end of his arc, the ropes broke, or became unfastened, and the man took a wrenching header into a pile of old furniture. As he lost consciousness, he said later, he heard a kind of hoarse, maniacal laughter from a darkened corner of the building. The fall almost put him out of commission; when he recovered he threatened to sue Fields, but the comedian paid him off, with a small bonus, and he left peacefully.

Magda Michael, Fields' secretary for twelve years, who stayed on the job as executrix of his estate, first went to his house at Toluca Lake in 1934 to help him with a dictaphone he had bought. The comedian had decided to capture, for posterity, the mental gems that visited him as he loafed around the premises. To transcribe his first notes, the dictaphone company suggested Miss Michael, not only because she was notably competent at secretarial work but because she had a philosophic disposition, not likely to be ruffled by the eccentricities of genius. When she arrived, she found her employer's affairs in a remarkable state of dishevelment. He had a desk almost identically like one that had turned up in a film he had recently made. The scene probably represented a dream of Fields; in it he was seated at a huge roll-top desk which was stuffed to bursting with papers of every size and shape, a picture of hopeless confusion. Fields, bent over, working with his hat on, was approached by a cringing client who asked for "that deed we were talking about a couple of years ago." Without looking up, Fields reached into the mess, withdrew a yellowed paper, and handed it over.

Miss Michael could recall no such miracle on the occasion of her first visit. The fact is, Fields, after shuffling through the desk for ten minutes, was unable to find his dictaphone rolls, and it took him the better part of the morning to locate them in an icebox, where he had absently placed them beside a jar of martinis. He seemed a little sheepish about the pearls he had collected during the past week, looking especially uncomfortable about one passage that referred to the musical daughter of a high government official as "a horse's ass," a designation by no means cleared up by its context, which dealt with the general subject of picnics.

The dictaphone company's sending Miss Michael to Fields turned out to be one of the great boons of his life. For the most part, his experiences with the other sex had been costly and disappointing. It was refreshing to him to meet a brisk, efficient woman who was both attractive and companionable but who had no romantic interest in him and no designs on his fortune. He found himself chatting with agreeable freedom; besides, he began to have that rare and wonderful feeling—a presentiment of lessened responsibility. "See here," he said on her next visit, by which time she had copied off unconstructive comments on sea gulls, butlers, other comedians, trespassers, income-tax officials, marriage, bankers and temperance, "why don't you come out here and take over? Obviously, things are going to pot." Miss Michael, who had just been apprised that thirty-two bankbooks in one corner of the desk had not been sent in for interest computation in more than twenty years, replied that she would as soon work for the comedian as anybody else, and he promptly took on a calculating look.

"So, so," he said. "Well, we'll strike a bargain. I'll pay you ten dollars a day for every day I need you. But mind, now, not a dime when you're not here."

Fields' establishment seemed an interesting and even an educational place of employment, and she agreed to his terms, not without amusement. Their relationship proved happy, and she acted as his secretary and all-around adviser off and on until his death. During the twelve-year period he handed over ten dollars at the end of each day's work, though she was frequently there every day for weeks in a row. From the day of her appearance at Toluca Lake, he addressed her only as "Mickey Mouse," and he never bothered to explain why.

Another important member of Fields' household in this phase was Carlotta Monti, his companion, friend, and practical nurse for fourteen years, a pretty, volatile girl of Mexican and Italian ancestry. The comedian and Miss Monti met when he was working for Paramount in *Million-Dollar*

Legs and she, as a bit player and dancer for the same studio, was asked to appear in some stills with him. Like Miss Michael, Miss Monti, from the start, found Fields a worthy subject for study, and she preserved a mental catalogue of his foibles. On the occasion of their meeting she sensed that the comedian would have liked her phone number but that he had too much ego to ask for it. He walked her to her car, making genteel, courteous conversation. On her part, she essayed a few slender jokes, at which he laughed without restraint. She once estimated that they were among the last jokes of hers he ever laughed at. Fields was often deferential to people until he came to know them, after which he relaxed. Miss Monti, an alert, good-natured girl, thoroughly enjoyed his fumbling efforts to become acquainted. She recalled that he said, "I hope you live conveniently near the studio?"

"Oh, yes," she said, "right in Hollywood."

"Very clever of you. South end of town, eh?"

"Well, no, more on the order of the middle, or north end."

Fields let a cane he was carrying snag onto a bush, and he killed two or three minutes unhooking it. Then he said, "It's a tough life—they don't care when they rout you out, any time of the day or night."

"Yes, they call me, too," she agreed. "On the telephone."

"A wonderful invention," said the comedian, and opened her car door, unable to voice the direct question. The Machiavellian byways of his mind prevented anything so simple as asking for a phone number; he had to resort to something devious. Two days later, he sent a writer they both knew to pick her up and take her riding after work. By an elaborate, unconvincing accident, the man made a beeline for Fields' place and said, "Well, what do you know! We're right here next to old Bill Fields'. Why don't we drop in and say hello?"

Such was the surprising nature of their visit that Fields had assembled a fancy cocktail spread and was waiting on the lawn, all dressed up. He came forward with characteristically hollow expressions of amazement, meanwhile making signals to a butler he had secreted in the shrubs. The party got under way. By another coincidence, the writer shortly recalled that an aunt of his was about to undergo an operation for eczema and he left for the hospital.

Miss Monti and Fields hit it right off. He was attracted to her because of her good looks, her ebullience and her generous nature, though his face fell slightly when he learned that she was an ardent spiritualist. She, on their second meeting, glanced at him suddenly and exclaimed, "Why, you look like a little Woody!" (rhymes with "moody"), an indescribable denizen or object known only to Miss Monti and her God. She never had any hints as to the origin of this term; the comparison must simply be put down as one of those divinations that come to those in communication with the spirit world. In any case, Fields agreed that his resemblance to a Woody was, in fact, strong, and the amenities flourished. The friendship between the comedian and Miss Monti—warm, fitful, therapeutic—was of great benefit to both of them. On her side, she gained an education that is denied to all but the privileged few, in addition to being mentioned in his will, and he found in her a dedicated attendant who stuck unselfishly by him until the sad, bitter end.

Fields' subsequent attitude toward the writer who had brought her out is of passing interest. Thenceforward, he never had anything to do with the man at all. Presumably, Fields took the notion that the writer might have conceived designs on Miss Monti during the brief car ride. Whatever the reason, he spoke of him in the most distrustful terms from then on out. The comedian was suspicious and jealous of nearly everybody. In the family circle (Miss Monti moved in and took up her duties soon after their introduction) Fields preferred to dominate the conversation, and he brooked no loose compliments, or even any references, to other funny men. Miss Michael often stayed overnight, if her work had piled up. She stored up vivid impressions of the group clustered around the radio, searching for something not likely to irritate the master. While Fields listened to the radio a good deal, he also damned it eloquently and burlesqued it for home consumption. Miss Michael and Miss Monti agreed that he gave splendid shows, of artistic worth rivaling that of his paid performances—a compelling tribute to his preoccupation with the medium.

At the bottom of Fields' radio list were operatic divas. During programs in which these ladies rode the air, he stuffed a pillow in his shirt front and walked around the house braying like a jackass. His gestures, his expressions, occasionally even his tones, had striking verisimilitude, and his single-handed portrayal of *Carmen,* a many-faceted effort in which he took note of several parts, including those of the fidgety heroine, the toreador, Micaela, a number of gypsies, several soldiers, and the bull, established new peaks in this kind of work.

Fields was very keen on advertising, especially that of the tobacco hawkers. He often tried to ferret meaning out of sentences like "More doctors smoke Cubebs than formerly," "Repeated tests have proved that Corn Silks are not responsible for 67 per cent of bad breath originating in the mouth," and "Your Y-Zone is safe with Hempies, the middle-sized cigarette." He was ever on the lookout for additions of valuable new ingredients, such as Latakia and chloroform, and he marveled that almost every cigarette was far outselling its competitors. In the windup, he realized that the ultimate end of the fight for mildness was no tobacco at all, and he quit smoking in response to advertising of this sort.

Now and then, when he had finished a successful movie, Fields ventured to listen to other comedians. On one memorable evening he announced to a stunned household that Jack Benny was a very accomplished performer. "The boy's got real timing, and I've always appreciated that talent," he said. The following Sunday, Miss Monti turned to the Benny program, and Fields jarred the radio with an accurately thrown volume of Martin Chuzzlewit. "I never heard such claptrap in my life!" he roared; then he turned to a musical hour which he detested.

During the second world war he was a passionate follower of the course of events. He listened to all the commentators, cursed and railed at the Japs and Germans, and bought a gaudy map, into which he thrust colored pins at odd, erroneous places, such as Madagascar and Peru. The war bit into Fields deeply. He discussed it at great length one afternoon with Lionel and John Barrymore, Gene Fowler, and John Decker, the artist. Their hatred of the foe provoked them to have quite a few drinks, and the drinks increased their hatred of the foe. Around four o'clock, in full battle humor, they got in a car and drove down to enlist. At the time, besides being fairly well along in both years and alcohol, most of them were suffering from some incapacitating illness. For example, it was thought best to take Lionel Barrymore's wheel chair along, in case they got an immediate overseas assignment. His colleagues assisted him from the car to his chair, after which they pushed him in. The girl at the recruiting center, after her first shock, had them fill out several forms, upon which she noted many doubtful entries. John Barrymore gave his age as nineteen, Fowler outlined somewhat more military experience than General Pershing's, and Fields requested duty as a commando. The girl looked them over carefully, then made what all of them cherished as a supreme example of extemporaneous government wit.

"Who sent you?" she said. "The enemy?"

CHAPTER TWENTY-FIVE

OF ALL Fields' houses, the one he liked best was a big Spanish place on a high hill in the center of Hollywood. The area is known as Laughlin Park, a quiet, faintly aristocratic collection of green knolls that struggle up above the glamour and neon. A handful of fine old houses, remindful of the leisurely but perhaps unphotogenic dons, has resisted the onward, indigenous march of redwood and glass; ringed by hedges, shaded by palms, they stand almost unseen on their inessential hills, tourist-free and forgotten in a city restlessly expanding.

Fields leased his house for five years in 1940, obtaining it by some mischievous device for $250 a month, which included a worn Japanese gardener, who presumably was installed on the property with the shrubbery and plumbing. Soon after the transaction the war talk thickened, prices went up, and the owner repented his hasty grant. He came around and asked Fields to hike the rent, out of common humanity. The response this provoked—peals of wild, triumphant laughter—set off one of the great real estate feuds of the century. Fields felt that he had put a lot of anxiety into the house; he intended to cling tight to his gains. His old friend William Le Baron had previously rented the place, and during a period when the producer was desperately ill, Fields had been torn by agonizing emotions. Many days when the mansion seemed almost within his grasp, Le Baron had miraculously rallied and checked the comedian's plans. After reading one cheerless newspaper report, Fields called Le Baron's hospital and talked to his nurse. "Are there any late bulletins?" he asked in a bereaved tone. "Mr. Le Baron is much better," said the nurse. "His physician is optimistic for the first time."

"It's a lie!" roared Fields. "He isn't going to pull through. Damn him, I'll get that house—you wait and see."

The nurse reported this solicitous exchange to Le Baron, who rallied enough further to laugh weakly.

"I don't think Bill actually wanted me to die," he said. "But he was a practical man, and he sure planned to get that house if I did die. As it turned out, I moved and he got it anyhow."

Fields always kept the telephones warm when his friends were going through a crisis. One time when Gene Fowler was involved in a terrible automobile accident, and lay at the point of death, Fields, having just got the news, called the hospital in the early hours of the morning. He was put through to a flustered nurse.

"How is he?" asked Fields.

"We're not sure—the doctors told the reporters he may be going," the nurse replied.

"Is he conscious?"

"Yes. I can deliver a message, Mr. Fields."

"Then tell the son of a bitch to get up from there and quit faking," said the comedian. A few minutes later, one of his household found him downstairs, sitting in a corner and swabbing away at his eyes.

Fields' house was on De Mille Drive, a circumstance that irked him. The pioneer movie maker of that name lived just across the road, on somewhat higher ground, an elevation disparity that also bothered Fields. Because of the name, and his subordinate sea level, the comedian took a raspy dislike to De Mille that appeared to be without any other foundation. Hearing De Mille's car start up, he would peer balefully through the shrubs and snort. If the weathered gardener was working near by, he would grab his arm and point.

"There he goes," Fields would cry. "Confound him! *Look* at him! Now what do you think of that?"

"Yamgatso moo toya?" the gardener would say, or something equally puzzling. At no time during the five years Fields had the house did the two exchange a single understandable scrap of conversation. It was likely, several people felt, that the Jap didn't know the house had changed hands. Both his origin and his tongue were obscure; reliable authorities claim that his utterances were garbled not only to Americans but to Japanese. Nevertheless, Fields continued to talk to him as though they had some means of communication. *"Yamgatso moo toya?"* the gardener would repeat, with a look of mild inquiry, and Fields would answer:

"De Mille. It's that damned old director. Look at him, look at that car. Where do you suppose he's going?"

"Negato yum ramsaky fui," the Jap might say, and perhaps laugh.

"Well, I tell you what we'll do. We'll sneak over there tonight and build a Burmese tiger trap on his lawn. Drat the old devil—we'll fix him up good."

The gardener would look comprehending, then hand Fields a potted plant, and they would retreat to the house, each talking volubly, neither getting through, each busy and satisfied on his own mysterious circuit.

Fields' staff thought that in some secret recess of his heart he had a grudging admiration of De Mille; the ranting was designed to cover it up. Certainly when the two met, the comedian was perfectly courteous. He would lift his hat, smile, call out a cheery "Good morning," and step along as briskly as if his house were as high as anybody's. Later, at home, he would report fictitious chats with his neighbor, upon which occasions he referred to De Mille as "Cease," a comradely abbreviation of "Cecil."

"Talking to Cease out there a minute ago," he'd say. "We're going to put a gate down on that lower end to keep out the picnickers."

Deanna Durbin, the melodic child star, lived on a nearby hill for a while, causing Fields great distress. He was worried sick that she might come out and sing in her yard. Against this awful contingency he prepared several measures. For a while he figured that he would have her arrested; later, he thought he might get a dog and train it to howl at the sound of feminine melody; perhaps the severest of his statements was that he would "get a good bead from the upstairs balcony and shoot her."

The house on De Mille Drive was entered after a long walk down a red-tile lane overhung with trellises. On either hand, carpetlike lawns sloped off steeply; they rolled and dipped with the contours of Fields' private hills. On one side of the house they formed an irregular bowl, whose face was as sheer as an alpine pasture. In the center was a lily pond, upon whose rippled surface a toy sailboat, given him by Magda Michael, steered to and fro in the shifting ocean breeze. It was to be the scene of an episode that Fields never quite got over.

The house had cavernous rooms, many of them paneled in rich oak or walnut, and long, broad stairways. Fields' décor, though interesting, was a sharp departure from that of most Spanish houses in Southern California. In the center of his living room, beneath an elegant chandelier, he had a pool table in pretty good condition, and in the drawing room he had a ping-pong table. Around the walls of both rooms stood high-bottomed chairs such as are found in most pool halls, and a further attraction of the living room was a small bowling alley. A low-ceilinged balcony, of impressive feudal appearance, circled part of this chamber; from its place of vantage Fields often watched pool games. He made a pretty picture, reminiscent of a mellower age—the squire of the manor, glass in hand, shouting encouragement to the lords: "Eight ball in the side pocket, Joe—reverse English! Reverse English!"

In another of the downstairs rooms Fields had a barber's chair, with a number of towels, aprons, and so on.

The comedian had his hair cut off the premises, as being fifty cents cheaper, but he needed the barber's chair for sleeping purposes. During the time of his joyless youth he had found haircuts among his principal luxuries. After a night huddled in a frozen doorway and a morning selling papers on an icy corner, he would squander a quarter for the privilege of sinking deep into warm black leather, steamed cloths and bottled, upper-class scents. As his middle years advanced, his sleeping became an increasing problem. He discovered that by re-creating the snug impressions of his early trims he could doze in occasional peace. Many afternoons saw him stretched out in his chair, the aprons and towels tucked all around, dreaming of the old, brief comforts. His regard for his barber's skill was such that he kept trying to persuade the fellow, an Italian, to leave his brain to the Moler Barbers' College.

Upstairs, Fields had his exercise room, a large, sunny chamber filled with things such as rowing machines, stationary bicycles, Indian clubs, and steam cabinets. To this room came Bob Howard, the trainer, several times a week. He undertook the overhauling of Fields after rescuing from West Coast erosion such notables as Lady Mendl, Cole Porter, Myrna Loy, Jon Hall, Irving Berlin, and Harry Richman. By comparison with Fields, this spirited group, together with his other clients, began to seem like lambs, but Howard hung on, determined to put the comedian in shape or join him in a sanitarium. After a fashion, Fields followed instructions, but he always added what struck Howard as an unnecessary touch of his own. For instance, he would, as directed, dress in a sweat suit and mount the stationary bicycle for a long ride, but he generally drank several martinis en route. He would pedal along stolidly, now and then honking a handle-bar klaxon he had installed "to break the monotony," and sip from the glass resting in his free hand. His rowing machine provided one of Fields' favorite exercises. He would place a drink about two feet from the rear end of the device, then, backwatering desperately, pretend to chase it as racing greyhounds chase a mechanical rabbit. "I'm gaining!" he'd cry at the disgusted Howard. "This is wonderful—these workouts are going to increase my liquor consumption 2 or 3 hundred percent." Often, as he rowed along, he would sing sea chanteys or bawl profane instructions to an imaginary crew. He developed into a good oarsman. No matter how rough the water, he always caught up with the drink. For some reason that Howard was unable to explain, Fields preferred highballs while seated in his steam cabinet. With weary resignation the trainer would zip him up (in a special electric-steam cabinet of his own design), leave his head and one arm free, and hand him a drink; then he would sit by while Fields carried on about the wonders of physical culture.

Howard, a fine athlete, occasionally boxed with Fields on the lawn. He found the comedian fast, strong, shifty, and utterly untrustworthy. After feigning severe fatigue, the former juggler was likely to loose a crushing uppercut, then offer windy expostulations that it was "a regrettable accident." Howard learned to keep his guard up and watch him closely. Fields hated to be bested at anything. In his off time, Howard was given to reading Shakespeare and other weighty authors, and he engaged his client in intellectual conversations. After a few sessions of this, Fields contrived ornate countermeasures. He would sit up late at night, with volumes of miscellaneous information. After memorizing a long string of facts, he would be all primed when the trainer arrived the next morning. He steered the conversation to his pets indirectly. "Hear old Bing won himself a couple of races yesterday," he'd say, with a pleased chuckle.

"That so?" Howard would murmur, and go on, "No doubt you recall that passage in *The Merchant of*——"

"A curious thing," Fields would boom, admitting no competition, "about that notion that horses were first discovered in Arabia."

As a rule, Howard fell into the trap, and Fields' morning was made. He had two names for his trainer; one, "The Learned Professor," was a tribute to Howard's erudition, the other, "Horizontal Howard," was a kind of envious sneer at his sleeping ability. The fact that the trainer was able to take naps at odd times nettled Fields; he himself, if he was lucky, often could get to sleep only after Howard had exercised and massaged him into a state of limp exhaustion.

With all their petty bickering, and despite Fields' many infractions of the course, he benefited greatly from his formal attempts to stay in training. His consumption of alcohol, instead of increasing, lessened for quite a while. Howard lectured him constantly about drinking hard liquor, and even cut a hole in Fields' shower curtain to police him during the sequestered period of his baths. Prior to the peephole, at the end of a morning's moderation, the comedian would often come out of his shower singing and in rare bloom. Suspicious, Howard investigated the soggy chamber and found a miniature bar hung on wires beneath the soap dish.

It was Howard who persuaded Fields to switch to red wine and soda for several months. The trainer's solicitous inquiries about how it was working all provoked the same answer: "Rotten." When the comedian decided to give up the wine, which he said was too rich for his blood, he had iceboxes placed in nearly every room in the house. He had thought it best to return to the less dangerous martinis, and martinis, he said, should be kept cold to preserve their medicinal powers. His additions to the house, of whatever kind, were all done at his own expense. As prices continued to climb, and he steadfastly refused to boost his rent, the owner understandably balked at making the slightest improvement or repair. The house more or less went to seed. Parts of the downstairs ceiling became loosened, and huge strips hung down several feet. One of the largest was directly over the pool table, making it hazardous to play. As games nevertheless progressed, chunks of plaster and wood occasionally fell down and had to be brushed aside before the players could continue.

Fields' ideas of improvements were frequently bizarre. Without much hesitation the owner declined to install a system of dictaphones, or bugs, throughout the house during a period when Fields felt that his servants were plotting. The comedian went ahead and had the system put in himself. It was expensive, but he placed the machines everywhere, even in the pantry and over the front door stoop. Upon this program Fields brought to bear all his furtive ingenuity, suggesting such hiding places as in chandeliers, behind pictures, in the bottoms of chairs, and under washbasins. The master panel of all this foolishness was on the outsize desk in Fields' study, a large upstairs room, with a balcony, that served as the pilothouse, so to speak, of his domestic ship. On days when conspiracy seemed thick in the air, he stayed close to his panel, hoping to pick up mutinous scraps. Since all the servants soon knew about the dictaphones, and because they had no plans to mutiny, the tidbits he collected made pretty dull listening. Nevertheless, he remained alerted, his face lit up in vindication, as he struggled to read sinister imports into remarks like "We need some more salt" and "I wish he'd quit leaving magazines in here."

Also on his desk (which was the apple of his eye) Fields had a spyglass, with which to sweep the lawn for trespassers, his horse pistol, with which to shoot them if they proved intractable, writing materials, a stack of newspapers, and a pot of paste and a pair of scissors. He spent a great deal of time at his desk, creating an atmosphere of bustling importance. Periodically he would step out on the balcony, taking his spyglass and pistol, and search carefully for felons. On one such occasion, after a quiet morning with the dictaphone, he actually spotted a formidable boarding party headed his way down the red-tile path. It was a meek group of nuns distributing pamphlets urging some charity, but Fields, springing into action, mustered all possible strength to repel them. He decided on Plan D, involving use of the dictaphone, whose door-stoop branch he switched on immediately. Holding the microphone close to his mouth, he launched a hair-raising and profane domestic argument, taking the parts of both husband and wife and touching on the most delicate aspects of marriage. The nuns hitched up their skirts and ran like rabbits, jettisoning pamphlets right and left, to add that marginal soupcon of acceleration which so often means the difference between freedom and capture.

Fields was always courteous to religious people unless their broadsides were aimed in his direction. It was a maxim of his life.

The paste pot and scissors on his desk were for deleting and affixing to letters pertinent items from his newspapers, most of which were house organs of well-known penitentiaries. The comedian liked to keep up with the prison news; he pretended that he was following the careers of many old friends. When he encountered a squib that amused him, he would clip it and mail it, with some appropriate comment, to one of his unincarcerated companions. Fields kept his friends posted about all sorts of developments that interested him. A more or less typical observation was one he sent Gene Fowler on November 16, 1939. It read, in its entirety:

Dear Mr. F.

Mr. Claude Millsap is now associated with the Baldwin Shirt Company of Glendale. He left his card with me this morning. I thought you would be glad to hear of his progress. Claude has been working in socks and underwear for years and we are all happy to know that he has made the grade.

Your loving Uncle William.

Magda Michael did his dictation, sitting in a chair on a somewhat lower level than her employer. Fields' desk was deliberately situated, Miss Michael believes, in the frowning manner of Jack Oakie's in *The Great Dictator,* when, as Mussolini, he contrived a physical eminence to gain moral superiority. Fields dictated ten or fifteen hot letters a day, raising hell about something, with prejudicial attention to the government. In the interest of coolheadedness, he kept the letters four hours before mailing them. Then he threw all of them in a wastebasket and cleared his desk for the next day's peeves.

Fields was a keen political observer. Actually, his personal politics were simple: he was violently against whatever government was in power and felt affectionate toward any and all people who belabored it. Fowler dropped by his house one election day and found the comedian on his way down to vote. He was shabbily dressed, so as to not give government people the idea he was rich, and his expression was fierce.

"Who are you going to vote for, Uncle Willie?" asked Fowler.

"Hell, I never vote *for* anybody," cried Fields, incensed, "I always vote *against.*"

He had a pretty good idea that governments were organized chiefly to separate him from income-tax money, and he spent several weeks of each year trying to think up ways to forestall this separation. Both Miss Michael and Miss Monti recalled that income-tax month was a severe trial for everybody in the house. Fields' manner was irritable and conspiratorial in the extreme. Miss Michael often helped him with his return, as Grady had done, but her counsel was largely ignored. She remembered suggesting, at one point, that no good could accrue from his deducting depreciation on a borrowed lawn mower, and another time she demurred at his construing twelve cans of weed killer as a professional expense. One year he deducted his bill for liquor, which he said was a necessary tool of his trade.

Westbrook Pegler came to visit Fields one day, and the two conversed at length on the general subject of vice-presidents. Pegler suggested, and Fields agreed, that a movie built around a typical Vice-President of the United States might be funny. They decided to concentrate their research, in the main, on Henry Wallace's speeches. Fields accordingly wrote Wallace a letter asking for copies of some of his speeches, explaining that he had a hobby of filing the public utterances of government officials. In reply, Wallace promptly sent him copies of all the speeches he had made while in office, and added a personal note of the warmest kind. He had always revered Fields' comedy, he said, and hoped that he would have, in the future, as many delightful hours of enjoyment from it as he had had in the past. Thereafter, Fields' attitude toward Wallace and all vice-presidents was guarded. He seemed to lose interest in the project with Pegler, and whenever he heard anybody damn Wallace, he would say, "Well, now, I wouldn't go that far. Mr. Wallace is a highly intelligent man, a sound man in many ways."

Fields' favorite dictation was done in collaboration with his pal Sam Hardy. They would set up shop in the comedian's study, looking very serious, and send for Magda Michael. Then, without changing expression, they would dictate horrifying letters, profane and blasphemous, to the most notable figures in the land. It was tragic, Miss Michael felt, that these scenes were lost to posterity. Fields and Hardy played them with all the artistic finesse at their command, and each sharpened the other's skill. "Sit down, will you, Miss Michael?" Fields would ask gently, his tone full of significance. "Thank you, Mr. Fields," she would reply, with a good idea of what was coming. Fields, wearing his bathrobe, its pockets stuffed, as usual, with thousand-dollar bills, would shuffle through his papers, then consult Hardy in an undertone.

"Do you have those notes we prepared?"

Hardy was an impressive-looking man, and his demeanor on these occasions would automatically have got him bids to many corporate boards. "I believe I returned them to you, Mr. Fields. Some of them were carried over from our last meeting."

"Ah, yes," Fields would say. "Here they are. Will you take a letter, Miss Michael? To Mr. Henry B. Meyer, Moronic Pictures, Hollywood, California." He would go on for a few minutes, perhaps breaking off for portentous whispered conversations with Hardy, then say, "Now, let's see, will you read that back, please?"

Miss Michael, whose expression also had not altered since the session began, would clear her throat bravely and read, "Dear Mr. Meyer, you ignorant son of a bitch, I wish to take this opportunity to tell you what I think of your goddamned movies. If I ever catch you out on the street, you thieving horse's ass, I'm going to break both of your legs. Of all the low-down bastards—— You stopped there, Mr. Fields."

"On bastards?"

"Yes, Mr. Fields."

"Read all right so far?"

"It's very well composed."

"Punctuation sound throughout? Comma after bitch?"

"Everything's in order, I believe, Mr. Fields."

"Then let us continue."

Fields' and Hardy's repeated attempts to crack Miss Michael's composure were unavailing; they finally sent her a telegram saying, "We're defeated. We take off our hats to you."

The comedian used to tell Miss Michael that he'd always wanted to be a writer. "What a wonderful trade!" he would say. "All you need is your head and paper and pencil." Elaborating on his frustration, he said he wanted particularly to be a crusading writer. "What would you crusade for, Mr. Fields?" his secretary asked, and got an answer like Fowler's on election day. "I'd crusade against everything," he said firmly. At other times, his urge was to write something "simple." "They overdo everything," he complained. "It's all complicated and significant." Although he seldom read modern best sellers, or book club selections, he read constantly from his old favorites, the English romanticists of the last century. To keep abreast of the times, he subscribed to several magazines. *The New Yorker,* the then magazine of humor edited by Harold Ross, was one of his special delights, and he went through each issue of *Time, Newsweek* and Wesley Stout's traditional, dignified *Saturday Evening Post.*

He loved the trappings of writing. His ritual with Miss Michael, on days when he was to work on a script or write something else, made him feel important. Humming cheerfully, he would lay things out, either on his desk or in a lawn swing where he liked to work. His style was extravagant, florid, influenced in large measure by Dickens, whom he knew by heart. "Despite his love of simplicity, he could never say, 'Hit him on the head,' " Miss Michael said. "He always had to make it 'Conk him on the noggin.' "

Some time before his death he was working on two major writing projects. One was a movie satire called *Grand Motel,* with which she was helping him, though they were not getting very far—Fields kept trying to switch the locale to a delicatessen. The other was an article for a magazine which had asked for his views as to how to end the war. Fields, in all seriousness, was expounding in careful prose his long-cherished plan to put the ringleaders of each country in the Rose Bowl and let them fight it out with sockfuls of dung. It was Miss Michael's theory (which proved to be correct) that the piece was not likely to get published.

Only infrequently did Fields' real comic genius shine through his writing. For the most part his material had a tendency to sink progressively deeper into the ridiculous, shedding all meaning, and most of its humor, in the process. He wrote one book, *Fields for President,* which ran serially in *This Week,* and one chapter of which, *My Views on Marriage,* was reprinted in several collections, such as *Tales for Males,* edited by Ed and Pegeen Fitzgerald, the radio breakfast clubbers. After a long, wheezy passage about how he had once tried to impress a woman named Abigail Twirlbaffing (by playing "The Whistler and His Dog" backward on a cornet) he outlined a daily regimen for model wives, one which he genuinely approved. It went as follows:

7 TO 8 A.M.—Arise quietly, shake down furnace, stoke it, prepare breakfast—eggs exactly four minutes, two lumps in the Java.

8 TO 9—Awake husband *gently,* singing *sotto voce.* My preferences would be "Narcissus" or "Silent Night."

9 TO 10—Drive husband to station, do marketing for dinner, and be sure not to order anything husband might decide to have for lunch.

10 TO 12—Mow lawn, wash clothes, iron husband's shirts, press his suits, paint screens, weed garden, swat flies.

12 TO 2—Clean cellar, wash windows, tidy house, beat rugs.

2 TO 2:15—Eat simple lunch.

2:15 TO 5:30—Spade garden, darn socks, wash Rover, put up jelly, polish car, burn rubbish, wash woodwork, paint garage, clean side walls of tires.

5:30 TO 7—Drive to station for husband, shake cocktails, cook dinner, serve dinner, wash dishes.

7:00 TO 12—Keep busy—keep smiling—for, as every man knows, the husband is tired.

The book, published by Dodd, Mead & Company, had only a moderate sale. Fields mentioned it wistfully in a note in October of 1941 to Gene Fowler: "I received a letter just this morning from Mr. Dodd saying he did not think it would be wise to reissue my book, which has a great deal to do with liquor. You very wisely shunned the horrid stuff in your classic on Barrymore."

Unencouraged by his success with books, Fields threw his best literary effort into his letter writing, which was marked by the same majestic hyperbole that characterized his other literary works. "Dear Dago," he usually addressed missives to La Cava, and in one of them, in 1937, he spoke of dining with Fowler and his "unholy family." Fowler's youngest son, Bill, Fields said, smoked black cigars and drank whisky until it ran out of his ears. His daughter, the letter went on, chewed tobacco, and spat tobacco juice on Fields' clean shirt front, and the eldest son "tried to roll me for my poke." In a letter to Fowler, when the comedian was in a sanitarium, Fields commented on a tidal wave which had recently struck the California coast. Their mutual friend, La Cava, said Fields, passed over his cottage and dropped a bottle saying he was headed for San Gabriel dam. He had a couple of "oars," according to Fields, and was doing his best with them.

Dictating and probing his lawn with the spyglass kept Fields content through many a dull day. He wrote a lot of letters, but he seldom spotted interlopers, to his great regret. On one memorable afternoon he brought into focus a whole party of men running across his front yard. His first instinct was to shout a blood-curdling warning and then, if they persisted, to reach for his gun. But something in their faces, a strain of desperation, caused him to turn and dash down his stairs. For a big man, Fields could move with surprising rapidity when he chose; he scrambled to the bottom of the bowl-like slope just as the party were lifting two-year-old Christopher Quinn, the son of Anthony Quinn and the grandson of Cecil B. De Mille, from his lily pond, upon whose surface they had seen him floating. White and shaken, Fields sat down and held his head in his hands as Quinn heartbrokenly tried to revive him. Fields, the parents, the De Milles, and several others kept a sad vigil beside the pond long into the twilight, while the police sought to return the child to consciousness with a pulmotor.

The next day, Fields took out the toy sailboat, of which he had been extremely proud, and burned it in his incinerator. Then he drained the water from the pond and never went near it again as long as he lived in the house.

CHAPTER TWENTY-SIX

FIELDS' HOME LIFE was colorful and robust. He enjoyed his household, even when he thought the members were after him. For a man who was basically anti-social, he had many recreations. High on his list was picnics. He was at his sharpest when organizing an outdoor jaunt. On these occasions all his caution about money vanished; everything he did was in the richest tradition of Diamond Jim Brady. Miss Michael recalled one idea the comedian had for a trip northward up the coast. It was a fine, blue morning, and he had, for a change, slept soundly. He came downstairs early, drank two double martinis on the terrace, then lit into an unusually large beaker of pineapple juice. "Let's have a picnic," he said to Miss Michael, Carlotta Monti, and her sister, Susie, who had stayed overnight. "I'll tell the chauffeur to tune up the big Lincoln."

He began to bustle around giving orders and urging everybody to hurry. "He had to do everything *right now*," Miss Michael said. "Once he had an idea, he couldn't put if off for a second. Even if he'd decided to buy some bud vases, he had to get in the car and go right after them." Within a few minutes he had his colored cook, Dell, laying out big wicker picnic hampers, making sandwiches, hard-boiling eggs, and stuffing celery with Roquefort cheese. He himself got out his ice buckets, including a red one that was often referred to in newspaper accounts of his drinking, and filled them. He had a built-in refrigerator in the silver-plated Lincoln, but he wanted to take no chances of running short. When the ice buckets were in shape, he unlocked his liquor room (which was then secured by two

iron bars and four padlocks) and carried down a case of
Lanson '28. He added to the champagne several bottles of
gin, half-a-dozen bottles of imported burgundy, and half-
a-dozen bottles of a fine, dry sauterne. Fields disliked
sweet wines. He put a case of beer in the Lincoln's refrigerator; then he had his chauffeur drive him and the three
girls to the Vendôme, a fancy catering establishment.

He bought about a hundred dollars' worth of black caviar,
pâté de fois gras, anchovies, smoked oysters, baby
shrimps, crab meat, tinned lobster, potted chicken and
turkey, several cheeses, including a soft yellow Swiss
cheese he was especially fond of, and some strong cheeses
like Liederkranz and Camembert, a big bottle of Grecian
olives, and three or four jars of glazed fruit. Back home, his
cook had made sandwiches out of water cress, chopped
olives and nuts, tongue, peanut butter and strawberry preserves, and deviled egg and spiced ham. She had also baked
both an angel food and a devils food cake. "What we've
missed we'll pick up on the road," Fields said, and he ushered his passengers to the car, which the chauffeur had
rubbed down with a chamois and vacuumed on the inside.

Fields sat in front. In the glove compartment he kept his
martini glass, which he passed back every half-hour or so
for a refill. They drove up Hollywood Boulevard, cut over
to Sunset and followed the winding, busy artery through
Beverly Hills, past the Beverly Hills Hotel, the Westwood
turnoff, Sepulveda, and into Pacific Palisades. The chauffeur, by direction, drove slowly, so that Fields could point
to many features of interest, including the homes of
movie notables, and damn them all. Instead of following
Sunset through Pacific Palisades, they turned left at Chau-
tauqua and followed the steep hill down into Santa Monica,
where they picked up the beach road and headed north
toward Santa Barbara. It was eleven o'clock now and the
sun was high overhead; the first bathers were making their
nests on the beach. A light but steady breeze had brought
out scores of sailboats, some of them with red, yellow, or
blue sails, and altogether it looked like a perfect day for an
outing.

Passing Malibu, Fields spotted Gregory La Cava in front
of his beach house, watering his insatiable lawn, and pulled
up long enough to call him "a Dago bum" and offer him a

martini, which La Cava refused with an exclamation of deep disgust. Fields waved amiably, cursed him some more, and they drove on. They had a late lunch in a grove just outside Santa Barbara, beside the ocean. For their table he picked a lot of wild flowers, or semi-wild, since the municipality had planted them several years before with some hope of permanency, and he walked around as they ate, exclaiming on the beauties of nature. He had opened a bottle of champagne, and after the others had sipped a glass or two, he finished it. Before they left, he went down to the sand, where he pointed out the loathsome surf, as if he were exhibiting some natural phenomenon for the first time, and described in detail his sapping employment as a drowner at Atlantic City.

Driving back to Santa Barbara, they decided that the afternoon was too far advanced to continue in comfort, so they stayed overnight, Fields engaging a suite for everybody at the Biltmore. They dined in the hotel that evening and went to a movie, a Western, one of the few kinds in which he could find no trace of competitiveness. On this night he even made the expansive observation that the comedian, an elderly whiskerando whose sole comic device was directing tobacco juice at a spittoon which rang like a gong, was "a terribly funny fellow." What this opinion meant, as his companions realized, was that he had analyzed the tobacco-juice trick and felt that nothing important would ever come of it.

Fields got everybody up early the next morning by rapping on their doors and calling out, to the indignation of other guests, that "we've got a big day ahead." They were on the road not long after sunrise, again heading north, into the big redwood country. In this precocious garden patch Fields tarried for hours, studying the trees, quizzing the guides, buying literature, and boning up on statistics, which he intended to use later on Bob Howard. They had another drawn-out picnic, in the course of which he undertook, on the sly, to carve their initials on one of the giants. But the project was too tiresome; he gave it up. They drove on to San Francisco. There, as in Santa Barbara, he got them all hotel suites, at the St. Francis. Then he consulted a travel office, to get a list of civic attractions and work out an itinerary. During the following day the party visited most of the monuments, bridges, monasteries, public buildings, pieces of high ground, bronze plaques, and bizarre quarters in the metropolitan area. "It's important to stick to the simple things," Fields said. "We have nothing finer than our ordinary tourist customs." For some reason, he showed no interest in Alcatraz.

Their return to Hollywood, down the winding, rugged coastline, was accomplished in luxurious torpor. The sun was hot, the motion and the springs of the big car were irresistibly lulling, and the ocean with its slow, even rhythm exerted a sedative effect. They picnicked in isolated coves; twice they paused for naps on shaded banks of sand. So deliciously soothed did Fields apparently feel, so removed from the stress of his career, that he began to buy gifts for the party at opportune places. "Mr. Fields usually bought everything in half-dozen quantities," Miss Michael said. "Whenever he found something he liked, he usually felt that he'd better get quite a few while they lasted." At Carmel he inexplicably had the chauffeur pull up beside a big jewelry store, into which he proceeded and bought a dozen electric clocks. These he presented to the members of his party. The purchase required a good deal of room; the chauffeur, though grateful and in an excellent position to keep track of the time for thirty or forty years, was hard pressed to get the bundle into the luggage compartment. The jeweler (who acknowledged in an aside to one of the group that the store hadn't put in such a day since his grandfather, a Spaniard, founded it not long after the gold rush) came out to see them off. "Thanks a lot, Mr. Fields," he kept saying. "Come in again—we've got a nice line of fountain pens, desk sets, silver-mounted brushes——"

For reasons best known to himself, Fields preferred to maintain a fiction of anonymity. "My name," he interrupted testily, "is Oglethorpe P. Bushmaster, of Punxsatawney, Pennsylvania. I am not acquainted with anyone by the name of Fields."

"Of course, of course, Mr. Bushwhacker," cried the jeweler, noting the California license plates. "Come back again, Mr. Fields. We also got some nice loving cups, dinner trays, carving sets, knock down a nice cut-glass centerpiece——"

"Bushmaster!" roared Fields, and to his chauffeur, "Drive on!"

When they got home, Fields told the group that, as picnics went, it had been very satisfactory, almost as good as the one he had gone on years before when he left Long Island in the middle of the night and regained consciousness in Ocala, Florida.

Often, after an expensive sortie, and especially if he weren't working, Fields felt a strong financial reaction. He would examine the household accounts, make a lot of mysterious figures in a notebook, and then announce, with terrible gravity, that "we've got to cut down around here." His favorite expression to describe the sudden reversal in his fortunes was, "We're scraping the bottom of the barrel." At the time of these utterances he had about a million dollars in cash lying idle in various banks. Nevertheless, the day after his return from the San Francisco picnic he was crouched in the shrubbery again, on this occasion checking up on the chauffeur. The comedian had a small secretary's memo pad, upon which he kept track of all his cars' mileage. Noting a big jump in the figures for the silver-plated Lincoln (possibly as a result of the picnic) he said of the chauffeur to another servant, "That bird's using those cars for a taxi service and by God it's got to stop!" Sure enough, around eleven o'clock he saw the chauffeur step quietly to the garage, start up the station wagon, and drive off. Fields checked his watch and waited. The man was gone eighteen minutes, just enough time to pick up a fare on Hollywood Boulevard and deliver it to, say, the Beverly Hills Hotel. As the car turned into the garage, Fields skipped out with a wild look in his eye. He held up one hand and said, "Ha!"

"Sir?" said the chauffeur, applying the brakes.

"Big tip?"

"Pardon me?" asked the chauffeur.

"Exactly where have you been?" said Fields.

"Cook asked me to pick up three cans of sardines and a loaf of pumpernickel," said the chauffeur, exhibiting a basket.

"Sardines, hey?" said Fields keenly.

"Yes, sir."

"What brand?"

The chauffeur examined the cans and said, "Norwegian Little Dandies—packed in mustard."

"What store?"

"Fleishhacker's Friendly Delicatessen."

Fields made some rapid calculations on his pad; then he said, "All right this time—drive on." He went up to check the story with the cook, and was chagrined to find nothing actionable.

Carlotta Monti supervised the buying and much of the preparation of food in the Fields household. Her genius in this line was exceptional; after his death she acted as special kitchen overseer for a number of first-grade restaurants. In consequence of her ministrations the comedian's meals were always gourmet's delights, although he himself often did little more than nibble at them. Miss Monti and Miss Michael also helped him decorate rooms, an enterprise for which he had great enthusiasm. His bedroom was done in blue, his favorite color. They went on expeditions to pick out drapes, at which times Fields bargained shrewdly, displaying expert knowledge of textures, dyes, and other important features. The centerpiece of his bedroom was an enormous fourposter, which Miss Monti bought him. Because of his cussedness with the landlord, his screens gave out, and neither he nor the landlord would buy new ones. For a few weeks bugs came and went freely through gaping, rusted-out holes in the wire. Fields then conceived the idea of replacing the wire with cheesecloth, to the raucous scorn of Bob Howard. "It won't work," the trainer told him. "The first good rain will fix them." Fields went ahead and bought about fifty yards of cheesecloth and spent several days tacking it up around his windows. The makeshift screens became a symbol of the striving between him and Howard. Fields won; they remained steadfast in the stormiest weather, and he found some way to allude to them in every argument with Howard.

During the fourteen years Miss Monti and the comedian knew each other, they interrupted their friendship several times. Like all the great attachments of history, theirs was bumpy. Fields had undergone certain hardships with female companions; he was wary of encroachments. Miss Monti sang, a circumstance that bothered Fields terribly. She spent hours taking auditions, consulting band leaders, practicing arias, and talking about music. He often asked her to give it all up, and at the same time he begged her to quit eating peppers, something else that irritated him. He once mentioned both of those annoyances, which he regarded as about equally aggravating, in a letter to her when, under the name of Ramona Rey, she was taking time out to sing with a band in Santa Barbara. "I'm sorry I get excited when I talk to you on the phone about singing," he said. "You have made up your mind to sing and eat peppers because you like them and to hell with the consequence, and why I should interfere with you I do not know unless it is that I am cuckoo."

Fields' communications to Miss Monti were filled with both lectures and mild, curiously impersonal endearments. He began one of them by saying that here was another of those "schoolmarm letters." Then he went on to denounce her indicated plan to sing for soldier and sailor camps, calling it an adventure of exhibitionism and saying that he had a "deeper interest" in her. At the end of the exhibitionism, he said, he wished to know that she would have a place to eat and sleep in case something terrible happened to him —something terrible meaning "kicking the bucket." As the letter progressed, Fields' interest took a paradoxical twist, for he announced that he was having his bank discontinue her weekly payment of twenty-five dollars. Instead, he said, he was going to deposit twenty-five dollars in her account until he thought it was time to cease. Her singing in "saloons," he went on, was a more expensive hobby than playing golf, polo, "and I was going to say horse racing." She repeatedly told him how she suffered, he said, but she still continued. She was a masochist—deriving pleasure from making herself suffer, and he was not going to be a party to such "goddamned nonsense." Fields wound up this billet-doux with a melancholy "Amen," adding that if she wished to be a martyr she could do so at her own expense, and signed himself "Father Favania Fields."

Fields covered broad terrain in his letters to Miss Monti, but the questions of money and her career never eluded him for long. Throughout, she remained one of the least mercenary of girls, but he worried that she might conceive delusions of privilege. Often he inserted small, protective legal phrases among his advices. "Now you are making $60 a week which is ample for anyone even in these days to live on," he told her in 1943. "You insist on emoting on the radio gratis. Your voice reaches very few people—I might add very few people of consequence—that would help you in your career . . . However, I shall open an account for you at the [Security First National Bank] and at the end of the year you will have something to show for getting all hot and bothered and nervous and sick headaches. This is not obligatory on my part and can be discontinued at any time.

"I'm sorry you are not feeling so well, but that daily grind, the twice nightly performance, trying to get new material, rehearsing and altercating with the union and the orchestra leader will drag anyone down," he went on. "I have never had much time for unions or orchestra leaders or anyone, for that matter, that confines themselves entirely to music. They feel so god-damned superior and have so little interest in anyone or anything else in the world but their lousy music. (Pleasant company always accepted) but I do like folks who scatter their interests."

Fields scattered his interests, or complaints, in all of his letters to Miss Monti. She was, for example, made privy to his rows with the studios. "I have asked the studio [Paramount] to call off my contract which amounts to $300,-000 and percentages," he told her in one hand-written document covering several pages. "It seems a weird thing to do. But when you have the Director, Supervisor* and writer trying to run the picture, you know you are headed for oblivion. I do not think they will accept my suggestions. If they do, I will be happy. If they don't I will be happy because I can then make a new contract, be my own supervisor, and I hope then to have full charge of the picture, unless some unforseen circumstance shows its ugly head. In any event something very big and important is bound to come of it. I have them by the clock-weights and I am not going to let go until they say uncle or spit tobacco."

Fields enlarged this theme soon afterward, saying, "I have partially patched up my fight with the writers and with X at the studio. Everything may come out right after all. I wish some day I could go in and make a picture the

---

* Note: Fields' distaste for producers was so ripe that he could seldom bring himself to utter the hateful word; he preferred to coin a synonym.

way I want to without having to lick everybody from the gateman to the President of the Company." This problem shelved in his mind, he shifted to a lyric vein touching on horticulture: "The lawn here has been fertilized and the grass is beautifully green. The flowers are in bloom, the poinsettias are at least twelve feet high. The eucalyptus trees are bearing a beautiful very pale blue flower and it looks like spring rather than the death of summer . . ." He concluded, though, with his usual piece of philosophical counsel. "You may still make the grade," he confided in a burst of muted optimism about her career. "From the beginning I have always considered it lost motion. But I am not always right. Then what? Well, you can be independent —define that. Do something, if you are capable and fortunate enough to find that that something will make you happy. The only happiness or consolation I have ever found is to be satisfied with what you have. Make the best of it and keep trying to climb a little higher. But never throw away the dirty water before you get clean . . ."

In almost none of his letters to Miss Monti did Fields permit himself so much as a "hell" or a "damn," and his subscriptions were those of a schoolboy writing to a cherished sister. During his life, the comedian had intimations of a sheriff's posse close behind with shotguns, and his missives to many persons were weighted with plans for "getting away." "I feel certain I shall go to Rio this winter and then fly over to Santiago, Chile," he told a Hollywood friend after signing a contract to write magazine articles deriding temperance. "On the southern trip I will naturally have to go through the Canal, and returning north take a west coast boat if possible. Do you know of anyone who can speak Portuguese or Spanish, as I feel I shall need an interpreter. The following year I am going to China and Japan, with a day's stop off at Manila. I will then have seen every country in the world and I can come back here and lie back on my pillow and just write for my coffee and doughnuts. This is just a dream, but all of my dreams have come true up to now. So maybe I will really go. I haven't had a drink of hard 'liker' for over a week, but I am bending the Elbo on Amber brew and that is a cinch to quit. I didn't want to go off altogether too sudden, for that is what did the damage last time."

There are few samples extant of Fields letters which the writer signed by pen with his right name. He had superstitions about affixing his name to documents of any sort; usually he contrived a humorous alias or nickname. Even though his stationery—a gay blue like his bedroom—had a white longhand "W. C. Fields" engraved diagonally across the top, the name at the bottom often turned out to be something quite baffling. He was represented by several different handles to Miss Monti. One of his favorites was "Continental Man," which was appended to letters in which he addressed her as "Dear Chinese People." He was also fond of "Continental Claude," "Continental Person," and "The Great Man." For telegrams, Fields generally used the name "Ampico J. Steinway," badly confusing a telegraph girl in his neighborhood, who always recognized him if he came into the office. With wires of a straightaway, serious nature, such as "Leaving today. See you Monday," he would wind up, with a delicate flourish, "Ampico J. Steinway," and eye her belligerently, as if inviting her to make something out of it. "Your address, Mr. Steinway?" she would ask, and he'd say, "2015 De Mille Drive."

"The same as Mr. W. C. Fields?"

"He's my butler," the great man would reply, and sometimes give her a nickel tip.

Miss Monti and Miss Michael, between them, kept his house in order and made his life much easier. For long periods he would refuse invitations and confine his recreation to quiet dinners at home, or drives in his cars. The family dinners often included Bob Howard and his wife and Fields' occasional agent, Charlie Beyer, and his wife. "Mr. Fields got a great many invitations to go out," Miss Michael said. "He always accepted them, at first. Then, as the time approached, he got cold feet and began to think up ways to get out of them." Fearful of offending anybody, he usually presented, in the end, as many as six or seven excuses, most of them conflicting. They went out by various means. A day or two before the event, he might call up, in a faint, hoarse voice, and say he had just contracted double pneumonia and wasn't expected to live until morning. The next day, still worrying, he would send a telegram saying he had been called to Mobile, Alabama, on business and wouldn't be back until spring. Before the time of the function arrived, he always had Magda Michael telephone and add something even more fantastic. Once he was asked to speak before the Los Angeles Bar Association. Fields was flattered; he said immediately, in his most expansive drawl, "Why, I'd be glad to—used to be a member of the Bar myself, always had a warm spot for it." When the lawyer who invited him left, Miss Michael said, "Mr. Fields, you know you have no intention of making that speech."

"Nonsense," he said. "I'm going upstairs to write it right now." He scratched around at his desk for a couple of days, then he began to get anxious. Miss Michael stood by watching, offering no suggestions, curious to see how long he would hold out before running up the distress signals. On the second day before the meeting, he came to her and said, "I guess I'm just a worthless old son of a bitch. I can't make that speech—I'd be scared stiff."

"All right," she told him, "I'll get you out of it, but next time why don't you say no right at the start?"

"I'll do it, I'll do it," he agreed. "That's the way to handle these things."

She telephoned the lawyer and informed him that Fields was down with a serious case of influenza, but Fields, listening in the next room, sang out, "Tell him I'll make it at next month's meeting without fail!"

He liked to take Miss Monti and Miss Michael in the big Lincoln and park near the corner of Hollywood and Vine, where they could watch the people. He would keep up a running commentary for hours on the citizens that passed before their view. His remarks were wholly uncomplimentary. "See that fat one," he said one afternoon, "the old girl with the coal bucket on her head and the bundle under her arm? You know what's in that bundle? Lime. She's killed her husband, the poor devil had been working for forty years to keep her in ugly hats, and she conked him with an andiron two hours ago and put him in the bathtub. Now tonight, when it's good and dark, she'll drag him out in the back and bury him. For two cents I'd call a policeman. Oh, oh, here comes something—*Godfrey Daniel!* look at that beaver! Ten to one that bastard's wanted by the FBI . . ."

While Fields' characterizations of the people on the streets, and particularly the women, were uniformly scurrilous, he could form tender, disinterested attachments. Of one young married couple that called at his house, he kept saying, "Now aren't they cute? I certainly do enjoy seeing them together." He invited them back several times to the family dinners, and was gallant to both the bride and groom. "He would compliment the girl on little things about her clothes," said Miss Michael. "Mr. Fields often surprised women by being noticing about things men seldom see, and of course they liked it." In a few months, when the girl had a baby, he loaded her hospital room with flowers. "I'm going to keep an eye on that youngster," he told his household. "With nice parents like that, he's bound to go someplace."

"I think Mr. Fields saw something clean and simple about the couple he would have liked for himself, if things had turned out differently," Miss Michael felt. He was out in his flower garden a year later when he got news that the baby, who had meningitis, had died. He grieved for weeks, and on the following Mother's Day he suffered torments about the propriety of sending the young bride flowers. "Flowers are for the living," he said to Miss Michael, as he insisted many times on other occasions. He finally ordered four dozen yellow roses and sent them to the couple, with a card saying, "Thinking of you both on this Mother's Day." They called him up that evening; he left the phone blowing his nose and complaining loudly about "a rotten connection"—one of his regular peeves.

Fields' agonies over the chances of hurting people's feelings sometimes assumed strange proportions. J. Edgar Hoover, the head of the F.B.I., once asked permission to call, and Fields, when he arrived, was deeply impressed. Over a long evening they exchanged priceless discussions of their professions. Hoover's composure was not at all jarred by the fact that Fields, who had trouble with unridiculous names, kept calling him "Herbert." Later, when the comedian realized his mistake, he stewed about possible remedial steps. He started several explanatory letters, switched to telegrams, tore them up, and finally asked Magda Michael's advice. "I'd just forget it," she told him. "I'm sure Mr. Hoover didn't give it a thought." Fields seemed relieved, but he hoped Hoover would call again, "so I can relieve him of the Presidency."

The emotional implications of Christmas bothered Fields; he pretended to detest it. As a rule, he announced several days beforehand that he was going to be "away." He wanted no fuss made. But as the neighborhood took on its colors and sounds of the season, he fell uneasily into line. One Christmas on De Mille Drive, his household gave him a party. "You always pay the bills," they told him. "This year we'll take care of everything." They got fine wines and food, decorated a handsome tree, and bought him several costly presents. All day long he was bursting with pride. He even ate two helpings of turkey, by way of celebration, and sang Christmas carols into the night. "You know," he kept saying afterward, "that was fun. That was the best Christmas I can remember." But the next year he was as quick as ever to damn the "mawkish festivity" of a holiday which touched some wellspring of sentiment that he preferred not to acknowledge.

When Fields was feeling up to par, he enjoyed occasional recreations with his male friends. He, Fowler, La Cava, Roland Young, John Decker, Jack Oakie, the Barrymores, and a few others, often went to the West Coast football games; in fact, largely for this purpose he bought a trailer, with a built-in bar and refrigerator. The group would load up, roll off to some place like the Rose Bowl, set up on a handy stretch of greensward, and approach football in a proper, civilized spirit. They were devoted students of the game. They would go up in the stands and watch a few plays, then come down and take them apart over several rounds of a popular tipple. Comedian Guy Kibbee, who had a trailer, too, liked to follow along and park beside them. Rather than drink, he preferred to place his spectator emphasis on food, and he would join them, his hands filled with fancy sandwiches, cakes and pies. Kibbee had a tent which they would pitch, leaving the flaps up on especially hot days.

This sporting group also attended the fights, in Jim Jeffries' Barn, out in San Fernando Valley. Fields watched the papers carefully for announced matches of his favorite pugilist, a scrawny, attenuated man named Claude Nesselrode, who seemed to spend an unconscionable amount of time on the canvas. The comedian would call Fowler, say, "Claude's fighting tonight," and Fowler would reply, "Who's his opponent?"

"The Burmese Crusher."

"What's the odds?"

"Morning line was 38 to 1 against Claude."

"Well," Fowler would say, "we'd better go out and give him a hand."

During the afternoon the trailer would be iced and provisioned, and evening saw the happy band rolling toward another feature attraction in Fields' cavalcade of sports. Once at the arena, they would get ringside seats, after some preliminary banter with Jim Jeffries, who had mixed feelings about their patronage. The old-time champion liked them all, but he sometimes wondered if they had the reverent regard for the game that ringsiders ought to have. For example, as their hero came stilting down the aisle they might chant, "N-E-S, Nes; S-E-L, Sel; R-O-D-E, Rode— that's the way to spell it, here's the way to yell it—NES-SELRODE!"

"Claude," Fields would tell the beanpole, having left his seat to creep to the fighter's corner, "play it smart. Let him hit you for a few rounds. Tire him out. Keep coming in— every time he thinks he's got you, shove that chin forward again."

Nesselrode's chances were ordinarily quite slight, but they were seldom improved by his cheering section. By the time he reached the center of the ring, his eyes were glazed and he was pretty well marked up mentally.

Undoubtedly Fields' happiest sport was golf. He was an expert player, whose game was improved by cheating. His most frequent opponent was La Cava, but they both belonged to a little group known as the Divot Diggers, whose members kept trying new courses. Fields' and La Cava's friendship was strained on the golf course. They both went around in the eighties, and they bet heavily. La Cava believed that, during the years they played together, Fields availed himself of every advantage possible to a competitive golfer. To begin with, he kept careful track of La Cava's professional life and always called about golf when the director had just finished a picture and was physically and emotionally exhausted. In this way, Fields was able to win two Lincoln sedans from La Cava.

On the course itself Fields had many devices to protect his interests. He carried a pocketful of change, which he rattled noisily when La Cava was putting. He was also given to paroxysms of coughing and wild, unexpected slaps at non-existent flies. As La Cava drove off the tee, Fields could usually be found scrubbing up a ball with raspy, irritating vigor. Of all the golfers who had ever played the game, he probably got the most consistently good lies. If his ball was in a hole or other disadvantageous spot, he would point to a fictitious airplane then roll the ball over with his club. His juggling grace enabled him to avoid being caught. One day, smarting under this style of play, La Cava blew up and said, "Look here, damn you, we'll play these things where they lie from now on. I'm going to get two caddies—one for me and another to watch you."

Fields said he would get two caddies himself. They returned to the clubhouse, hired the additional caddies, and started out again. From the first tee La Cava's ball hopped into a gopher hole. "What am I supposed to do about that?" he asked.

"Too bad, too bad," said Fields. "You'll have to play it."

La Cava took a number-seven iron and in eight strokes unearthed the ball, together with some old bones and rock formations. He finished the hole in thirteen, in a very dusky humor. However, two holes later Fields sliced over a fence that marked the club's boundary and into the city dump. They located his ball in the center of some discarded bedsprings.

"I'll throw out and count a stroke," he said.

"You'll shoot out if it takes till midnight," said La Cava.

Fields pointed up, cried, "Wild geese!" and rattled the springs with his club.

"Lying two," called La Cava cheerfully.

Fields broke a new mashie on the bedsprings without moving the ball, and went back to the clubhouse, where La Cava found him an hour or so later, seated in a deck chair on the lawn and with a colored waiter standing by holding martinis.

On one of the group's golfing trips, to Del Monte, La Cava made the mistake of sharing a room with Fields. The two were to be matched against each other the next day. After dinner, La Cava took a walk around the grounds;

then he returned to their room, planning to get some sleep, so as to be fresh and in top form for tomorrow. Fields was seated in one corner with a washtub full of iced beer at his feet. "I got the management to bring this up," he said. "We'll make a night of it."

"We'll do nothing of the kind," said La Cava. "I engaged this room to sleep in."

"Well, I'm going to drink beer in my half," Fields told him. Because of his insomnia, he needed little sleep, and he had fixed on a sure way to get a good handicap. As La Cava tossed and turned, Fields came and went throughout the night, always carrying a beer bottle. He exclaimed rapturously over the dawn. "Get up, get up!" he yelled at the director. "What a sky!"

"Would you mind shutting up?" La Cava said. "I haven't had an hour's sleep all night."

"See the sunrise," said Fields. "You're a movie director, you're supposed to like beauty, get up and look at the sunrise."

"Describe it to me," said La Cava.

During the match that followed, La Cava was obliged to sit down for ten-minute stretches under palm trees. He was beaten handily.

Fields' sporting group had a sad but interesting time when John Barrymore died in May of 1942. The family arranged a big funeral, as befitted a public figure of Barrymore's stature, and the undertaking company in charge spared no pains to see that the last, bereaved tribute should be memorable. Producer Nunnally Johnson, who attended, recalled a peculiar cleavage among the mourners. On one side of the chapel sat the Barrymore family and certain elderly friends, people long devoted to restrained behavior; on the other side were grouped the departed's rowdy boon companions. There was evidence of hostility between the two factions. One was in favor of preserving the traditional solemnity of funerals, the other made known its wishes audibly from time to time with statements like, "Let's step outside for a drink— Jack'd want it that way," and "We've got to carry on!"

"The first thing I saw when I walked in was old John Carradine sittin' there rockin' back and forth and keenin' so you could hear him all over the church," said Johnson, whose speech retained a slight, attractive Southern accent.

At the conclusion of the service, Fowler, who was close to the Barrymore family and had attended in a mortician's limousine, walked outside and bumped into Fields.

"Don't be a sucker," hissed the comedian, motioning with distaste toward the lugubrious black carrier. "Ride back in my car with me." They got into the rear seat of Fields' Lincoln, and the chauffeur wheeled slowly into the long line of moving vehicles. Fowler was impressed by the fact that, although the day was excessively warm, Fields had most of the rear interior, including their feet, protected by a fur lap robe. When the procession had gone about a mile down the avenue, Fields leaned forward and said to the chauffeur, "This will do."

"Here, sir?" the man asked.

"The vacant lot off to the right."

They pulled up and Fields threw aside the robe, revealing a large icebox containing beer, bottles of gin and vermouth, and several tall tumblers autographed by movie stars and bearing the legend, "Earl Carroll's Restaurant."

"What will you have to drink, a beer or a martini?" he said.

"Both," replied Fowler.

"A very wise decision," said Fields.

The comedian made the martinis by pouring gin and vermouth into the tumblers and shaking the mixture against the palm of his hand. He made two double ones, opened two beers, then told the chauffeur to drive on. As they stopped for a light, a pair of patrolmen in a prowl car, bent on enforcing the Los Angeles law against drinking in automobiles, pulled up beside them. Fields leaned out of a window and regarded them sternly. He said, "Sorry, my fine public servants, but I haven't enough of this nectar to pass about willy-nilly." To his chauffeur he shouted, "Drive on!" The patrolmen, confused, let them go.

At the next stop light they drew up beside one of the undertaker's machines and noticed Earl Carroll, a lone, huddled mourner, seated in the back.

Fields said to Fowler, "There is an old program boy. I've known him for years. What is your pleasure?"

"I'd offer a man like that a drink," said Fowler. Fields

nodded and they called to Carroll, who climbed out of the limousine with great alacrity and into Fields' car. Not bothering to greet him in any way, Fields mixed a third martini in one of the showy tumblers. Carroll took it, examined it gravely, and drank the cocktail without comment. They continued down the street in the sun. Near his mansion, Carroll said, "Come and have a drink with me." Once inside, he went to his bar and mixed some martinis, which he poured into three beautiful crystal glasses. Handing the glasses to his guests, he observed a trifle acidly that "These weren't stolen."

From Carroll's they went to the home of John Decker. By a remarkable coincidence, Decker made drinks for them, and for Tony Quinn, Herbert Marshall, Roland Young, and several others, in glasses that bore the inscription "Club Eugene." Fields felt much better; later on he confided that before he saw Decker's glasses he had been on the point of returning Carroll's tumblers.

That night on the way home he stopped by Fowler's briefly, and the next morning Fowler noticed that he had left a new hat—an expensive black fedora, size seven and a half, from Desmond's in Beverly Hills—hanging on a peg in a closet off Fowler's study. Informed by telephone where the hat was, Fields said, "I left it there on purpose. I bought it for the funeral and I never want to see it again."

It continued to hang there untouched, dusty like the little toy dog, for more than twenty years.

CHAPTER TWENTY-SEVEN

IN THE MIDDLE 1930s Fields' rocklike constitution began to crumble. The prodigious quantities of liquor which he consumed could not have failed to take their toll. His resistance to disease weakened, various of his internal organs became impaired, and at length, in 1935, he went to Seboba Hot Springs, a health resort, for a season of recovery. He had been ill throughout the filming of *Poppy,* an illness brought on when he injured his sacroiliac in reaching for an impossible tennis shot on his Encino court. His struggles to avoid collapsing on the *Poppy* sets aroused the admiring wonder of everybody making the picture. Oddly enough, at these times he tried to perpetuate the myth that he was drunk. "I'd rather have people think I was drunk than sick," he told director Eddie Sutherland.

"Bill was only in a few scenes," said Sutherland. "We had to use his double, Johnny Sinclair, in everything but the close-ups." One scene required Fields to crawl out from under a sink. By this time his equilibrium had gone bad and he was scarcely able to walk. But he got under the sink, then, with his jaw set, began the torturing process of trying to stagger out, half crawling and half walking. He couldn't make it. As the others watched, anxious not to interfere and hurt his feelings, he got up and fell down three times. "Bill," said Sutherland, "let Johnny under there— he's an old plumber and knows how it's done."

"Sure," said Sinclair, "I never really feel at ease anywhere else."

Sinclair played about 75 per cent of the scenes that supposedly featured Fields: Fields authentically appeared in the other 25 per cent. Though sick, he was no less autocratic, mulish, and irritating. He had fixed on a new word (he often carried a pocket dictionary to look up words with which he was unfamiliar), and had adopted "redundancy" as having agreeable possibilities of articulation. To the dismay of the script writers, about every fifth line he lifted his hat and, with a pleasing sneer, cried, "Pardon my redundancy," apropos of nothing. Fields in this period was approaching an almost fatal illness, and he had never been funnier. His condescension, the spurious bereavement of a man once used to elegance, as he approached a hot-dog stand with Rochelle Hudson, was a kind of key to his whole stage character. "A little *fois gras,* something to spread on it?" he asked the counterman, after viewing the naked wiener. And when he heard the snarling reply,

"What's that, brother?" he hastily exclaimed, "Pardon my redundancy," and took a forlorn, ignoble bite.

Sam Hardy accompanied Fields to Seboba Hot Springs. Both Magda Michael and Carlotta went along, too, and arranged themselves in cottages at the resort. Fields had been told that the continued use of liquor would hamper his recovery, so he stepped up his daily consumption about 20 per cent, in an effort to make liars out of the doctors. He failed spectacularly. His soul rebelled at the necessity for hiring doctors in the first place, and he never lost an opportunity to insult them. To the curious press he issued bulletins explaining how he passed his time. "I'm preparing a movie called *The High Cost of Dying*," he was quoted as saying. Sam Hardy drove back and forth between Seboba and Hollywood, where he lived with his wife. In his solicitude for his old friend he probably gave little thought to his own health. Hardy's wife called the resort one morning to say that Sam wouldn't be out that day; he was having some pains in his chest. Late that night the owner of Seboba Hot Springs walked into Fields' room, with a downcast look, and started to speak, but Fields saved him the trouble. "Sam Hardy's dead," he said.

He fretted that he was unable to go to the funeral. He sent Magda Michael, and when she returned he wanted details. "How did Sam look?" he said. "I hope he had on his blue suit—that was his favorite." The comedian seemed relieved that Hardy had looked spruce and lifelike, an unusual reaction, since Fields detested the idea of funerals. Not long afterward, another of his old friends, Will Rogers, died in the airplane crash with Wiley Post. Fields was hard hit by these two tragedies during his illness. He talked about them, and recounted many anecdotes from the lives of both men. He kept saying, "You know, the last newspaper piece Will wrote before he died was about me."

As Fields continued to drink, and to disregard other basic rules for invalids, his condition worsened, and some weeks later he was removed to Riverside Hospital, with a critical case of pneumonia and many complications. For a considerable time he lay at the point of death, in an oxygen tent, fighting, the physicians thought, an uphill and losing battle. In the bleakest hour of his travail, several of his intimates—Eddie Sutherland, Fowler, and others—came to the hospital. They were admonished to be quiet and were admitted to the sickroom. Fields had been unconscious, but he suddenly opened his eyes and summoned them with a feeble gesture of an index finger. The group approached and Sutherland leaned forward. "Oh, ye of little faith," whispered the comedian, and straightway began to rally.

When the pneumonia had subsided, he left Riverside Hospital for Las Encinas Sanitarium, still a very sick man. He told Magda Michael he regretfully must let her go for a while, and she returned home, but Carlotta Monti stayed with him at the sanitarium for months. At first he was in a private room and with two nurses in attendance; later he was moved to a cottage, where Miss Monti could be within call of his bedside. The long addiction to alcohol had overtaken him at last. He had many of the traditional symptoms of delirium tremens—hallucinations, grotesque visitations, nostalgic evocations. Once, as Miss Monti sat holding his hands, he screamed that watches were materializing between all of his fingers. Much later, when he had recovered, he alluded to this fancy in a letter to Miss Monti, taking the opportunity to combine it with a lecture on her singing, as usual. He asked if she remembered when he was in Las Encinas and suffering from paresthesia, then recalled that he had remonstrated with her for not gathering up the watches that he believed he was pulling out from "betwixt my fingers." The letter went on to thank Miss Monti for her kindness in telling him the unvarnished truth about his condition, and he said he wanted to "reciprocate" her kindness. She had fooled around for five or six years without obtaining even "a modicum of success," he said, with the result that she had "suffered and your friends have suffered with you."

Fields often made his shortcomings the basis for stern moral admonitions to others. At the same time, he never forgot Miss Monti's devotion when he was stricken. Among other ways of showing his appreciation, he had a doctor flown to her when, a year or so afterward, she was on location working in a movie in the northern California mountains and was laid low by what was diagnosed as chipmunk fever, said to have been the second such case in California history. He was acutely grateful for the visits and other expressions of loyalty by his friends and acquaintances.

Fields was always similarly grateful for fan letters; he would brag about them, and he tried to answer them all personally. Mrs. Fowler frequently made cakes and sent them to the sanitarium. Dave Chasen took him the choicest edibles of his extravagant kitchen; Grady sneaked bottles in to him; and many additional well-wishers responded variously. In a letter to Fowler, Fields mentioned that Franklin Pangborn had just been out; an attached clipping, a news photo of an officer of the anti-Negro Columbians, bore the penciled comment: "If you do not believe in Darwin's theory that man emanated from the animal, look at the figure on the left."

There were times, at Las Encinas, when only reminders of the changing moods of nature could soothe him. Perhaps of all the natural phenomena, rain pleased him most. He loved rain; often, when he was well, he would go out bareheaded and stand in his yard when showers came. Miss Michael believes that rain conveyed a feeling of isolation and a sense of mankind's insignificance to Fields. "He felt that somehow a moratorium was declared on all his troubles when it was raining," she says. California, while a very cornucopia in some other respect, is a vexatious place for rain lovers. There are long stretches of each year when rain is not only non-existent but many citizens are laying bets that it is not likely ever to rain again. Miss Monti overcame this deficiency, if deficiency it be, very neatly. She bought a garden hose, attached it to a handy tap, and sprayed water on his cottage's tin roof. He responded well to the treatment; usually he went peacefully to sleep, his mind purged of whatever torments were assailing him before the rains came. A little later, when he could go outside, she rigged up a lawn umbrella, and while he rested beneath it she sat in a chair somewhat removed and pelted his retreat with the hose. It made an interesting sight for visitors to the spa—the famous comedian reading under his make-believe shower, the pretty Mexican near by playing God.

Both Magda Michael and Charlie Beyer, his agent, went out frequently to keep him posted on matters mundane. He was always glad to see them, though Beyer sometimes irritated him, as he did in other places. The agent had a harmless speech habit, a trick of greeting acquaintances with, "Hello, what's new?" and Fields regarded it as the essence of foolishness. Beyer would breeze into the sanitarium, give an affable, extroverted wave of the hand, and cry, "Hello, Bill, what's new?" Fields would rise up from his bed of pain and yell, "How the hell would I know, you half-wit? I've been in a hospital for three months." He was so incensed that he once had Miss Michael bring out a dictaphone, which he hooked up in an unobtrusive spot. When Beyer arrived and performed the inquisitive rite, Fields played the record back to him. "Now, how does that sound to *you?*" he said.

Fields' relationship with his agent was as peculiar as it was with most people who served him. As the comedian saw it, Beyer's function was to act as errand boy. Fields kept him hot on the trail. If negotiations were afoot, Beyer was obliged to run back and forth to the party of the second part and deliver all manner of insults from his boss. "He won't take a hundred thousand, he'll take two hundred thousand, and he said to tell you that you're a goddamned sneak and a cheap grafter" was a typical message from Fields. Throughout their association, Fields spent most of his time trying to beat Beyer down from the customary 10 per cent to five.

Even when his life was running lowest, Fields retained clear fiscal impressions. He was disturbed that his accommodations were so costly—at one time he was reputed to be paying the sanitarium $500 a week—and on occasions, after a pathetic rally, he would raise his head slightly and gasp, "We're scraping the bottom of the barrel." Once he dispatched Miss Michael and Beyer to a certain office he had rented, under the name of Felton J. Satchelstern, wherein lay ten thousand dollars of his capital. "Here's the combination," he whispered. "Go to the safe and get the money—it's urgent." Mystified but obedient, they drove to the hideout and opened the safe. They found various papers—prison notices, marked items that Fields intended to blast in letters, and other mementos of his personal life—but no ten thousand. They went back and reported that the bills were missing. "It worked," Fields cried feverishly. "The man was telling the truth," and he leaned back and laughed till the tears came. It developed that the safe had a secret compartment, invulnerable to thieves, as advertised by the fellow who sold it. Later on, Fields took Miss Michael and Beyer to the office, and after a good deal of mumbo jumbo uncovered the cash.

Though Fields put up a brave show of good spirits at Las Encinas, he suffered the tortures of the damned. Miss Michael remembered a sad afternoon when Jim Tully was in the sanitarium, with the illness that was to end in his death, and was wheeled over to visit his old friend. Both men were so sick they had no heart for conversation. Tully at length smiled weakly, and Fields just nodded in agreement. "I couldn't help thinking," Miss Michael said, "that here were these two famous men, with all the rewards life could give them, and either one would have given it all for a little health and peace."

At one stage of his illness Fields had a dreadful seizure of polyneuritis. His whole body was sensitized so that the lightest touch was torture. It was necessary to chloroform him to cut his fingernails and toenails. Even the weight of a sheet caused him agony. A new nurse coming on decided to change his pajamas. For some reason, she got mixed up and tried to pull a pillowcase, instead of the pajamas, over his feet. The pillowcase understandably refused to come up, and she tried to solve the problem by yanking it. The pain was so numbing, and the cause so senseless, that Fields was more angry than injured. He sat up and gave the nurse such a flagrant cursing that he bragged about it forever afterward. "I knew then I was all right," he said later. "I was going to get well."

Convalescent, he began to think again about his work. With Miss Michael and Miss Monti he went over script ideas and at odd times wrote down scraps of dialogue and skeleton plots. Some of the movie people were organizing a radio jubilee for Adolph Zukor, and they asked Fields to broadcast from his sickroom, a request that started the comedian on a successful venture in yet another medium. His voice came over the air with such resonance and comic effect that, when he went home in a few weeks, the Chase and Sanborn Coffee Company wanted him for a series of broadcasts with Edgar Bergen and his wooden dummy. For two years his asthmatic feuds with Charlie McCarthy were an important part of the Sunday night scene, like querulous youngsters and cold chicken.

For the series with Bergen, Fields reportedly got $6500 a week. The New York advertising agency that handled the program, J. Walter Thompson, sent a radio writer, Dick Mack, out to help Fields. Like the other Fields' collaborators, Mack had his troubles. He would send a prepared script to Fields' home around the first of every week for "editing." But with Fields, editing took the form of throwing out all the lines assigned to him and substituting creations of his own. He and Mack had spirited wrangles. Fields never altered a word in another actor's lines; his attitude was that if an actor wished to trust himself to anybody as freakish as a writer, it was on his own head. After the comedian had read the script, Mack would drive out to his home and they would square off, then go over it together. Rehearsals were held at the studio on Saturday and again early Sunday. Fields was driven down by his chauffeur, arriving with a retinue of secretaries, butlers, nurses, and others, amid great pomp. On Sunday night the production staff always displayed agitation over his script, to which he clung doggedly. "Any changes, Bill?" they would say, and the comedian would reply, "No, I'm going to do it just as it is." In an aside to Miss Michael he would add, "We won't show the damned thing to them—the hell with them." The production people would explain that the final version must be on file at "the New York office" before the show. At that stage, Fields had no idea what they meant by the New York office, and cared less. When it came time to do the program, he just said what he pleased, without worrying about J. Walter Thompson, Chase and Sanborn, the National Broadcasting Company, or even radio in general. By extreme good fortune Bergen was a man with an exceptionally nimble mind, and he made out skillfully without cues.

Fields' radio employers had to handle him with kid gloves. As he had grown older, his speaking tempo had slowed down, and he sent them into prostrations of nervousness by dragging the show. When they remonstrated, he would say, as he had said to Mack Sennett, "Well, you'd better get yourself another boy." The production staff eventually depended upon Magda Michael's influence. She could often lead Fields to the trough, and even make him drink by simple tricks of psychology. The basic principle of her method was flattery. If she wished to speed him up, she first spent ten minutes telling him how faultlessly, how stunningly he had done the passage. "It was probably the best reading anyone has ever heard on radio," she would say. "You have no idea how they admire you." Then she might add, in an elegiac tone, "Of course *they'd* like to make it slower, but I'm inclined to agree with you that a trifle more speed might get even more of the essential *you* in it." Fields would nod sagely, muttering, "You're right, you're right. The devil with them—we'll speed it up."

He continually maintained that he was unable to find writers to suit him, but he tried to change everything they offered, no matter who they were. At one point he was dickering with Bugs Baer, who writes the column of newspaper humor, and with Gene Fowler, who had no intention of writing for him. In February of 1938 he told Baer that "Chase and Sanborn have discovered that they are not ruining as many livers as they would like to and would like me to run off at the mouth on the radio every Sunday for a few months." He wanted Baer and Fowler to "share part of the loot" with him, by writing him some ten- or twelve-minute scripts. "I'll make them do a thing that hasn't been done on the radio to date," Fields said. "I'll make them, at the conclusion of the performance, give credit to whosoever has written the material." As usual, he said he'd reserve the right to "collaborate upon and edit" the material on its arrival. "My present bite is $5000 a week, less commission," he told Baer, and that "would net either of you around $1200."

Why Fields gave the figure $5000 is something of a mystery, since his intimates, including Miss Michael, who was comparatively familiar with his finances, have agreed that his weekly check was $6500. In any case, the offer came to nothing, for neither Baer nor Fowler, though they loved him, ever wrote him any material.

Fields' lack of reverence for radio and everything connected with it, not excluding the advertising agencies, was notable. He was always involved in a squabble over money, material, time, personnel, or some additional aspect of his employment. He probably couldn't have stayed happy otherwise. In a letter to Fowler in 1937, he said that J. Walter Thompson objected to his burlesquing "that counterfeit" who talks through one nostril, advising child movie actresses not to play squat tag in asparagus beds. They also objected, he said, to his references to Walter Winchell, on the ground that he was too big to imitate such persons. Fields remarked that he didn't know how to take that. Later on he told Fowler that he and J. Walter Thompson had arrived at a definite agreement, "amenable and compatible to either side," which hinged on a colorful, unworkable system by which the agency could dispose of its "delicious coffee in its hermetically sealed, dated bags."

Chase and Sanborn and J. Walter Thompson were able to swallow Fields' unremitting insults for two years, and after that he went over to Lucky Strike, for $7500 a week, out of which he was to furnish his own material. Here again he ran into arguments, the crux of which was that Fields wished to lampoon advertisers, somewhat in the manner of Henry Morgan's gibes later on. After a series or so of broadcasts for the tobacco people he quit radio, mainly, he said, because it was too much trouble to find writers and he was too busy to do the whole job himself.

Fields lived at the sanitarium off and on until the spring of 1937. His condition had improved greatly, but his restlessness had grown painful. To Fowler in March of that year he telephoned that if he were well enough he would write him a funny letter. "Every time I get what I think is a funny idea," Fields said, "the goddamned croaker sends his bill in with nurses and room rent attached. Then Uncle Whiskers sends his insult from Washington, claiming everything you've got and an extra pair of pants as his share of the season's loot. Sure, I'm a good citizen."

When he again set up permanently at home, he went over his bills with tremendous anxiety. His long illness had been expensive, and he fought bitterly with his doctors. One of them, Dr. Jesse Citron, finally sued to force Fields to pay his bill of $12,000. The comedian considered the charge unreasonably high, and so did most of his friends. Thinking it over, he became so outraged that he filed a countersuit of $25,000, maintaining that his recovery had been impeded by narcotics Dr. Citron had given him. The actions seesawed expensively through the courts, as lawsuits do, and if the doctor's original solicitude had been worth $12,000, his legal ministrations perhaps canceled the good works out, for Fields was obliged to drag into court day after day, though he felt wretched and spent. At one point in the proceedings, the lawyers and judges expressed an interest in the comedian's income. "Come into court with all your records of the past year," they told him, or words to that effect. Fields appeared the following week without any visible impedimenta, and when he had ascended majestically to the stand, they said, "Where are the books?" From his pocket he withdrew a used check, on the back of which he had penciled a couple of sentences that gave, in a general, confused way, what his income had amounted to during the year past. Then he eyed the judge vindictively, his manner suggesting that he would be pleased to step into the alley and fight it out. The judge, who had different ideas, allowed the valuable Dr. Citron his $12,000. Fields never got to first base with his countersuit about the narcotics. Like many laymen, he was hopelessly lost in the dark labyrinth of an archaic legal system for tangling the civil affairs of man.

After the long illness, Fields' sleeping became an acute problem. Many nights he never got to sleep at all. His household could hear him, pacing the length of his padlocked room, seeking fatigue, calming his nerves, fighting the black despair of the insomniac. His discovery of sleeping pills tided him over the worst spots. On a little memo pad beside his desk he had written, "First pill 9 P.M., second pill 10 P.M., hope for best thereafter." Always it was his desire to spend his time profitably, and he read hundreds of books during the lonesome watches of his sleepless nights. As he read, he took detailed notes, largely for the purpose of extracting useful ideas. He went through newspapers, marked objectionable passages, sometimes pretty well covering the entire paper, and made reminders to write letters about them. Some nights he scribbled over dozens of sheets with dialogue, which he hoped to incorporate into movies. As often as not, he tore them all up the next morning. Once in a while, if feeling extraordinarily bold, he would arm himself and "make a search" of the grounds. During some of these excursions, as he frequently did in his room, he conducted a bluffing monologue, to indicate that he was not alone and that an intruder, if he didn't cut and run, would shortly find himself in a sorry mess. One of the comedian's servants, on a night when the moon was bright, saw him tiptoeing along, this time as silent as his shadow behind him, now stopping to listen, again feeling around bushes or birdbaths, the pistol high in his hand, the accusative nose uptilted at the old, familiar angle.

With Miss Monti and Miss Michael he liked to make week-end trips back to Seboba Hot Springs, to rest up and get away from his telephone. Because of his patronage, and the publicity it got, the place became popular, drawing from the city many other people suffering from faulty nerves, and some who hoped to acquire faulty nerves by fashionable exposure. Fields resented the progress of the resort. "The joint's getting crowded," he began to say, repeating his ancient refrain. Though his illness was abated, his mind, so long chafed by sick nerves, was more than ever subject to suspicions. One night as he sat on the porch of his bungalow, talking to his companions, two prize fighters came up and said, "Good evening, Mr. Fields." Their intention, as they sought relief from the monotony of their training, was nothing more sinister than to observe at close hand a man who had always delighted them. Fields, however, construed their presence as a plot to kidnap him. He had been expecting it for months, and he only wondered what had held them up. He jumped nimbly to his feet, ran inside, and came back out with his pistol. Aided by Miss Monti and Miss Michael, the fellows persuaded him of their harmless design, and Fields relaxed enough to converse with them for an hour or so, but he kept the pistol cocked and ready, on his lap.

The onset of his illness had brought from New York his wife and son, who moved to California, it was said, in order to help him in his hour of need. A story had gone around Hollywood, and even reached a few newspapers, including the column of Leonard Lyons, that Fields had refused the son admittance to his home. A visitor to Seboba one week end, William Le Baron, sounded Fields out on this rumor. "There wasn't anything to it, was there, Bill?" he said, probing gently.

"An unidentified youth put in an appearance at my gate," replied Fields with austerity.

"What happened?"

The youth had rung his bell, Fields related with pleasure, and had asked to see his father. This request, relayed

to the comedian by his butler, resulted in the butler's returning to the gate to ask for credentials. "I haven't got
anything but my driver's license," the young man said.

"I'll take that, sir," the butler told him, and carried it
in on a salver.

"He could have forged it," said Fields. "Go back and ask
him for additional proof."

"Well, I *know* he's my father," insisted the visitor a minute later. "I know it because I'm his son."

In the face of this deadly logic, Fields told the butler to
admit him. "I'll take a look," he said.

"Hello, Father," cried the young man, when he got inside. "How are you feeling?"

"Have a drink?" said Fields.

"Oh, fine, Father. Let's have a nice drink together."

"What'll it be?" asked Fields.

"Make mine a coke," said the youth in an abandoned
tone.

Fields opened his mouth and roared for the butler.
"Throw him out," he said. "He's no son of mine."

At the conclusion of this narrative, Le Baron said,
"Well, now, damn it, Bill, you ought to feel proud—a
grown son, a fine boy from what I hear, coming to see you
and all."

He watched Fields' face carefully in the moonlight, and
thought he saw a softening of the expression, even a hint
of moisture in the belligerent eyes. But the shifting palm
fronds play strange tricks with the moonlight, he concluded a moment afterward, for Fields suddenly opened
his mouth and gave vent to a raucous and disparaging
Bronx cheer.

Later on, Fields said that he had investigated the visit
and that the boy was not his son at all. "It was another
fellow entirely," he said. "I misunderstood the whole business."

Fields' friends believe that if he ever did deny any of
his family, it was because he felt that they made him seem
old. During the war, when his son's wife had a child, the
fact that Fields was a grandfather was advertised by Walter Winchell. Fields was gloomy. "I'm rooked," he told
Fowler, using one of his favorite terms. "It dates me." He
was always touchy about having his age mentioned; Mack

Sennett used to ruffle his feelings by saying, "I saw you juggle when I was a kid, Bill. You were wonderful."

"That's a lie, you old fraud," Fields would yell. "You're old enough to be my father." Now and then Fields told reporters he was single, a statement to which his son took pardonable umbrage. The son once forced a retraction from a national magazine which had quoted Fields on his unmarried state.

By request of his wife, Fields transported his new grandson from the hospital to his son's home in Beverly Hills, the son being away in the Navy. It was a singular trip. The chauffeur drove them—Fields, the estranged Mrs. Fields, his daughter-in-law, her mother from Massachusetts, and the babe in his swaddling clothes—in the big Lincoln. Fields devoted the trip, to his wife's horror, to a detailed explanation of how one could drink martinis without that fact being suspected from one's breath. He had two flasks, one containing martinis and the other containing a popular mouthwash. "You take a snort, like this," he said in the friendliest way to his son's mother-in-law, "and then you gargle with mouthwash. After that you spit out," and cranking down a window he gave a misty blow. His manner indicated that he hoped the visitor was chalking up the trick for future use.

Fields' sickness gave him a permanent worry about food and other shortages. He heard of the bitter malnutrition in Europe, and he took measures to ride out the scarcity. During the war he began to buy canned goods in large quantities. Once bought, they presented a serious problem of storage, which Fields solved, he thought, very ingeniously. What it boiled down to was that, at the time, he had among his servants only one, a maid, whom he trusted. It was in her room, therefore, that his stockpiles of commodity goods were heaped. At the outset of his hoarding, she and the others thought that his diligence would soon wane. But as the months went by, her situation became critical. To get to her closet, she had to shovel cans aside like a miner moving coal, and the nightly trip to bed was accomplished over shifting dunes of salmon, tuna, peaches, corned beef and carrots. The likelihood that Fields would ever eat any of this material, even if he was starving, was slight,

but its possession bucked him up. He was crestfallen when
the maid came forward with a badly injured shin and said,
"Mr. Fields, I don't think I can make it any longer. Up to
this week it was all right, if I took it slow, but that last load
of succotash is more than I can handle."

"Can't get to bed, eh?" said Fields.

"No, sir—I fell down twice last night," and she thrust
out the shin again.

"Well, now, we'll think of something, don't you fret,"
said Fields soothingly, afraid she would sue him. He
weighed the problem for several days, meanwhile holding
up on purchases, and finally announced that he had worked
everything out wonderfully. The only thing to do, he said,
was pick out a couple of items and keep them in *his*
room. For some reason he settled on beets and apricots.

The rumor once reached Fields' friends that he was planning to visit a black market. They determined to stop him.
John Decker obtained the address of the place, then drove
there and struck a deal with the proprietor. By the time
Fields arrived, with a commodious carrier for his acquisitions, the artist was dressed in a white apron and was wearing a false beard.

He came forward with cringing servility and said, "Wish
something, sir?"

"I'm having a look around," Fields told him.

"Make yourself at home, sir," said Decker, and followed
along behind. He kept muttering as they walked down the
aisles, and Fields looked back sharply from time to time.
He made out occasional words that sounded like "rich old
bastards" and "no-good capitalist cheats." He grew increasingly nervous as his inspection drew on and the phrases
became more insultingly distinct. Finally he blew up and
turned around, ready to do battle. "You're selling the stuff,
aren't you, you goddamned gangster?" he yelled. He set
up a noisy tirade of abusive language directed at "grafters
who take advantage of those fine boys fighting out there."

Decker pulled off his beard and said, "Glad to hear you
say so, Bill. We feel exactly the same."

Fields was in no mood for cordiality. He left in a huff.
Later on he was heard to say to another friend, "I was
surprised to hear that John Decker was seen frequenting

one of those dirty black markets." He himself never entered another one, so far as his friends or servants knew, as long as he lived.

CHAPTER TWENTY-EIGHT

Now, with his illness halted, Fields was ready for his last performances, the priceless but all-too-brief series he made for Universal. Except for *David Copperfield,* for which he was loaned to Metro-Goldwyn-Mayer, his pictures had been done for Paramount, but money disputes and other frictions caused him to seek another sponsor.

He was beginning the fresh decade of his sixties, one that he would not complete, and he was at the height of his powers. His illness, his troubles, his suspicions, his worries and frights had only served to sharpen his genius. He was at once at the twilight and at the climax of his career; he had brought into co-ordinated focus more than half a century of wonderfully varied research into the elusive organism of comedy. He knew what was funny, and scarcely a day went past that he failed to inform Universal of that fact. His four starring films for his new studio—*You Can't Cheat an Honest Man, My Little Chickadee, The Bank Dick,* and *Never Give a Sucker an Even Break*—made between 1938 and 1942—were distinguished by the same quarrelsome racket that had set his previous pictures apart. Toward George Marshall, the first director of *You Can't Cheat an Honest Man,* Fields was so steadily disagreeable that the company was split into two parts, Marshall to direct Edgar Bergen and the dummy, and Eddie Cline being brought in to direct Fields. With the hapless Cline he set marks of high-handed truculence that the movie industry

may never see equaled. Cline had been an actor of the old
school, and Fields, unfairly pouncing on this, regarded every suggestion he made as a pure distillate of obsolescent
corn. Walking onto a set, Cline would play in vigorous detail his version of how a scene should go; Fields, immediately afterward, would parody the performance cruelly.
He danced and capered with much lifting of the eyebrows,
flinging about of capes, and additional gestures not greatly
exercised since the heyday of Edwin Booth. In general,
Fields' parody had no relevance to Cline's suggestions,
which, everybody else agreed, were quite sound.

A saying went around Universal that if they'd thrown
the picture away and filmed the byplay between Cline and
Fields, they would have produced one of the all-time masterpieces of motion-picture art. As it was, the footage they
kept turned out satisfactorily. The idea that an honest man
can't be cheated had some vast, secret attraction for
Fields. When the picture was released, he would see the
title advertised on marquees, and his face would glow with
whatever strange merriment the words brought to his
mind. A rough synthesis of his friends' opinions on this
point is that he intended to convey just the reverse of the
statement. They felt that he considered himself almost the
model of the honest man and that as such he had been
cheated with regularity throughout his life. In any case, it
was his favorite slogan, much dearer to him than "Never
Give a Sucker an Even Break," a sentiment he never really
supported, and he was filled with joy when he talked the
studio into using it. The basis of Universal's reluctance to
promote such a bizarre title was twofold; besides the
fact that it was mechanically troublesome, being suited to
no ordinary marquee, it had the vaguest connection with
the film.

"How does it tie up, Mr. Fields?" asked one of the Universal heads.

"Ha!" exclaimed the comedian with a meaningful glance.

"Which character did you have in mind, Mr. Fields?"

The answer, as obscure as the connection, was a ringing
shout of wild, private laughter. The studio officials decided
at length that maybe it would be better all around if they
let the title's significance remain clouded. "I don't even
want to know," one of them said.

The role of Larson E. Whipsnade, the shoestring circus owner of *You Can't Cheat an Honest Man,* pleased Fields. By browbeating the production unit, he was able to insert many scenes that jibed harmoniously with his views. He later spoke feelingly of the scene in which his daughter, played by Constance Moore, introduced him at the upper-class party of the Bel-Goodie family, whose son she hoped to marry. Fields made a big impression. He had a colored roustabout drive him to the party in one of the circus chariots. He was wearing full dress, except for a button-up, sleeveless sweater and an opera cape whose white silk underside proclaimed in large letters "Larson E. Whipsnade's Circus Giganticus." His lordly air, as he rapped on the family's majestic door with a gold-headed cane, was typically synthetic. His expression was hollow, tired; he was a little bored with the wealthy circle in which he moved. When a butler opened the door and presented a salver, Fields started and gave a forgetful smile, then dug in his pocket and came up with a dime, which he sportingly dropped on the plate. He followed the butler in, removed the odious cape, and tried to spread it blatantly over a chair, "to get a little break on the advertisement," he explained, with precious enunciation of the rolling word, and accenting its second syllable.

Amid an embarrassing hush, the Bel-Goodies and their guests, including Miss Moore and her swain, were awaiting the elder Whipsnade in the drawing room. His entrance was stately, but he was patting his stomach with both hands and seemed to be in some pain. "How are you, sir?" asked the white-haired and courtly Bel-Goodie in rich tones, and Fields replied, "Not too good. Those olives they put in martinis give me a stomachache." The guests murmured polite sympathy, and he maundered on, seizing the opportunity, and the audience, to tell a revolting anecdote about rattlesnakes. The best efforts of the agitated group failed to get across to him that Mrs. Bel-Goodie had a dangerous allergy to even the mention of snakes, and he continued his discourse. The room was in an interesting uproar. Every time he said "snake," the hostess shrieked and fell over in a faint; the noisy attempts to revive her had no effect on the anecdote, which droned on to its senseless climax, in which the snake somehow saved Fields' life: "the little beggar stuck his tail out of the window and rattled for a constable."

Altogether, the scene may have represented Fields' idea of the general course that all upper-class parties should take.

So many people had commented adversely on his eating habits that Fields introduced a little joke at his own expense in this movie. At one point he entered his ticket wagon, found a thermos opened and on its side, and began to rail in a complaining voice, "Somebody left the cork out of my lunch." A moment later the emphasis had shifted to his lifelong heckling by children. "Larceny Whipsnake! Larceny Whipsnake!" called a wreck of a Western Union boy, and Fields, leaning out of his window, looking injured, tried to summon him.

"Street gamin," he cried, with an ingratiating leer. "Street gamin." When the boy approached, he said, "Larson *E.,* and it's Whip*snade,* not Whipsnake."

"All right, snake," the boy replied cheerfully, and Fields made the mistake of throwing a big handful of tickets at him. As the crowd scrambled for free admittance, he eyed the child with the special malevolence he had reserved so long for the young.

In some ways, *My Little Chickadee* and *Never Give a Sucker an Even Break* will probably stand up among the worst movies ever made. This scarcely detracts from their over-all worth; *The Cabinet of Dr. Caligari* and *The Great Train Robbery* were filled with flaws, but they retain elements of classicism. Neither of the two Fields pictures had what might even charitably be called a plot. The "story line" of *Sucker,* as the master preferred to think of it, previously outlined in Chapter One, was as grotesque a travesty of a plot as he could contrive in the brief time allotted to him. *My Little Chickadee,* with Mae West, finally resolved itself into a simple duel of ad libbers. The screen play was credited to "Mae West and W. C. Fields," but they mostly made it up as they went along. There was a good deal of professional antagonism between the two authors. The part called for such extravagances of wooing on Fields' part that he couldn't shake it off between takes. His voice took on the permanent note of endearment, and he pranced around, holding his preposterous hat, like an adolescent. His style was enriched by frequent doses from the flask. The bouncy quality of his conduct began to get on Miss West's nerves. One afternoon on the set she said, "Bill's a good guy, but it's a shame he has to be so goddamned cute." The subject of her analysis had just waltzed over, planted a kiss on her forehead with his thumb and index finger, and addressed her as "My little brood mare."

By misfortune, Fields' happiest inspirations—the view of him traveling through the cow country on a litter dragged by an Indian riding an underfed pony, his entrance into the bridal chamber with his sheriff's badge pinned to his pajamas—were subordinated to the labored exchanges between him and the co-star. The scene in which he was installed as sheriff of the lawless Western town was of interest. Fields was happy to be identified on the side of the law for once, particularly since he had succeeded to the office by fraud, but he was convinced that, in real life, if the opportunity had arisen, he still would have been slighted in some way. Consequently, at the banquet to celebrate his taking over he found himself seated, at the lower end of a fifty-foot table, in a closet. Moreover, the ends of a feather boa kept drifting down into his plate. He made repeated stabs at them with a fork, finally pinning them temporarily to the wall. Altogether, it was a pretty scraggly-looking company and a banquet scene dismal enough for all ordinary purposes, being laid in a run-down saloon, but at the head of the table, Joseph Calleia, the outgoing sheriff, was making an emotional speech in which he reminded the diners that "all this" had been made possible by the incoming Cuthbert J. Twillie. His remarks prompted a certain amount of boozy applause, but Twillie, in his closet, was occupied in staving off the boa.

The head of Universal's publicity department, Danny Thomas, has remembered how Fields used to arrive on the set each morning, at whatever hour suited him best, usually with Magda Michael, who helped him with his lines, and carrying his hampers, shakers and laprobes. He had insisted that the studio equip his dressing room with a front porch, an innovation of star temperament, and he took rests there in a rocker on sunny days. When a violent dispute arose over the story, every hour or two, he would retire to his rocker, withdraw miles into his shell, and be, for all practical purposes, incommunicado. The directors could plead, abuse, storm, and threaten, and he would continue to rock silently, his little frosty blue eyes distant and unfriendly. When Fields blew up in his lines, his answer was always that he had "a poor memory." This was an old and specialized lack, for his memory about other things was faultless. Sometimes his bosses would persuade him to try a scene their way, as a "dry run," just for fun. But he always inspected the cameras first, to see if they were loaded with film. "No tricks," he would warn them. "Keep those cameras empty."

Strangely, he was a marvel of co-operation to the publicity boys. For one thing, his publicity stills were the delight of the studio photographers. His controlled expressions somehow managed to convey every facet of his humor, and it was unnecessary to add much promotional material to his photos. Thomas drove out to Laughlin Park one day to confer with the comedian about a release. Fields received him affably, on the lawn, and showed him over the grounds, taking careful note of the flowers and shrubs. Before Thomas left, a watch salesman Fields had summoned arrived with a big sample case of his wares. Ever since the hallucinations at Las Encinas, Fields had showed an unusual interest in watches. He looked these over slowly, handling them, and holding them up to the light. At length he selected several for himself, and asked Thomas, "Do you see any others I ought to have?"

"I like the gold oval one there, Mr. Fields," he said.

Fields picked it up, held it out to him, and said, "It's yours. A little gift from one of your grateful charges."

Fields got $125,000 for each of his pictures at Universal; it took him approximately two months to finish one. This amount was swelled by the $25,000 he required and got for his "stories," which were nothing but scrambled notes. He never wrote a screen treatment or anything else that took time or effort. His literary offerings for the cinema were bare outlines of plots, situations, all of them troublesome and some downright impossible to film, such as his plan to parachute off a mountain with an umbrella. Most of his pictures made money for Universal, despite their unconventional outlook on life. By the time of his employment for that studio, he had a large and definite,

even hysterical, following, and its members could be counted on to see each new release over and over again. Fields
was always curious as to why his pictures were not shown,
on their first run, at the massive palaces, such as the Radio
City Music Hall. He pointed out, ruefully, that *Never Give
a Sucker an Even Break* opened in New York at the Rialto,
a small pleasure center usually given over to the exhibition
of "horror" films. When the officials explained, with great
patience, considering everything, that audiences in the big
theaters demanded the usual ingredients of Hollywood films
—well-barbered stars, a plot with a strong emetic quality,
and painful, saccharine, often ungrammatical dialogue—
he said, "Well, damn it, aren't my pictures rich in those
things?"

"Yours are mostly about cheating and robbery and terrible people, Mr. Fields," they had to tell him.

The truth is that Universal, as well as Paramount and
Metro-Goldwyn-Mayer, despite their general hewing to the
outworn and failing American movie line, were deserving
of considerable honor for the boldness, forbearance, and
latitude which characterized their handling of a difficult
comedian for so many years. With a good deal of courage, they continued to turn out products of his that defied
every law of the industry, and sometimes netted a minute
financial return.

Of the movies that Fields used to square old, and sometimes imaginary, accounts, *The Bank Dick* was his special pet. He was given a free hand in its construction, and
he had a frolicsome time. He received a screen credit for
the story, under his alternate pen name of Mahatma Kane
Jeeves. In many particulars it was a thrilling plot. To begin with, it resulted in the only known movie to date in
which the hero was wholly unregenerate throughout and
still reaped every possible reward. Fields cast himself as
Egbert Sousé, ("accent grahve over the *e*"), an improvi-
dent husband in a town called Lompoc, which by a wild coincidence spells "Cop Mol" backward. His wife, Agatha
Sousé, played by Cora Witherspoon, represented Fields'
idea of the typical housewife—a nagging slattern who kept
her mother constantly at her side. He had various prog-
eny, one of whom, a daughter, hit him in the back of the
head with a rock before the film was five minutes old. His

effort at retaliation, an attempt to kill her with a concrete urn, was frustrated by the family.

The problem Fields found himself confronting, and it was a ticklish one, was how to talk his prospective son-in-law, a bank clerk, into embezzling $500 of his employers' money to invest in a beefsteak mine. To this end he had an admirable stroke of fortune. A pair of robbers, Repulsive Rogan and Filthy McNasty, stuck up the bank; in making a getaway one of them, carrying the loot, stumbled over a park bench where Sousé was reading the Lompoc *Picayune-Intelligencer* and knocked himself cold. Fields picked him up, modestly explained to the town that he had cowed him into surrender, even though the man had "pulled an assagai" on him, and collected his idea of a bank's reward —the institution's new calendar, entitled "Spring in Lompoc." He was also offered the job of bank dick, or policeman.

The scene in which he went home with the good news of his capture was Fields' definitive picture of American home life. His wife, his eldest daughter, Myrtle, and his mother-in-law, Mrs. Hermisillo Brunch, were playing cards in the living room. He walked in with an expression of self-conscious pride. He was smoking a cigarette, wearing a straw hat and a ratty Windsor tie, and carrying a newspaper with a splashy account of his fake heroics. "Captured this bandit," he said, grinning sheepishly, as if he wished to disclaim credit, which was not remarkable, since he'd had nothing whatever to do with the capture. "They've got a story here," he said in a louder voice, but his wife seized the paper without looking up and flung it into the fireplace. At this point his mother-in-law stuck a finger in her mouth and began to make puffing noises. Then they all jumped on him about smoking in the house. Watching them, browbeaten, Fields started toward his room on the second floor, but in his preoccupation he missed the stairs and ascended a hassock, a chair, a table, and a bookcase, upon which he found himself bumping at the ceiling. As he climbed ignominiously down, his family gave him the respectful attention they would have accorded a criminal lunatic.

When he left the house shortly afterward he had regained his aplomb. And by a lucky accident he was able to do a favor for an elderly lady and her chauffeur, whose limousine had broken down near by. Fields lifted his hat, waved the perspiring chauffeur aside, reached under the hood with a dainty gesture, gave a single turn to a screw, and the whole engine dropped down into the street. He lifted his hat again, this time somewhat more briskly, and made off down the sidewalk at a pretty rapid clip. The incident had no bearing on the plot; it was one of those irrelevancies which Fields had always cherished, and which had started so many ulcers in the movie industry. A few months after the picture was released he told a friend that the automobile skit had been taken from his own life. "People were always offering to help me out like that, with about the same results," he said.

His old grievance against banks produced the next scene, one of the most satisfactory in the entire picture, Fields felt. He entered the bank to collect his reward and meet the president, Mr. Skinner. But every time he reached a teller's window, after standing in line, he was told to "Move aside, please, and let the next man up." This went on for several minutes, as Fields meekly obeyed, with the crushed mien of one accustomed to rough handling in banks, and then he finally got his message across. Mr. Skinner received him with enthusiasm. The banker, impressed, asked about some details of the fortuitous capture. He expressed particular interest in the assagai. In evading this issue, Fields launched a windy account of a knife fight he'd once had with a colored midget named Major Moe. "He was using a small knife, about an inch long," the hero related.

"An inch long?" asked Skinner in a baffled voice. "I don't believe I've ever seen a knife that——"

"It wasn't so much a knife as it was a razor," said Fields, and rambled on to other exploits.

Mr. Skinner broke in to give him the reward—"Spring in Lompoc" and "my heartiest handshake." When he mentioned the bank-dick job, Fields looked concerned and asked what the hours would be, roughly. "The bank opens at ten sharp," the president told him. "Well, that's all right," said Fields. "I think I can make that." He appeared in an ill-fitting uniform the next day and took up a stand in the lobby. In almost no time he demonstrated the wisdom of Skinner's appointment: he sneaked up on a small boy playing with a cap pistol, grabbed him by the neck, and shook him roughly.

Fields' opportunity with the beefsteak mine came to him by chance. In one of the abruptest scene changes on record, he rushed in to his favorite lounge, The Black Pussy Cat Café and Snack Bar, and, badly agitated, said to the bartender, "Did I spend a twenty-dollar bill in here last night?"

"Why, yes, you did, Mr. Sousé."

"Thank heaven," said Fields, mopping his brow. "I thought I'd lost it."

He relaxed and ordered a "depth bomb," with some water on the side. He drank the potion and washed his fingers carefully; then he called for another round, including a fresh glass of water. "Never like to bathe in the same water twice," he confided to a neighbor, an emaciated ruin that Fields often had standing around in his movie scenes. When he finished, he wiped his fingers with a napkin, rolled it into a ball, and tossed it negligently into the air; when it fell, he boosted it into a spittoon with his heel. Even in his juggling days he had never been in better form.

In the saloon he met J. Frothingham Waterbury, an investment counselor, a man with the composite impressiveness of all the salesmen who had tried to peddle Fields stock for fifty years. Waterbury described the mine and the probable results of investing. "You'll have a country place," he said, "with a beer river running through it, and all you'll have to do is sit in a rocker, wrapped in a Paisley shawl, and sign checks."

Fields' interest was aroused by the implications of this story. "You mean I'll have a fountain pen by then?" he asked, elated. Pressed for cash, he started to work on his prospective son-in-law, Og Ogilbie. "Don't be a fuddie duddie, don't be a moon calf," he told the reluctant youth. "Invest in the beefsteak mine. You'll have a country place, with your old grandmother's Paisley shawl running through it. A rocker, a beer river——" and in his emotion he became incoherent, a little indistinct.

Ogilbie capitulated, and the abstraction was accomplished, but the bank examiner, J. Pinkerton Snoopington, turned up unexpectedly and Fields was obliged to divert him. Franklin Pangborn played the part of the examiner, a performance which was in some measure effaced by the brilliant light of the star. Fields had always considered Pangborn a very funny man; as Preston Sturges did, he used him whenever possible. The byplay between the worried Sousé and the conscientious Snoopington has been mentioned as outstanding among the gems of Fields comedy.

His first effort to prevent Snoopington from reaching the bank took the form of showing him around the town. Passing a hardware store, Fields urged that the examiner weigh himself on a sidewalk scales. "The proprietor's a friend of mine," he said. "I can get you weighed free." Snoopington declined, and Fields steered him, over some protest, into the Black Pussy Cat. "Is it possible to get a light rye highball in here?" asked the examiner nervously. "You can get anything you want," Fields told him with municipal pride. "The place is a regular joint." To the bartender he called, "Have you seen Michael Finn lately?"

"I think I can find him for you, Mr. Sousé," the bartender answered.

Snoopington was seized by a violent illness during his second drink. Filled with solicitude, Fields hurried him to his room at the New Old Lompoc House and called a physician, "Dr. Stall." As he telephoned, he absently plucked some crockery grapes from a table piece and crunched into them with a painful racket. Fields at this time was fresh from his own medical wrangles, and he worked hard to present the physician of *The Bank Dick* in a proper light. In his office, as Stall answered the phone, was a male patient, nude to the waist but with a hat on, standing in an attitude of moribund dejection. "The first thing you'll have to do is cut out all health foods," the doctor was saying. "That'll be ten dollars. You'll get your clothes with a receipt."

In Snoopington's room, the doctor advised the examiner against all exercise and prescribed some pills about the size of golf balls that he'd brought in a jar. "Take these three nights running and then skip a night," he directed.

"But I thought you said no exercise," gasped the patient.

"The doctor's right, the doctor's right," Fields assured him, with an awful mockery of a bedside manner.

When the doctor left, he offered to get some food for

the nauseated sufferer. "Some nice pork chops fried in grease," he suggested, "a couple of cold poached eggs?" Snoopington dived for the bathroom, and Fields left, looking nonplused.

Through machinations almost too devious to follow, he captured the second bandit, again by fraud, earned the wild acclaim of the town, got a permanent job with a movie company, sold an "original movie story" for ten thousand dollars, and impressed his family into subordinate devotion. His manipulations of Snoopington also worked: the distraught examiner was sick as a dog for three days, in which time a bonanza vein was struck in the beefsteak mine, and the money was replaced.

The final scene, and a great comfort to Fields, saw him seated at the dinner table of his sumptuous new house. At his wife's request he was finishing "a second noggin of café baba au rhum." He arose, kissed them all good-by, then struck out for an evening's entertainment, after a little trouble at the door, during which he put his hat on his upthrust cane by mistake and searched for it all over the floor. He paddled off across the lawn, his expressive hips conveying high self-esteem, and turned, humming, in the direction of the saloon. His self-esteem was forgivable; he had just completed one of the great classics of American comedy.

CHAPTER TWENTY-NINE

THE EXPENDITURES of energy that went into his Universal series caused Fields to step up his drinking. As before, he was never drunk, but he found that even alcohol was losing its sedative magic. He became listless and dispirited, and his old illness, at the best only arrested, began putting forth new, small shoots. On his sixty-fifth birthday, in 1944, he told one of his household, "All of a sudden I'm a tired old man"—a curious revelation, for never in his life had he been known to complain of physical pain. During the acutest tortures of his polyneuritis, his only reaction was to swear and make jokes about it. As his health began its final dissolution, the movie companies were reluctant to sign him to contracts. His idleness took its added toll; he fretted, and worried, and, for the first time, added up the balances in his bankbooks.

"I have been trying to get into the movies these many months, but I can't seem to consummate the deal," he wrote Roy McCardle, an old friend of his Ziegfeld days. "I've cut the bite almost in half but I still have no takers." A little later he told McCardle, "I'm in a dither to know just what has happened. Maybe I've kicked too many of the chosen people in the can. There's a Nubian in the fuel supply and I can't locate him."

He lost the house on De Mille Drive. Much as he loved it, he refused to increase the rent when his lease expired, and the landlord promptly evicted hm. "Will you rent another place, Mr. Fields?" Miss Michael asked him, as they sat in his lawn swing after receiving the fateful notice. Despite the turbulence of the day, his face, she thought, showed an odd kind of repose. "No, no," he said easily. "I think it's back to the sanitarium for the nonce."

"We both knew what he meant," she says. "This was his last house—he would never leave the sanitarium."

When they got up to walk back to the house, she noticed that his legs were unsteady. His motor impulses had been failing for weeks. His fingers had grown so arthritic that he could no longer juggle, and he frequently stumbled and fell. His sleep, fragmentary and shallow for years, had become wildly restless. He often tumbled out of bed. So disturbing was this symptom that he bought a gigantic antique cradle and substituted it for his four-poster. Many times in the night, Miss Monti would tiptoe in to see that, in thrashing about, he had not flung himself over the sideboards of even this sturdy bunk.

Before they left the house for the last time, Fields made the old inspection tour of his grounds. The day was fine, everything was in order—no trespassers in sight. In his flower beds he appeared to be searching for something; at length they saw him scramble down the slope to his lily pool—a painful feat, since he could scarcely walk on level ground—and toss the largest of his red roses onto the waterless stone bottom. Then, gleaming with sweat, he came up to the car and they drove off toward Las Encinas.

Once again he was established comfortably in the sanitarium. Miss Monti went with him; Miss Michael visited him several times a week. He made light of his condition, but he wanted his affairs put in order. In the past, in his talks with Gene Fowler, he had always referred to death, for some reason, as "the fellow in the bright nightgown." Now, in a humorous tone, he said to Miss Michael, "None of us, sick or well, can tell when the fellow in the bright nightgown's coming to pay us a visit." He spent his days reading, dictating letters, seeing a few close friends, and sitting outside in a rocker, his eyes fixed on the same distant horizons, his expression as fiercely belligerent as ever. During one period of improvement he made an album of records, having to do mainly with the calamities which had attended his mistakenly drinking a glass of water. On September 10, 1946, he wrote Fowler saying that Franklin Pangborn—"J. Pinkerton Snoopington"—had been out again, with suggestions that Fields, to steady his gait, buy one of the new "Phantom Crotches." On the phone the next day he said to Fowler, "I want to wish you and yours a Merry Christmas and a Happy New Year in case I take off suddenly for the Far East after reading *The New Yorker* article on the atomic bomb."

Fields was in truth preparing for a journey, but he had reversed his directions. He was growing much worse. Like his friend John Barrymore, he now had a badly diseased liver and a dropsical condition which embarrassed his heart. As the fall deepened into winter, approaching the holiday season which he professed to loathe, he had periods of delirium. Occasionally he cursed and railed at things that Miss Monti and Miss Michael had never heard him mention previously, and once, out of a blue sky, he sang what appeared to be a kind of love song, called up from some experience of his youth that had been long forgotten by his conscious mind.

On Christmas Eve, Fowler telephoned the sanitarium to arrange a visit for the next day at eleven. Ordinarily, Fields slept until ten, then had a massage and "breakfast"—some fruit juice followed by martinis, if he could get them. Fowler was told that the comedian was under treatment and would not be able to receive callers until after the first of the year. "It was the first time I'd suspected how serious his condition really was," he said.

Late into the night of Christmas Eve, Fields' room was full of doctors and nurses. Both Miss Monti and Miss Michael were there, waiting for the answer to what was plainly his severest crisis. After sixty-six years of the most damaging kind of abuse, his life stream was ebbing out. Shortly before midnight, Miss Monti took his hand and began calling to him. While she pleaded, he opened his eyes, and, noting the people in the room, put a finger to his lips and winked. A few minutes later, as bells over the city announced the arrival of Christmas morning, he suffered a violent hemorrhage of the stomach. The blood bubbled thickly out of his lips, he drew several long sighs, and lay still. The fellow in the bright nightgown, so often frustrated before, had finally come for W. C. Fields.

Christmas noon, Dave Chasen and Billy Grady were approaching Fields' cottage. The fact of his death had not yet been announced. They were dressed up in funny clothes; Grady had a couple of bottles and Chasen had a hamper of delicacies. At the gate, an undertaker and several assistants passed them carrying a basket. "Somebody dead?" asked Chasen, a little addled.

"Mr. Fields died early this morning," said the undertaker.

Chasen, a mild, gentle man, grew white and his legs started to buckle. Grady helped him to the ground, then uncorked one of the bottles and gave him a drink. He took a drink himself. They sat there half an hour or so, blowing their noses, swiping at their eyes, and finishing the bottle. They noticed at last that it was raining. "It's a rainy day," said Grady. "Bill would have liked that fine." Much relieved, they got up and went home.

A period of confusion followed the comedian's death. It is perhaps best to draw a curtain of charity over much of the shoddy fuss that followed the reading of his will. Miss Michael, as executrix, faithfully discharged her duties when the physicians pronounced him dead. She called Mrs. Fields and her son Claude. They came to the sanitarium with the greatest dispatch, and took charge of his effects. Fields' will stipulated that his body was to be taken to a cemetery and immediately cremated, and that under no conditions was he to have any sort of funeral. He had three. First, Mrs. Fields and Claude had a good-sized public one, of a generally non-sectarian nature, at which Edgar Bergen officiated. Bergen made a brief, unemotional talk. "It seems wrong not to pray for a man who gave such happiness to the world," he told a large crowd of friends and film people. "But that was the way he wanted it. Bill knew life, and knew that laughter was the way to live it. He knew that happiness depended on disposition, not position. . . . We simply say farewell."

Mrs. Fields indicated that she would overrule the comedian's wish about cremation, on the ground that such a procedure was contrary to her religious doctrines. No mention was made of Fields' doctrines. Commenting on the service, the Los Angeles *Times* said, "When the family departed, Carlotta (Monti) tried to go to the crypt. A cemetery attendant stopped her. On orders of Mr. Fields' son, she was not to be admitted until the crypt was sealed." After the first funeral Mrs. Fields had another, a Catholic service. Then Miss Monti had a third funeral, a spiritualist reading, presided over by the Reverend Mae Taylor, a leading Hollywood practitioner.

The will left Mrs. Fields and Claude each ten thousand dollars. It mentioned trust funds of seventy-five dollars weekly for Fields' brother, Walter, sixty dollars weekly for his sister, Adele, and twenty-five dollars weekly for Carlotta. Various other friends, relatives and employees were bequeathed sums of a few hundred or a few thousand dollars. The remainder of the estate, which was appraised at $800,000, in cash, was to be used for the establishment of the "W. C. Fields College for Orphan White Boys and Girls, Where No Religion of Any Sort Is to Be Preached." Gene Fowler recalled that some time before his death Fields had intended the orphanage for colored children. His decision to switch was caused by the insolence, or imagined insolence, of a colored servant he employed. During his lifetime, Fields' affections for races and sects veered sharply from day to day. In general, however, he bore all groups the same considered animosity. And from start to finish it was entirely superficial. Even after his change of heart about the orphans, he paid off a $4000 mortgage on the house of his Negro cook, and he once ordered from his premises a man who used the word "nigger" within earshot of his staff.

Mrs. Fields' and her son's answer to the will was to file suits that, in effect, would convey almost the entire estate to them. Mrs. Fields, in claiming half the $800,000 as automatically hers under the California community property law, appeared likely to make out, as the widow, very comfortably; the future of the orphans looked dubious. Among her other suits, she claimed that Fields, during his life, "gave away" more than $400,000 to women, and she was entitled, she said, to half of that sum, too. The lawsuits, involving the usual congress of attorneys, dragged on, and the estate, accumulated so bitterly by one of the world's hardest workers, dwindled. In the meantime, the court directed Miss Michael, as executrix, to pay Mrs. Fields $600 a month. For a long time, at least, Miss Monti never received any payments from her minute trust fund, the court not having reached a decision on it.

In the scrapping over his money, Fields himself was largely forgotten. Two years after his death he lay in an unmarked grave—an anonymous crypt in an ornate niche at Forest Lawn, a pretentious burial park that he frequently derided. Miss Michael and Miss Monti often went out with the flowers he loved, hoping on each trip that somebody might have gotten around to putting a simple identifying inscription on what promised to be his final resting place. Miss Michael, reflecting on all the turbulence that harassed her employer, sometimes thought of a question she once asked him. "If you had your life to do over, what would you like to change, Mr. Fields?" He thought a minute before answering. "You know," he said, "I'd like to see how I would have made out without liquor."

It seems doubtful, as Bergen told the funeral crowd, that he could have brought any more happiness to all the people he delighted for so many years. It is almost certain, though, that his personal life would have been more normal, less painful, what he had probably dreamed for it in the cruel time after his flight from home. But if George Sand was in the right, in her letter to Gustave Flaubert, then *"L'homme c'est rien, L'œuvre c'est tout"*—the man is nothing, the work is everything—and Fields had brilliantly discharged his debt to society.

The night of his death, several of his friends gathered at Chasen's restaurant for a wake. There, beneath John Decker's famous painting of the comedian as "Victoria Regina" —squatting lumpily with a doily and a silver salt cellar perched atop his head—they talked about his life and why they had liked him. Toward morning they put it briefly into words, and phoned it to the Hollywood *Reporter,* where it appeared as a page ad on December 27, 1946.

THE MOST PREJUDICED AND HONEST AND BELOVED FIGURE OF OUR SO-CALLED "COLONY" WENT AWAY ON A DAY THAT HE PRETENDED TO ABHOR—"CHRISTMAS."

WE LOVED HIM, AND—PECULIARLY ENOUGH—HE LOVED US.

TO THE MOST AUTHENTIC HUMORIST SINCE MARK TWAIN, TO THE GREATEST HEART THAT HAS BEATEN SINCE THE MIDDLE AGES—W. C. FIELDS, OUR FRIEND.

> *Dave Chasen*
> *Billy Grady*
> *Eddie Sutherland*
> *Ben Hecht*
> *Grantland Rice*
> *Greg La Cava*
> *Gene Fowler*

Requiescat in Pace

Ⓢ

Other SIGNET Titles You Will Enjoy

☐ **I CAN'T WAIT UNTIL TOMORROW . . . 'CAUSE I GET BETTER LOOKING EVERY DAY by Joe Willie Namath with Dick Schaap.** The one-and-only, authorized story of Namath's rapid rise to football fame. Chock-full of frank confessions and very personal anecdotes about Namath's private life—his buddies, his broads, his booze and football! (#Y4308—$1.25)

☐ **LIFE WITH PICASSO by Francoise Gilot and Carlton Lake.** An intimate view of the great artist's personality and art, as seen by the woman who was his mistress, his model, and the mother of two of his children. (#Q2772—95¢)

☐ **LENA by Lena Horne and Richard Schickel.** A great entertainer relates the dramatic story of her rise to stardom and her victory over fear and loneliness. (#T3015—75¢)

☐ **ACT ONE by Moss Hart.** The famous playwright and director tells of his early life, from poverty-stricken boyhood to his first big Broadway success, in this fascinating bestseller. (#Q2833—95¢)

◯

Recent Bestsellers Now in SIGNET Editions

☐ **SONS by Evan Hunter.** By the bestselling author of **The Blackboard Jungle**, this is a powerful novel about three generations of Tyler men, portraying grandfather, father and son; their changing world and values.

(#Y4288—$1.25)

☐ **THE NUN OF MONZA by Mario Muzzuchelli.** This historical story about a young nun who fell in love with an Italian nobleman, and bore two children by him will soon be released as a major motion picture starring Anne Heywood.

(#Q4242—95¢)

☐ **THE PRETENDERS by Gwen Davis.** The exciting bestseller about the jet-setters is a masterful portrait of their loves, lives and fears.

(#Y4260—$1.25)

☐ **JENNIE by Ralph G. Martin.** JENNIE, the Life of Lady Randolph Churchill, has been on the bestseller list almost since publication. Ralph G. Martin, successful author and recognized authority on the Churchills, has created a vivid picture of an exciting woman.

(#Y4213—$1.25)
